THE GLASS SLIPPER

THE GLASS SLIPPER

Women and Love Stories

SUSAN OSTROV WEISSER

RUTGERS UNIVERSITY PRESS
New Brunswick, New Jersey, and London

Library of Congress Cataloging-in-Publication Data
Weisser, Susan Ostrov.
          The glass slipper : women and love stories / Susan Ostrov Weisser.
                    pages cm
          Includes bibliographical references and index.
          ISBN 978–0–8135–6178–3 (hardcover : alk. paper) —
          ISBN 978–0–8135–6177–6 (pbk. : alk. paper) —
          ISBN 978–0–8135–6179–0 (e-book)
          1. Love stories—History and criticism. 2. Women and literature. 3. Women in
literature. 4. Love in literature. I. Title.
          PN3448.L67W37 2013
          809.3'85—dc23

                                                        2012051437

A British Cataloging-in-Publication record for this book is available from the British
Library.

Visit our website: http://rutgerspress.rutgers.edu

Manufactured in the United States of America

For Madeline, Liam, Oscar, Leo, Alex,
and Juliet: the stars in my sky

Some people would never have been in love,
had they never heard love talked about.
—La Rochefoucauld

CONTENTS

PREFACE

> The woman in love feels endowed with a high and undeniable value.
> —Simone de Beauvoir, *The Second Sex*

The original impulse to write this book came from teaching young women who face a peculiar double bind. These students consider themselves the most independent and self-determining generation of women in history, yet their expectations of love do not seem to match their real-life observations and experience of romance and marriage, and they're not sure why. Magazine articles, self-help books, and psychology studies quoted on TV and the Internet tell them how to find the right man but seem to have helped very little.

Though most of my female students rhetorically reject the traditional feminine motive of economic security in marriage, they often worry that they won't be seen as desirable if they project independence and self-interest. The lure of being chosen by the desirable man who pursues, and the fear of not being seen as a desirable object worthy of emotional attachment, are more powerful than the threat of what they might lose through submergence in a relationship. So the old idea of a woman's value as defined through her ability to attain the love of the high-status man lives on to a surprising degree. Courtship is still celebrated in movies, novels, magazines, and TV as the most special time of a woman's life, as opposed to a man's.

Though Simone de Beauvoir published *The Second Sex* in 1949, well before the Second Wave of the women's movement in Western nations, it seems to me that many women still seek to be adored in love, perhaps more than ever. De Beauvoir claimed that women both want freedom and fear giving up the privileges of dependency. I would argue that in a society in which there are suddenly greater sexual freedoms than ever, women counter their anxiety about continuing sexual exploitation by clinging to romantic love as a kind of emotional affirmation that they are worth more than the exchange value of their bodies. The ideal and hope of being adored, protected, and given lifelong emotional security becomes insurance against the increasingly heavy demands for a kind of sexuality that is still devalued for women, though paradoxically it's also encouraged and inflated. In other words, women react to the pressure to be both super-desirable (literally adore-able) and yet strong and independent by holding on to the Victorian split between the good woman, who is loved, and the hypersexual woman, who may be exploited. If they're loved, they feel they must be good.

How do young women meet their desire to find someone to love while not compromising a strong sense of self? There aren't many role models or guides for that, and so romance has become an unexamined area where many women remain squeezed between unappealing options. Heterosexual women often live with anxiety about the price paid for condemning "men," which includes the "good" men and the desirable mates. My students resent critiques of romance as "man-hating" and radical or extreme and are anxious to assure me and themselves that they are not cynical or hostile . . . unlike feminists. Or they may define their own feminism as the power to get what they want, and vigorously endorse using their desirability as a kind of power tool. These conflicts around romantic love parallel women's similar ambivalence and anxieties surrounding beauty, youth, sexuality, and motherhood.

As the recent work of psychologists Laurie Rudman and Kim Fairchild has shown, both women and men perceive feminism and romance to be in conflict.[1] Overwhelmingly, the "postfeminist" young women I encounter reject Second Wave feminists' analysis of love as a power dynamic. They see romance as a semi-magical space of perfectly mutual and enduring feelings; if there is an imbalance of power, in their view, it isn't "real" love in the first place, and everyone will find "real" love eventually, so there is no problem to discuss. After all, they argue, if I need you and you need me, there is no power issue: it does not occur to them that desire, need, and dependence can assume a variety of forms that don't necessarily harmonize or equalize.

I see this topic as timely and important because romance is an area of life that informs most Western women's choices, in a way that is evolving along with modernity. While the Glass Ceiling limits female executives or members of Congress, the idea of the Glass Slipper directly affects ordinary women of all groups and classes in our culture in far greater numbers. Romantic love is intensely personal (yet also deeply social), and all the more potent for being ordinary. We have made romantic love so important in contemporary society that how we think about the promises and experiences of romance has an enormous role in shaping the direction of our lives: where we go, how we behave, who we expect to become, what we are willing to do to be loved.

Over my twenty-five years of teaching, students have shared these ideas and many of their experiences in love as well. This book is not concerned with the practice of love, however, but rather the way these experiences and beliefs are represented in the structures of storytelling. I hope to show how Victorian ideas and stories about women's sexuality, femininity, and romantic love have survived as seemingly protective elements in a more modern, feminist, sexually open society, confusing the picture for women themselves. Love stories, ranging from traditional fairy tales to the classic *Jane Eyre* to the reality show *The Bachelor*, tend to be conservative in their appeals to women, using themes and images from the Victorian age. My intent is to explain why we cling to these old stories of gender and romance, linking these to modern women's anxieties about their value in the emotional marketplace.

I am as grateful as I should be to those who helped me through the writing and editing process these last three years. First among these is Leslie Mitchner, editor extraordinaire at Rutgers University Press, whose skill is well matched by her creativity and kindness. I am grateful to the terrific staff at Rutgers University Press, especially India Cooper, my copy editor. I would also like to thank the following for their contributions, from expert suggestions and good conversation to help with information and other tasks, undertaken with a good heart: Roni Berger, Jerome Bruner, Marsha Darling, Maeghan Donohue, Diane Della Croce, Sarah Frantz, Bernard Gendron, Jessica Harris, Eric Heinemann, Dora Keller, Elayne Rapping, Sonia Jaffe Robbins, Edwin Troeber, Robyn Warhol, and Sokthan Yeng. Adelphi University supported my research with released time; I greatly appreciate the assistance of former dean Stephen Rubin. Thanks to Barnes & Noble Inc. and Maney Publishing for their kind permission to reprint previously published portions of my work. And not least, I know how fortunate I am to have a ruthless professional editor in the family: many thanks to Cybele Weisser for her patient, unpitying (and unpaid) aid when the going was rough.

THE GLASS SLIPPER

INTRODUCTION

Women and the Story of Romantic Love

"I believe my Prince Charming is out there somewhere."

These words were tearfully spoken by rejected "Bachelorettes" in the ninth season of the popular reality TV show *The Bachelor*, in which dozens of beautiful women compete for "the heart" of a coveted male. This time around, *The Bachelor: Rome* (2006), whose overwhelmingly female audience numbered over eight million viewers a week, featured an actual prince from Europe, thereby invoking many breathless references to fairy tales. The tale of Cinderella, with its beautiful but undervalued woman and the instant recognition she garners from the prince, is of course the quintessential romantic story. As even a six-year-old can tell you, its climactic moment centers on the perfect fit between the mistreated Cinderella's dainty foot and the highly improbable shoes that she wore to the ball. And as a feminist literary critic will tell you, the Glass Slipper is a trope for the "perfect fit" of the romantic couple and particularly women's wish to be chosen as the One, whose value is at last recognized and rewarded at the moment she is discovered as perfect for him.

It's well known that the *Bachelor* series rarely works as a route to romantic happiness for its participants, though this lack of success apparently doesn't prevent the audience from enjoying the fantasy. We may take this odd fact as a metaphor for the cultural view of marriage as a safety net for the domestic happiness of young women. In 2005 newspapers trumpeted a new trend in American society: for the first time, married women were in the minority of all U.S. women. Marriage has been decreasing in the United States, slowly catching up to a trend that has been prevalent in Europe for quite a while. Even as gay activists campaign for marriage rights in America, all couples are marrying later, divorce is common and increasingly acceptable, and more women remain single after being widowed or divorced.

1

But the story of "finding" or being chosen by the "right guy" still has enormous power over many women's lives. Feminism or no feminism, romantic "chick lit" is mushrooming, date movies still dictate the ideal lifestyle for women, and Valentine's Day is like a national holiday requiring levels of spending surpassed only by Christmas. It's a fascinating irony that Harlequin novels began publication at the same time that feminists were engaged in a forceful critique of romance and marriage as oppressive and weakening to women.[1]

A quarter of a century later, the popular romance industry has gone on to become phenomenally successful, while my college students are irritated by Shulamith Firestone's 1970 pronouncement that "men can't love" and laugh at Germaine Greer's formulation that romance is "dupe for dopes." At the same time that there is widespread anxiety and cynicism about marriage today, there is also more and more hope, envy, and desire among young and old for the kind of romance that will make a woman feel . . . well, womanly. Though it's no longer true, thanks to the postwar explosion of women's participation in the workforce, that getting the right man to marry you is the only golden ticket to the good life, as it was for my mother and earlier generations, it still seems widely and unquestioningly accepted that romance is essential to personal identity, and that women in particular can't get enough of it.

We might say that, in a way, romance is the new marriage. The irony is that romance is most often defined by the kind of love that leads to marriage—whether or not the marriage "works" in reality. One way that romance triumphed is in seeming to take seriously feminism's advocacy of equal gender roles, leading to an egalitarian partnership or marriage.[2] I will argue, however, that a strong wave of nostalgia for traditional ideas of gender informs what might be called the master narrative of current romantic literature, as a hidden agenda masked by the modern ideology of love's democratizing power.

At the height of the feminist movement in the 1970s, Colette Dowling's analysis of the Cinderella myth, *The Cinderella Complex: Women's Hidden Fear of Independence*, was a best seller because it spoke to women's new expectations for their lives, including the exciting possibility of breaking through the Glass Ceiling. But the Cinderella story is only one of many stories of love that surround us. More and more, we have become a culture of romance: stories of all kinds shape the terms of love, from classic novels to modern films, Harlequin romances to reality television and the profiles of Internet dating. Narratives make life, including our own particular lives, readable, in the sense of coherent and intelligible. The more incoherent romance and marriage become, the more the stories of romance proliferate and assume an ever more pivotal cultural role.

There is an odd paradox to this: while romance is more popular than ever in contemporary Western society, increasing layers of crassness, skepticism, and anxiety about it have grown alongside the intense romanticism about love.[3] The two views, sentimentally reverent on the one hand and cynical on the other, weirdly coexist in tension. And as love has become a fixture in popular media, as well as a near-universal expectation in modern Western life, we have become increasingly reluctant to engage the question of whether women benefit personally and as a gender from romance.

This is partly because contemporary heterosexual popular romances model a kind of postfeminist femininity, one that supposedly encompasses both social progress and traditional plots for women.[4] The emotions and behaviors of men versus women, sometimes called Mars and Venus, are readily available as explanatory myths for gender problems, as are popular psychological recipes for "taking control" of relationships in a "healthy way." But underneath all this rhetoric and representation is a long history of conflict over the validity of women's desire, pleasure, and power that is not often articulated.

BACKGROUND

The problems and values of the past haunt us even as they change in shape. We might say that the past is not so much a cradle of the present as the dream that we can't entirely shake, often taking the form of pleasant lies. The modern dream of love is a story still immersed in Victorian ideas about women's nature and roles.

The love story in Anglo-American culture has evolved with the changing conditions of women's lives since the Victorian era by adapting new forms after the Second Wave of feminism. My thesis is that the romantic story, whose trope is the Glass Slipper, has adapted to women's anxieties about these developments, yet continues to be a medium for transmitting Victorian gender values. This allows romance to have both progressive and conservative aspects, allaying the uncertainty that modern women may feel about extraordinarily rapid changes in work, social roles, and intimate relations.

"Man is intellect, woman is love. Man is mind, woman is heart," cried the *Monthly Religious Magazine* in 1862. The Victorian view of gender turned on these important differences, and romantic love was often dramatized in nineteenth-century culture as a meeting point of "mind" and "heart," propping up perceived deficiencies in each sex. In the Victorian era, two important ideas concerning women can be traced: on the one hand, the "official" middle-class ideology that society requires women's self-denial and sexual purity, and on the other, the growing sense that meaning could be found in the individual pursuit of self-fulfillment in intimate personal life. These two messages appeared in dialectical tension in nineteenth-century culture, and the burgeoning popularity of romantic love as the reward for the selfless, sexually pure heroine seemed to support each side. In a previous book, I explored how romance, as the mediator between these two powerful, contradictory messages, filled a vacancy for women by acknowledging their secret craving for fulfillment.[5]

From the eighteenth century on, Western feminists have tried to sort out the impact of romantic love on women's lives, usually showing hostility either to romance as the basis of marriage (as did Mary Wollstonecraft) or to marriage itself as an unequal institution that hinders love (as did Emma Goldman in the early twentieth century). Second Wave feminists of the 1970s continued that tradition by attacking the pleasing role women are supposed to play in romance as just another instance of classic feminine passivity. They urged women to kick that Glass Slipper away, leave the hearth altogether, and go to law school instead. But while marriage and the suburban family were dissected and heterosexual romance sometimes indicted, feminist theory was largely silent about the emotional needs of the ordinary woman (often conceived as monochromatic and middle class) and how she was supposed to go about forfeiting, changing, or fulfilling them in her new independence. Women's sexual freedom was a shared ideal (though with disputes over what that implied), and loving other women usually applauded, but what they were supposed to do for emotional gratification if they were heterosexual was left unexplored.

This view of romance between men and women as politically incorrect has long since seemed cranky and unrealistic to most Anglo-American women, and has largely died away since the seventies. Feminism went on to successful activism in the decades since the Second Wave movement, bringing more parity in the workplace, legalized abortion, laws prohibiting sexual harassment and spousal abuse, and much else we can be proud of. Next to the Glass Ceiling, the problem of the Glass Slipper no doubt came to seem trivial, the feminist insistence that romance is "wretched cant . . . masking egotism, lust, masochism, fantasy under a mythology of sentimental postures," as Germaine Greer put it, over the top and a turnoff to both women and the men they want to love them.[6]

But though modern Western society has come to adopt a language of equality of intellect and mind between the sexes, women are still often depicted as, and see themselves as, the ones who are centrally concerned with and invested in romantic relationships, if not marriage. In other words, since women have entered higher education and professions in great numbers, men may no longer be automatically equated with "mind," but women *are still "heart,"* the creators of mass-media romantic fiction, the primary audience for romantic films and novels, and both subjects and consumers of bridal magazines and articles about keeping romance alive in marriage.

As a feminist, I am extremely interested in why this should be so more than a century after Victorianism. It is puzzling that a bizarre dualism has arisen in representations of romance between portraits of love in contemporary "serious" literature by men and women that range from skeptical to sardonic and the highly stylized mass-produced culture of romantic images and stories for a female audience. And in the twenty-first century, where the gains of the women's movement have been notably threatened, the political implications of this ambivalent view seem all the more problematic.

APPROACH

Rooted and submerged in subjectivity, love can be understood as a story, fiction or nonfiction, perhaps more than through statistics or abstractions alone. This book is about the varied forms romance can take as a narrative, whether or not the romance is imaginary, and what stories of romantic love say to and about women in particular, for whom they are often produced.

I am especially concerned with comparing romance in differing versions. For that reason, my chapters are diverse: they discuss topics in gender and romance over the last two centuries, in both high culture and low. I have tried to look at romantic stories from different angles, including (in chapter 10) how modern cultures of "reality" play with the story of love.

Given this approach, it must be acknowledged that this book is not meant to be a comprehensive examination of the vast and complex field of romance since the Victorian era. Obviously love is not *only* a story, and love does not involve or affect only women. In order to explore the meeting point of romance, women, and stories, we had better start with a look at the way each of these terms will be treated in this book.

Romantic Love: What Is Love, to Begin With?

What is romantic love? Depends on whom you ask: biologist, social scientist, psychoanalyst, songwriter, television character, the girl or boy next door. Many believe that like sex or parenthood, it's something you can authentically understand only when you have experienced it. Apparently there are almost as many ways to conceptualize romantic love, as the enormous and diverse literature on it proves, as there are to express and represent love. This is unquestionably part of the problem of defining it: there's no uniform and dependable "it" there to define. Romantic love is a slippery and confused notion at best on which to base a study.

Because of its complexity, love is a subject that lends itself to many disciplinary approaches. Yet the narrowness of isolated scholarly fields can get in the way of broader understanding, as when the psychoanalyst treats it as an individual adjustment to universal infantile desires, the scientist deals with it as a neurochemical phenomenon, the sociologist assumes it is socially adaptive, the philosopher addresses the phenomenon as an abstract concept, the historian focuses on its culturally specific development, and the literary critic analyzes the shape and thematics of the narrative itself. All of these seem at least partially right yet somehow also lacking a sense of the whole, like the proverbial parts of the elephant. Meanwhile, popular literature, songs, movies, TV, advertising, and so on address the subject as if there were a universal—yet also intensely personal—experience with ideal meaning.

Does this variability of explanation of love's nature, source, and rules mean that it is entirely socially constructed? Not necessarily. Or to the contrary, is it therefore best explained as a biological universal? Again, not necessarily: the capacity to *feel* romantic love (if you define it as a feeling) or the potential to *have a romantic relationship* (if you define love as a kind of relation with another) doesn't imply that everyone feels it or has a romance, though it's sometimes construed that way in the West, where its absence implies abnormality. Pop psychology says that if you are "emotionally available," romance will be your destiny, which then slides into the implication that if you don't feel romantic love or have romance, it must be your fault, a character defect or neurosis. In our society, there is a Tinker Bell approach to "believing in love": it authorizes itself, much like religious faith.

What makes "love" particularly difficult as a subject of investigation is that it is *not just* a construct or script with coded gestures and behaviors. Elucidating romance that way appears chilly, overly cerebral, and out of tune, something like citing a number to express how much you love someone. Romance may be a set of mores and a story for performance (a repertoire of moves, if you will), coded in a system of linguistic and behavioral conventions, as scholars would say, but it's also a vividly felt dream of transcendence through the body (or "soul," if you will) of another. Dreams are notoriously difficult to describe, especially those with profound emotional resonance. Students express this by saying that "love can't be defined" (when I ask them to do just that) because it's "mysterious." Examine its biological effects, and you have left out a world of meaning; discuss its representation in media, and students will claim that real romances are not like that, though they might hope and expect they will be; try to discover the principles of our common cultural understanding of romantic love, and they will tell you that "everyone has their own definition of love."

Moreover, love is a particularly challenging topic because its meaning is continually in flux through historical periods, a cultural fact many students don't recognize (until I get hold of them). A sense of history can anchor such questions as whether the *feeling* of romantic love or the *practice* of romantic relationships is universal (as some anthropologists and psychologists hold); as difficult as that is to answer certainly, we know that the representation of love relationships is not. For example, most of my students define romance as a mutual relationship, distinguishing between love that is "real" because it leads to a "successful" (by which they mean enduring) couple formation and "false" love, which does not. In other words, they believe *romance is constituted by the equality of loving feeling and commitment*. However, the medieval Provençal poets, often credited by literary historians with setting the terms for the Western concept of romantic love, would be surprised to hear this assumption, since so many of their love songs and poems are about passion for a cruel or indifferent beloved.

Then, too, students use a language of what they call "intimacy," a psychological sense of connection based on mutual self-disclosure and knowledge of the beloved over time, which doesn't square well with Romeo and Juliet's version of immediate love, or in general with the still-popular idea of "love at first sight." As for the prevailing idea of romance as self-development, the means to growth in psychological and emotional maturation (to become one's "best self," as Oprah would say), this modern concept, too, would be quite alien to many of our most famous authors. Would the ancient poet Sappho or even the nineteenth-century novelist Gustave Flaubert agree?

In our modernized version, we increasingly value intensity, individuality, and spontaneity (legacies of Romanticism) and love is an everyday glamour, like wearing costly shoes with ordinary clothing. In a society where we want ever more and newer forms of stimulation—extreme sports, unprecedented intrusions on (others') privacy, scenes of mass destruction, and a constant state of arousal by whatever is louder and bigger—love, supposedly available to and expectable by everyone, seems like a ready answer. Love is a kind of super-entertainment, but it also has serious social meaning: finding the One is connected to status and a sense of "arriving" in society. Yet since it has become attached to the everydayness of marriage or at least long-term emotional stability, it also promises the safety of the familiar and the strength of a legally and socially privileged institution.

The way my students talk about the subject of romantic love, you would think you could formulate an algorithm: let's say, $(s + f = RL)$, where sex and best-friendship combine to render "romantic love," a product somehow more powerful and meaningful than either of its two ingredients. But we know from the "friends with benefits" idea that it must be far more complex than that! Rather than the simple combination of two common human arrangements (sex and friendship) adding up to a certain category of love, romance often seems to be, at least in our modern rendering, a specific kind of emotional attachment that is used as a yardstick to measure something deep, valuable, or enduring against sexual relations that are more temporary or casual.

At the end of season 13 on the TV reality show *The Bachelor*, one of the final women, Jillian, made a speech about her idea of romantic love: it has to be based on being "best friends." The Bachelor, Jason, agreed, but then gave her the boot because he wanted "more" than a best friend. In the reunion episode, Jillian tried to argue this point, rationally countering that relationships based on friendship are better and last longer. He concurred with the idea but wasn't feeling it. Jillian then pointed out that there was also a lot of sexual attraction between them, which was proven by the scenes we saw on TV, where he seemed to be humping her in the pool with skimpy bathing suits on. He conceded that, too, but wanted "more" than both friendship and sexuality. Jason didn't need to say what "more" was missing from the equation, assuming the audience understood this. After all, if someone tells us out here in reality that he feels we are a "friend," we usually get what that means. There's no use making a case for how wonderful we are or how good we would be together.

What is interesting about this disagreement is the way it exposes invisible contradictions in the muddled concept of contemporary romance. At this reunion, Jillian, later a Bachelorette herself in a no-less-unsuccessful attempt to find the One, was indignant, even angry, as though Jason were purposely avoiding the rationality of what she was saying. Isn't that what everyone wants, she seemed to argue, best-friendship with sex? He seemed befuddled because he agreed with her logic but just didn't want to be with her, and couldn't explain why. It's as though they were incoherent to each other, speaking two different languages of (modern) love: on the one hand, there is "chemistry," the necessary-but-not sufficient magic factor emphasizing sexuality, desire, and longing, with or without compatibility and admiration, which motivates the relationship, and on the other, there is rational, "mature" love that sustains a relationship, based on the friendship model. The combination of these in love is treated as a form of fate or mystery. And it is mysterious, though perhaps only in the sense that it isn't easy to articulate or explain in any coherent manner.

The view of love as mystery is a much older idea of romance; in fact, it was intrinsic to the broader traditional sense of "romance" and "romantic," which alluded to a fabled world of imagination rather than what is "realistic." But when love and marriage began to become more firmly cemented together (the proverbial "horse and carriage" in the Frank Sinatra song), the relational view of love rose to prominence, as befitting a personal bond of enormous societal importance. In the Victorian age, the older view of love was often disparaged as trivial, immature, and even dangerous, the heart leading the head to make bad (often in the sense of sexually loose) choices. Gradually, the compromise position emerged in the twentieth century and beyond, aided by enormous breakthroughs in the status of women's rights and the increasing modern value of sexuality.

An analogy is the compromise effected (more or less around the same time) in the division between evangelical Christian and scientific views of the origin of life: most Americans do not reject one account for the other but simply put them together in a theory of stages; that is, God begins the story, then evolution takes over, presumably with His approval and guidance. Similarly, the value we now put on sexual pleasure requires that we validate passion as the starter yeast for the long-term relationship, with the "meant to be" narrative guiding the tricky transition from mysterious passion to rational choice. If it doesn't go well . . . you guessed it: it wasn't meant to be, to use a phrase my students are enamored of, though it's never quite clear who or what meant it to come into being.[7]

One view in our contemporary culture is to see romantic love as a necessary but not sufficient condition for romance—it's possible to love the wrong person, but then you must rationally exert your will to "move on" so you can free yourself to love the "right" person, someone who can fulfill the social/personal role of partner. The mystery of it is how romance—with the proper person who feels exactly as you do and for whom you fulfill exactly the same role forevermore—will supposedly happen to everyone who is not selfish, undeveloped, or neurotic.

The modern idea of romantic love involves vaguely commingling the mystery of passion with the knowledge and control that allow enduring affection to thrive in a permanent and primary relationship. We blithely live with these paradoxical convictions: on the one hand, the prevailing wisdom is that you "have to work at relationships," while on the other, love relations are "meant to be" in some mysterious way. There are whole sackfuls of clichés that support each of these ideas. My sophisticated students will readily mouth both unquestioningly; oddly, they may sneer at "fate" as an overly romanticized causal explanation, yet say that a particular relationship was "not meant to be" to justify or console themselves after a breakup.

The usual way we reconcile these two discordant principles is to see them as *serially* true, which I call the "stages theory" of romantic love. That is, "first comes the passion," then a more "mature" version of romance, which will develop out of the first stage, and which will be permanent if the object is the One. In other words, the magic comes first, and that *enables* the rational relationship. Few of my students seem aware that historically this is a rather novel idea. I am not so cynical as to say this cannot and does not work—but what is odd and unlikely is that it's expected to *always* work that way, by its nature.

The initial stage is supposed to have features very much like passionate sexual desire: intense, spontaneous, inexplicable, beyond control. The "mature" second act is more akin to friendship, stressing liking, mutuality, compatibility, and loyalty, or as one male student put it:

> What I had [before] wasn't true love. It was only a continuous emotional eruption, an insatiable desire. What I have now is true love. I would do anything for my current girlfriend, to keep her happy, to keep her safe. . . . I love her in a healthy way that allows me to complete my school work, or have time on my own that I need. We support and supplement each other. The main difference between them [first love and this love] is that my current girlfriend is my best friend.[8]

The two stages are not obviously harmonious, yet the whole package is assumed to be there from the beginning in some way if it's "real." One can see how this concept developed: it makes sense that when romance became hooked onto marriage, it was necessary to reconceive it as the kind of feeling that enables relationship. But we moderns don't want to relinquish passion—it's a popular theme of our culture, as in "follow your passion"—so the much older rhetoric of transcendent emotion and intense sexuality has had to be incorporated into our larger social system of marriage and family.

This evolution has had varied effects on ideas about romance. Some believe in "passion that lasts a lifetime," as when my students speak of their eighty-year-old grandparents who are "madly in love." Others, including many critics and experts, denounce passion as illusory, deceptive, or detrimental. The latter often want to handle the problem by relabeling romance; for example, the critic bell hooks denounces the destructiveness of the notion "that we come to love with no will and no capacity to choose. This illusion . . . stands in the way of our learning how to love." Hooks endorses making a list of qualities we want to find in a mate, then evaluating our needs. Passion "can only ever be a preliminary stage in the process" to "perfect love," says hooks, since we have to "learn to love goodness, not good looks, good sex or what someone can give us."⁹ (Note the stages theory here.) Similarly, the self-described "realistic romance guru" Mary-Lou Galician vows to teach readers to "empower ourselves" to resist the unrealistic expectations of romance in the media, since what she calls "real love" takes time and "shared values." Yet she also claims that being "realistic" does *not* mean "forsaking romance." It's all about setting "achievable standards," she claims.¹⁰

On the other hand, passion has an elevated status in our culture only under certain circumstances, such as ambitious talent and sexual desire that leads to coupledom. Two contemporary writers, the critic Laura Kipnis and the essayist Cristina Nehring, have trenchantly critiqued our practice of romance as both overhyped and yet also hollow, lacking in real passion.¹¹

In sum, then, how do we count the ways to define romantic love? It's an emotion, sometimes overwhelming; a story we tell ourselves and others; a template for behavior; a particular idealized perspective; a kind of spectacle with social codes as interpretive frame. I believe romantic love, like all love, is embedded in the brain as well as the rest of the body, but I also view it as a social concept, one with immense personal meaning, as is the body itself. Love is experienced as feeling—or rather multiple feelings, physical, mental, and emotional—labeled within a belief system and positioned within a social system.

Another way to put this is that love is the private enactment of a public script we might call romance. An assumption of my approach to love is that it is never either just individual emotion or public institution; each informs the other to create meaning. Love performs, both socially and emotionally, a biological impulse that is at some times, in some places, switched on and then channeled into social expectations and forms. The author Daniel Harris illustrates this when he defines romance as "both a stage show put on for others and an anxious attempt to regain lost privacy as our love lives have become opportunities for public display of assets."¹² There is more than one line of thought, more than one dialogue here, from passion and domesticity to longing and dependence, or mutuality and selflessness. Our experiences and their public forums shape each other but also conflict.

The Story of Love

Out of that conflict comes story. Romantic love often appears as a story in our culture (and in others as well, of course), even when the narrative is more or less implied in music or image. But the story itself differs from era to era: for example, it may be a source of comfort or excitement; a gesture of rebellion (as in Jane Eyre's speech to Rochester when she falls in love) or stability (the conclusion of *Jane Eyre*: "Reader, I married him"); an embodiment of elitism (only for the beautiful and aristocratic) or a putative expression of democratic impulse (everyone is entitled to feel like a princess.)

If love is a feeling that may appear (and be) natural, and entirely individual, it's one that's also subject to the formulations that are available to us as *romantic*. Romance as genre implies conventional form and style, along with familiar patterns, such as surrender to fate, the heroic rescue of a threatened woman, the psychological rescue of a damaged man, or the tragic pursuit of someone just out of reach. But genre rules and proprieties can contain inconsistencies within them. For example, while our egalitarian idea of romantic love implies that everyone deserves and can get love, love stories present a different picture: the ones who are lovable and are loved (not necessarily the same) are also represented as a privileged class, to be imitated or at least envied.

The critic Jan Cohn, among others, has written about the way narrative encodes a fantasized victory over real social conditions.[13] To understand the genre of storied romance, one must have a historical sense of what those social conditions are. Narratives are *for* something: ideology is reaffirmed or subverted, a field of terms is renegotiated, or conceptual confusion is made to seem normal, universal, and unitary. Consuming a narrative is a social act, even if done in the privacy of one's bedroom or on the subway with a Kindle. To live in a culture is inescapably to live out the dreams of that culture, even in resistance.

In the mass-produced formula romance, the fears and anxieties surrounding love are allowed to surface in the plot as problems because the genre creates a safe space in which to present them, since the clues are eminently interpretable and the ending certain. The conventions, known to the largely female and heterosexual audience, set the rules of engagement, so to speak, in which the shape of the struggle between the lovers may be differentially marked by gender. For example, in much mass-market romance, power takes the form of the heroine's ability to (unconsciously) manipulate the hero's emotions, while for the male hero of a spy novel or action thriller, power is marked by physical dominance, whose shape is the gun.

Narrative operates through setting up a tension between stability and instability, with a drive to resolution. By definition it has form: a beginning, selective sequencing, human or humanlike characters, some type of closure. The conventions provide the means to understand and resolve a problem ("resolve" does not necessarily imply a happy ending) or name and remove an obstacle. The appeal of stories, from autobiography to classic novels to modern articles about celebrity romances, is that they put a frame around our lives. They organize our focus, make sense of who we think we are and what we think we're doing. Whether or not the story has a clear "message," we are attracted to its explanatory power, the ability to both elucidate and possibly elide what is troublesome.

The term "story" implies structure, words or images of specific bodies moving through events in time in a coherent way that conveys a generalized idea. When the internal logic of the famous "beginning, middle, and end" applies to what we call a "love story," we expect a couple, if not coupling, but this has taken a great variety of forms in various cultures and eras. This book is mainly concerned with a dominant narrative of romantic love that still reproduces Victorian ideologies in many ways, alongside new or even opposing features, as I hope to show.[14]

Some of the features of this master narrative are the following: gender is generally stressed as *opposite*, for the most part excluding all other forms of sexuality in romance (the bodies must fit together in certain prescribed ways); "love" is equal and requited or it isn't "real"; there is an obstacle to the lovers' mutuality, often tied to gender, such as the fictional male's unwillingness to commit or marry, his lack of communicativeness, or his uncontrolled sexuality; the story tends to end when the coupling (or recoupling) is achieved—or not. When that fails, the story is tragic; when it succeeds, it may be either romantic drama or comedy, and a bright future of permanent monogamy is always at least vaguely implied. In either case, the narrative's ending defines the "realness" of the romance.

Then, too, because the audience for these narratives is often assumed to be female, the point of view in the master narrative is typically that of a woman who desires, and/or is adored from afar and doesn't know it. She is a heroine, and her youth, beauty, complexion, and middle-class tastes and lifestyle are as important as her innate goodness to her pivotal role in the story. If any of these particular features deviates from the norm (and rarely does mass culture risk more than one deviation at a time), the difference is invoked as a "quirk" that is absorbed into the coherence of the whole. Take, for example, the movies by Nancy Meyers featuring older (but comfortingly youthful and lovely) actresses: Meyers's 2009 film *It's Complicated*, with its middle-aged, well-off heroine and her problem choosing between two men who pursue her, is actually not at all complicated: it's the same old, same old.

Why does romantic love lend itself particularly well to story? The great critic Fredric Jameson observed about romance that it offers a transitional and imaginary solution to ideological contradictions.[15] One might speculate that the love story has taken off exponentially in the age of media because it coincides with an age of increasing tensions in women's most personal ways of understanding ourselves in the world.

Love stories are popular in many media because we crave the sensation of extraordinary phenomena, but we also want the artifice of narrative, a shaping and selection that allows us to process "meaning" in a simplified way as "message"—that we are lucky or unlucky, or good or bad, that what happens is right or not. Love *as a story* fills in blanks and gaps, colors dark places, and creates deeper meaning. How we make sense of that "depth" and decide *what* is meaningful, however, is not as obvious as it might seem.

Women and Romantic Love

In love stories, how does the power dynamic of gender interact with the power of love?

Whether romantic love is a sweet and gentle or overwhelmingly intense feeling, a performance or a kind of relationship, a template, script, or story, it has come to be a major source of personal identity in Western culture. But though our contemporary concept of love insists that feeling must be completely mutual in a relationship, romance is particularly embedded in *women's* identity as a powerful marker of value. For many, it is as much a negative marker of worth as it is positive: in its absence, it shows who you are not.

My book focuses on a master narrative in Western culture that is based largely on Jane Austen and the Brontës. I must acknowledge here (so that I need not tediously repeat throughout) that "women" is a convenient category that elides the variety of bodies, sexualities, classes, and subcultures that identify with that category. Though I make frequent use of the term "woman" as a shortcut, my aim throughout is to critique the gender binary in hetero romance, in pop culture and elsewhere. It's important to remember that there is no one type of "woman" in actuality, but you would not necessarily know that from consuming our culture's representations of love.

But, it would be fair to object, men also fall in love, and they are a necessary part of heterosexual romance. Why attend mainly to women? And for that matter, why focus on hetero women? Don't gay men and lesbians love, too?

Of course they do. Men in love, as well as gay and lesbian romance, are all important. But the difficult questions for feminists have always concerned the relations between men and women: Is inequality built into heterosexual romantic relationships, or is love itself the answer to inequality? Why do women still seem to value romance more than men do (romantic movies, magazine articles, and mass fiction, not to mention the wedding industry, are all aimed at consumption by women, not men)? Is women's purported greater desire for romance oppressive or a difference to be celebrated? Because of this one-sidedness, I propose to narrow my subject to romance between a woman and a man. I would suggest there's an odd imbalance: women have made more progress in validating their sexuality as equal to men's than men have in altering the modern association of romantic love with femininity.

I do not focus on gay relationships simply because those aren't and never were a real problem for feminist ideology; on the contrary, for twentieth-century postwar feminists, lesbian love, both for its own sake and also as the subversion of traditional hetero romantic ideals, often seemed to embody the values of feminism in action. But the greater acceptance and celebration of lesbian and bisexual love have not resolved the old questions about relations between men and women. As the sociologist Gabriele Schafer has written, "It is in hetero love that the politics of gender and sexuality operate most clearly."[16]

Though evolutionary psychology claims a biological basis for gendered behavior in love (men must spread their sperm widely to ensure the propagation of the species, while women look for monogamous and stable paternity; men "love the chase" because they are natural hunters, while women tend the home fire), Western literary history tells a different tale, since in major texts before the near-modern age, most often it was men who behaved more "romantically" than women. In Chrétien de Troyes's classic twelfth-century poem about Lancelot and Guinevere, when Lancelot approaches his beloved's bed, for example, he bows "in adoration at the holiest relic he knew." As for Guinevere herself, we are told that "It was Love that moved her/ And she loved him truly, but he/ Loved her a hundred thousand/ Times more."[17]

If women's connection to romance from about the eighteenth century on was based on their historical dependency on marriage, it remains to explain why this association has persisted after the feminist revolution and women's increasing economic independence. The idea that women's "job" is love makes for an uncomfortable dynamic in modern society, after all, where the woman has to seduce emotionally but not chase, the man should initiate and pursue yet resist emotional commitment, the woman ought to be both assertive and self-reliant (modern) yet still self-sacrificing (her traditional role), and men must be coolly "masculine" (traditional) yet "sensitive" to her needs (modern). Many contemporary Western women want independence and freedom, including sexual freedom, but are understandably reluctant to give up the power and privileges that love promises in such an unsettled emotional economy.[18]

If modern-day love, with its peculiar combination of passion and rational work, implies both mystery *and* rational control in one package, this may be especially appealing to women, who have a good deal to gain in social value from being loved and desired in a romantic context.[19] This seems to many women a *literal* good deal when being sexual in a nonemotional context can still devalue them, perhaps more than ever because good girls are now expected to perform sexually in all sorts of display—dress, language, and behavior—in everyday life. In the romantic story, women find the means to maintain their "mystery" while controlling what they have on offer to determine their future.

The result is that a huge number of modern Anglo-American women, having gone through an influential feminist revolution that changed many of the terms of their lives, are still enthralled with the old story of romance.

THE STRUCTURE OF THE BOOK

The structure of this book was determined by my desire to cross the line between "serious" texts (such as classic novels in chapters 1 and 2) that contribute to a modern paradigm of romance and the serious understanding and enjoyment of popular culture in the Victorian and modern eras. I intend to look at some of the ways stories of romance operate as both works of imagination (chapters 3 through 9) and forms of "real life" (chapter 10). This requires not only the triangulation of romance in classic novels, popular culture, and actual lives but also an examination of the way the past is woven into the present, encompassing both traditional notions (Victorian fantasies about women's nature) and present concerns (a popularized and sanitized feminist view).

All of these versions of women, love, and story invade, explain, and reproduce each other. I chose my topics to demonstrate the symmetry of both fictional and nonfiction texts about women and romance in traditional society (Austen, Charlotte Brontë, Victorian magazine culture in chapters 1, 2, and 3) and modern society (mass-media romance in chapters 3 through 10). Some very hoary ideas about women and love weave unexpectedly through the most diverse materials, even those that loudly proclaim their modernity. The final chapter (chapter 10) looks at representations of romance as they appear both in Internet dating and on a TV dating program as a kind of reality show.

Is my focus on shifts in views and representations of women and romantic love or on their continuities? Even in the nineteenth century, Austen and Brontë differ radically on the role of sexual passion in defining romance, a major development in modern views of love, yet also share the wish to preserve the legitimation of love by linking romance with noble values and principles. On the other hand, while sexual passion as the basis of love in D. H. Lawrence's twentieth-century work seems to place him at the opposite end of the spectrum of modernization from Austen, both authors represent the reformation of society in the formation of the ideal couple, based on their individual ideology of gender and romance. Austen and Lawrence bookend a time of significant transition in the meaning of love and its relation to women, a change also reflected in the difference between Victorian and modern magazines (chapter 3).

Turning to our own time, I hope to show that modern popular culture works both sides of the street, as it were: progressive when it serves the purpose, reactionary when that is necessary to soothe and sell. Movies for women and young girls, the development of a gigantic popular romance novel industry, and even the relationship of pornography to romance illustrate the way modern romance serves specific audiences with meanings that evolve with changing times and new problems in power relations. My point is that this same mixture of the wish to conserve and the wish to modernize continues to be reflected in our own ambiguous definitions of romantic love. And so, to answer the question above, our contemporary views of romantic love are reflected in both continuities with and shifts away from the Victorian era in the stories we tell.

THE GLASS SLIPPER

Our society has such blurred and ambiguous messages about both feminism and romance that we tend not to look closely at their relationship, preferring the easy explanations of simple biological imperatives and the universal nature of love. The stories examined here have a different meaning for me: that modern culture has found a way to erase uncomfortable contradictions and smooth over anxieties in new retellings of Victorian ideas about women and love.

My project is to recover the basis of the long-standing appeal of romantic narrative as it appears to, and appeals to, modern women, as well as examine its hidden contradictions and disappointments. I am not interested in patronizing or scolding the reader for wanting to love and be loved; this book is not a polemic, and I am very sympathetic to these desires. But I do hope to make sense of romance in a different way, attempting to understand and mediate the conflict between women's right to pleasure, romantic as well as sexual, and the feminist imperative to change the social forces that shape that pleasure at the expense of other rights and powers.

In this book the narrative versions of what I call the Glass Slipper are taken as seriously as the Glass Ceiling, as we see how their representations of romantic love are meant to inform women's beliefs and goals. My own goal is not to shatter the Glass Slipper but to see through it.

1

THE ODD COUPLE

Mating Jane Austen with D. H. Lawrence

It is *the* problem of today, the establishment of a new relation, or the re-adjustment of the old one, between men and women.
—D. H. Lawrence, letter of May 2, 1913

On the surface, you'd be hard-pressed to find two major British authors at further poles than Regency-era girl-favorite novelist Jane Austen and metaphorically muscular twentieth-century writer D. H. Lawrence. The first is popularly associated with clichés of prim convention and the cozy comforts of traditional moral convictions, the second with outrageous (some would say obscene or pornographic) sexual rebellion. Surely imagining them as a matched pair in literary history is only an occasion of absurdity; it seems preposterous at first to compare them in any way other than as authors at odds in what they do with a love story.

Their differences are not only notorious but supposed to be obvious: first, Austen is quaint, while Lawrence is (or was at the time, or at least thought he was) daringly modern; second, where she was (arguably) conservative and concerned with convention, he was (arguably) radical in his views of social life. Furthermore, Austen's writing is both brilliantly humorous and decorous, while Lawrence manages to be serious, preachy, and bawdy all at once. We may sum all this up by saying that *she* seems to belong wholly to a genteel drawing room, while fans of Laurentian love tend to think of . . . Nature.

Surely the admirers of Austen and Lawrence treasure what is distinctive about their styles, which feature Lawrence's hypnotic repetition, gloomy pronouncements, and undulating passionate prose, resembling mutterings during lovemaking, versus Austen's precise and elegantly turned sentences. Put them against one another, and who wins? Austenites would point out that *her* way with language is graceful, polite, sane, and exacting, while Lawrence has always struck some readers as cranky, rude, wordy, and often downright nutty. Whereas *he* is schematic and didactic, they would insist, *she* is light and bright and charming. Austen's style, combining sharply honed observations of character and social mores with finely calibrated wit, has been much imitated. Yet detractors see Austen as often rigid and didactic in her prissy way, while Lawrence's prose can be quite beautiful and poetic, something rarely said of Austen. I will confess that I adore them both, different as they are, faults and all.

But let's face it, the difference in their reputations so often comes down to sex: the much-repeated eternal opposition of restrained manners and desiring body. It's all too easy to pit the pop image of Austen, eternal virgin and respectable maiden aunt ("Jane Austen, chaste and clear," said the critic Rachel Brownstein), against Lawrence, the sexy bohemian guy with his intense love affairs and quirky marriage. We think of *her* restraint and *his* passion, she as the bonneted and he as the unclothed. All that brings them together, seemingly, is the extremity of reactions they provoke: worshipped by fans and reviled by those whose cup of tea they most definitely are not. Famous among Austen-haters was Mark Twain, who made a classic jab ("Every time I read *Pride and Prejudice* I want to dig her up and beat her over the skull with her own shin-bone"), as did the feminist Kate Millett a hundred years later while taking down D. H. Lawrence ("the transformation of masculine ascendancy into a mystical religion").[1]

But for intellectual fun, I'm going to make a shotgun wedding between the two, metaphorically speaking, on the usual matchmaking grounds that though the reluctant couple may not like each other much—or even know each other at all—they are more compatible than may first appear. I am confident that love will emerge in the end . . . or at least their mutual interest in love. And I hope to show that, for all that they may seem to be polar opposites (which in popular wisdom attract), extremes of their super-feminine and weirdly phallic reputations, they are oddly alike in telling and sometimes ironic ways.

One improbable resemblance is that each author developed a reputation concerning love quite contrary to the real themes of his or her writing. Austen attracts those who are nostalgic for life in a supposedly simpler time, when romance seemed opposite to sex, and when being a lady protected women from what the author Ariel Levy calls the "raunch culture" of modern society. Yet where so-called Jane-ites value Austen for her reputed moral certainties and fine gentility, a deeper understanding of her work reveals a layer of radical ambivalence about the values underlying romantic decisions, connected to her critically ironic view of modern society. More about that later.

As for Lawrence, no one ever accused him of gentility, fine or otherwise, much less prissiness. Rather, he has been viewed by many as liberating and revolutionary, on one hand, and by others as conservative, even fascistic, on the other. In general, Lawrence seems to be a writer whom readers either love passionately for the splendor of his best prose and the honesty of his provocative ideas or find overblown, absurd, and annoying because of his tendency to preach his eccentric opinions when we want the character and plot development so beautifully rendered in an Austen novel. It is safe to say that few readers find him bland. But where Lawrence was condemned by detractors (and celebrated by admirers) for his out-of-bounds view of sexuality, I will try to make the case that his critique of love in modern society turns out to be something close to an updated version of Austen's.

What joins the two in our admittedly odd coupling is that both attempted to resolve the contradictions of their literary imaginations through their own narrative versions of the ideal romantic couple. While he is more interested in love than you might know, she is less of an enthusiast of romance than you might think. We might say that while they are very different, they are similarly misunderstood. Many a marital coupling has been formed on more foolish grounds.

Though not far apart geographically (she born in an eighteenth-century English village, he from a coal-mining town in the Midlands, about three hours away from Austen's birthplace ... by car), our two authors came from different classes in society, middle-class for Austen and working-class for Lawrence. This can be problematic in matchmaking, it's true, even putting aside the difference in ages (I am referring, of course, to the one hundred years that separate the authors). We need to know more about their backgrounds before we assess their chances for marital harmony.

JANE AUSTEN: THE BRIDE

The real Austen, who left little in the way of biographical material (no diary has ever been found, and most of her letters were destroyed), is not quite the Austen of the contemporary imagination. It's the latter version that is the basis of cultish fan enthusiasm, which constitutes what the critic Margaret Doody calls "Aunt Jane-ism." My students often call Austen by her first name in a way they wouldn't think of doing with other authors: they feel they "know" Austen rather personally. Yet for a novelist so identified with romantic love, courtship, and marriage as literary subjects, Austen's life is notoriously bare of actual evidence that she experienced love or romance (there is no lack of copious speculation, of course, including a film about this very topic). In fact, her life was probably quite different than that imagined in the popular mind.

Austen has such enduring appeal that it is fair to ask why the writing of an unfashionable woman who rarely traveled and wrote mainly about local domestic and village life at the turn of the nineteenth century has remained so beloved. Some readers are clearly attracted by the difference between her world and ours, the depiction of a society that is not yet fully modern. It seems important that the Austenian world operates by the ground rules of traditional conventions, including those accorded by gender, though characters do break these rules from time to time (as when Elizabeth Bennett's sister Lydia runs away with her lover in *Pride and Prejudice*).

For many the novels have come to satisfy the yearning for an imaginary pre–Industrial Revolution England, an idyll of country houses, gentrified manners, and old-fashioned values. Clear moral standards signify an Old World apart from the chaos of our urban, electronic living and the struggle for modern capital. In today's confusing buzz of technological life, dominated by uncertainty, mass-market values, and the uneven breakdown of traditional gender roles, Austen's fictional cosmos seems to have the pull of sentiment for a life we think we would have liked, safe and comforting but also charming rather than tedious compared to our own. Many fans think of an Austen novel as one where nothing very bad ever happens, that is, nothing worse than the anxiety that a woman will not marry a man she loves; this is, to be sure, the very element that turns off her detractors.[2]

It is easy to see why Austen's novels have become a kind of cinematic fetish: film adaptations selectively focus on the clear trajectory of the courtship plot, the fine detail of a tightly enclosed, knowable, historical but seemingly apolitical world in which everyone seems to know his place. So solidified has this mythos become that there is a popular series of mystery novels by Stephanie Barron featuring Jane Austen as the amateur detective, patterned on Agatha Christie's spinster figure Miss Marple, solving fictional mysteries with pert wit and ingenuity in her quaint village, and in a 2011 novel by the esteemed mystery writer P. D. James, Elizabeth Bennet solves a murder at Pemberley. It is, frankly, a mystery to me why so many want Austen or her heroine-avatar to solve mysteries. More recently, Austen zombie novels became a publishing phenomenon, popular among my students, a kind of backlash to the hyping of Austen's propriety.[3]

Into this delightfully picturesque vision of genteel ways and village days, the imagined life of Austen was molded to perfection from the first published biographical sketch by her brother Henry Austen, emphasizing Austen's modesty, sweetness, and simple piety. Though concrete evidence for what Jane Austen was really like may be slim, the publication in the twentieth century of her early fiction and the letters that survived has revealed surprising layers that do not fit comfortably with the proper image that stubbornly persists. The short early pieces she wrote, dedicated to various family members and probably read aloud, are absurd, extravagant, and flippant in tone, rather than modest and moral. Just as the Brontës' juvenilia were melodramatic and hyper-romantic, Austen's earliest efforts at fiction surprise with the antisocial liberties taken.

Austen's letters, sharp-tongued and acerbic like the early fiction, shocked and even offended some readers when they were first published. Her nephew, writing before the publication of his memoir, cautioned that their "materials may be thought inferior" because they "treat only the details of domestic life. They resemble the nest which some little bird builds of the materials nearest at hand."

But actually they are filled with harsh, pointed, and dark wit: she calls someone a "queer animal with a white neck"; she writes that she "had the comfort of finding out the other evening who all the fat girls with short noses were that disturbed me" (letter of November 20, 1800).

Rather than Fanny Price's or Anne Elliot's "gentle manner" and "elegant mind" here, or the prissy, quaint, modest, humble Aunt Jane of the myth, the letters reveal a voice that does not shy away from the harsh realities of sexual and social life: "Another stupid party last night," comments Austen to her only sister and beloved confidante, Cassandra. And while at the "stupid party," she observes: "I am proud to say that I have a very good eye at an Adultress, for tho' repeatedly assured that another in the same party was the *She*, I fixed upon the right one from the first. . . . She is not so pretty as I expected; her face has the same defect of baldness as her sister's . . . ;—she was highly rouged, & looked rather quietly and contentedly silly than anything else" (letter of May 12, 1801).

This is hardly the Jane who would rather put on a servant's uniform than describe an actual kiss. Actually, she'd do very well as the smart-mouthed but good-at-heart best friend in a modern romantic comedy.

D. H. LAWRENCE: THE GROOM

By contrast, D. H. Lawrence, about a hundred years later, had an active, though not altogether satisfying, love life from an early age. You might assume, in light of his reputation for rebellious (if not obscene) fiction, that Lawrence was probably a merry sexual prankster, but in 1912 he encountered the woman he was to love and with whom he was to remain in marriage, however stormy, for life. Frieda von Richthofen, a distant cousin of the famous German World War I flying ace Baron von Richthofen, came from an aristocratic German family and was married with children when she and Lawrence began a passionate affair. In a startlingly short time, they eloped at Lawrence's insistence. In a way he was very like a romantic hero, ready to be transformed by love.

Lawrence really did begin a new life with Frieda, finally leaving England for Europe and other places abroad until his death. With Frieda at his side, Lawrence felt that he loved and was loved for the first time. Of Frieda, he wrote, "At any rate, and whatever happens, I do love and I am loved—I have given and I have taken—and that is eternal" (letter of August 19, 1912). His life with Frieda was the start of an extremely prolific period for Lawrence, who had found his subject: "The work is of me, and her, and it is beautiful," he wrote (letter of April 3, 1914). His marriage to Frieda was a dramatic one, filled with sometimes violent arguments, occasional separations, and a few infidelities, but it was also his emotional core and anchor. Though she often threatened to leave him, they never remained apart for long. "If I die, nothing has mattered but you, nothing at all," he said to Frieda near the end of his restless life.[4]

Lawrence's marriage to Frieda coincided with his developing the fictions that would eventually become *The Rainbow* and *Women in Love*, two of his master-pieces. However, his new confidence and radical experimentation with the sub-ject of sex got him in trouble with censors and resulted in denunciations that shadowed him the rest of his life. *The Rainbow*, published in 1915, was almost im-mediately banned in Britain, and the publisher was prosecuted under the 1857 Obscene Publications Act. Though D. H. Lawrence was always held in high criti-cal esteem by some, popular reviewers were as hostile as the law was: "There is no form of viciousness . . . that is not reflected in these pages," wrote the respected critic Clement Shorter of *The Rainbow*. "This whole book is an orgie of sexiness."[5]

PERSUASION AND *LADY CHATTERLEY'S LOVER*: THE TEST

Sometimes a prospective pair comes to a matchmaking attempt with children of their own. Taking a close look at a potential mate's child can tell you a great deal about the values and true nature of the intended fiancé. And if you arrange a play-date, you can see how well the children will mesh together, and that can be a crucial trial before concluding the union. To see the important similarities and differences between Austen and Lawrence, we have only to compare their last novels, Austen's *Persuasion* and Lawrence's *Lady Chatterley's Lover*, as love stories. Both works were created near the end of the author's life: Austen completed *Persuasion* but died be-fore it could be published (it came out a year later, in 1818), while Lawrence saw the publication of *Lady Chatterley* in 1928, only two years before his death in 1930.

Just as Austen is the favorite author of many discerning readers, *Persuasion* is the most highly respected novel of many Austenites. *Persuasion* is a type of novel we are very familiar with in the modern age: that is, it is a book about a young, unmar-ried woman, following the ups and downs of a courtship (here a courtship for the second time by a previously rejected suitor) and ending with the heroine's happy marriage. But unusually, *Persuasion* begins with loss, both emotional and financial, and slowly reverses the trajectory toward a renewal of romantic spirit.

Lady Chatterley's Lover, on the other hand, traces the evolution of a married heroine through her affair with a working-class hero. To be sure, the novel is a particularly vibrant example of what is both valuable *and* grating in reading Law-rence. He certainly can sound cranky and peevish when we contemplate the long list of what he indicts in the novel: movies, children singing, militarism, mastur-bation, promiscuity, public schools, motorbikes, very sociable people, and mod-ern art, among much else. He can be ridiculous in his fulminations about orgas-mic surrender for females and the exaltation of the phallus, and very odd indeed with ideas like his scheme for workingmen to wear scarlet trousers so they will attract women and think less of money. Yet as a serious work of fiction, the novel is in some ways astonishing. *Lady Chatterley's Lover* memorably embodies its large theme of regeneration in an unconventional (for its time) story of sexual love that reflects the way real men and women behave, in contrast to ideal depictions of romance in the Victorian novels that preceded it in the hundred years after Austen's *Persuasion*.

Yes, the difference is startling: Lawrence's novel centers on an adulterous affair, a situation that rarely rears its head anywhere in Austen's fiction (in spite of her interest in finding adulteresses at parties, as we have seen). And sexuality is described in some detail in *Lady Chatterley's Lover*, whereas even chaste embraces are not on Austen's textual radar. But isn't this just another way of saying that Lawrence is modern and Austen is not? Though sex is an obvious distinction, it is not just as a contrast in presence or absence. On the contrary, though Austen and Lawrence came to quite opposite conclusions about the relation between sex and love, their imaginative attempts to redefine love unite them.

The Ancestral Home

Where the bride's and groom's families reside tells us much about who they are and what they bring to the match. A great house is prominent in both Austen's *Persuasion* and Lawrence's *Lady Chatterley's Lover*, marking their heroines' class status and the telling problems accompanying it. Both novels trace the heroines' movement away from that house to new and contrastive dwellings as the trajectory of their psychological journey.

In *Persuasion*, the ancestral manor house that is the symbol as well as source of Anne Elliot's family wealth and privilege must be "let" because of financial troubles. Anne, her father, and her sister must separate from it but not entirely give it up, a condition that has metaphorical significance for Austen's view of class. At this point the heroine (along with her family) enters a kind of limbo in which she is a wanderer from the ancestral estate, privileged by birth but with a social and economic identity whose worth is uncertain and in flux. Though she is well-born, Anne's future will be determined by her value in the marriage market.

Constance Chatterley, heroine of Lawrence's last novel, resides, by contrast, in the great house her husband has inherited, a privilege that has become a prison. She has already made a "good" marriage, yet she feels disconnected and "restless." While Anne Elliot leaves her ancestral home reluctantly, and without a husband, a step that will lead her toward marriage, Connie Chatterley leaves her husband's ancestral home willingly. And that is the crux of the matter for each.

Becoming a Heroine

Modern as D. H. Lawrence's novel is in contrast to Jane Austen's, there is an unexpected connection between the heroines of their final novels. We might say that Austen's Anne, like Lawrence's Connie, is a kind of poor little rich girl. Not coincidentally, both Anne, daughter of a baronet, and Connie, who has married up to become Lady Chatterley, are upper-class yet neglected and unhappy (Anne is said to suffer from a "loss of bloom and spirits"). One way to approach the two novels is to look at the romantic tension that arises from the same paradoxical situation in each, where material comfort and emotional deprivation go together.

While one heroine is married and one is not, both *Persuasion* and *Lady Chatterley's Lover* center on the consciousness of a woman, still young but no longer inexperienced in romance, on the cusp of finding "real" love. The question in both novels is what we should consider "real," and how we are to know that.

Both our heroines are neglected and deprived in a sense, but Austen's Anne is hardly a Cinderella figure, and not only because she is well-born, of a better social rank than even the heroine of Austen's *Emma*. Though she belongs by "blood" to the elite class, Anne Elliot has more in common with Charlotte Brontë's Victorian heroine Jane Eyre in that she seems at first distinctly ineligible for the role of beloved, appearing to the world as apparently unlovable and without much physical charm. Anne, however, has none of Jane Eyre's ready temper, tongue, and fire; she tends to think and feel alone and in silence—except, of course, that we, her readers, share the literary mind she inhabits and see the world with her through her discerning eyes. Unlike so many girls in love stories, Austen's heroines are never just pretty young stick figures. They are appealing because of their intelligence, good sense, and decency, and often their verbal fluency and wit as well. In *Persuasion*, no other female character comes close to Anne Elliot, though Anne is one of the quietest of Austen's heroines.

Just as Austen's heroine is unlike those in the conventional romance of her time, the reader should also appreciate how different Lawrence's Lady Chatterley is from the conventional heroine of the nineteenth century. Connie, unlike Anne, is not particularly virtuous, selfless, or humble. Neither is she silent, nor at all modest and virginal. Lawrence describes early in the novel how, before her marriage to Clifford, the youthful Connie and her forward-thinking compatriots "took the sex-thrill as a sensation," using sex as a means to assert their will with their lovers. What a difference a mere century makes!

But here Lawrence demonstrates the contradictions of power relations in sex: though the young Connie and her circle see themselves as liberated from traditional notions of virginity, the act of sex itself is not sexy when the woman sees it in the old gendered terms of having something to "give" the man rather than experiencing it as her own deep desire. Connie attains a certain sense of dominance over the men who "insisted on the sex thing like dogs," but she shortchanges herself in remaining "free" of real feeling. Though sexuality plays an overt and important role in *Lady Chatterley's Lover*, unacknowledged desire is as much a problem for Connie as it was for Anne. And the stifling of their desires has a great deal to do with their position as "ladies" in their respective social contexts.

Then There Is the Hero

Not only are the heroines of Austen's and Lawrence's last novels both emotionally neglected rich girls, both their lovers are from a lower class. However,

Anne's suitor, Captain Wentworth, is a rising naval officer, not working-class like Connie's Oliver Mellors. The impossibility of imagining the pairing of a lady and a lower-class male in an Austen novel shows what made Lawrence a radical in his time. This similarity in the two heroines' beloveds is not just a random coincidence of plot point; it's the striking disparity in social and economic standing of hero and heroine that fuels the development of romance and the themes of each novel, opening a different world of possibilities and viewpoints to each of our heroines.

Anne's father, Sir Walter, is seen as a failure because his rank and privilege, to which he is entitled by inheritance, ought to be accompanied by responsibility to his estate and family. Austen generally tends to favor character over rank, especially in her heroine's eventual husband, but she also prefers the traditional and stable elements of society to its vulgar upstarts. On the other hand, the navy interested Austen as a place where young men could advance on merit and ability rather than on inherited privilege, as did her own brothers.

The proposed marriage of Anne and Wentworth implies a rejection of the traditional principles of stable and universal hierarchy, since Wentworth is, in that perspective, "a young man, who had nothing but himself to recommend him, and no hopes of attaining affluence, but in the chances of a most uncertain profession, and no connexions to secure even his farther rise in that profession."[6] This is why Anne's mentor, Lady Russell, has dissuaded her from marrying him before the novel opens (thus the title). Wentworth is the upwardly mobile talented young man of the nineteenth century, "full of fire and ardour" (22). He has only his own resources rather than privilege to fall back on, yet he is confident and proud.

By the time the hero and heroine meet again, Wentworth has done well for himself by earning "prizes," money gained from conquering enemy ships during war and selling their booty, and therefore has advanced by individual merit. The task of the hero, and the heroine who chooses him as husband, is to integrate solid social rank with character based on principles and family values. The critic Juliet McMaster has called these heroes "moral aristocrats."[7] This is not unlike the class difference harmonized with the superiority of middle-class character that we love in Austen's *Pride and Prejudice*.

The famous love affair between Lady Chatterley and her gamekeeper also crossed class lines, skipping over the middle class and joining together aristocracy and working class in an intimacy meant to threaten traditional sanctified hierarchies. This sexual union became so famous that "the lady and the gamekeeper" has become a kind of joke or cliché in modern literary culture. But Lawrence's hero, Mellors, unlike Austen's Wentworth, is *not* determinedly upwardly mobile. To the contrary, we are told Mellors deliberately left the army, where he had been rising in position through merit in a way parallel to Wentworth, to take up a working life doing physical labor. Where Connie's husband (like all his circle, and her first extramarital lover, Michaelis) is all talk, performed in front of company for ego and social power, Mellors tends to be silent and alone; where Michaelis is mannered, peevish, and graspingly ambitious for praise, fame, and acceptance by the wealthy set, the gamekeeper renounces common ambition to be simply and authoritatively himself, outside society.

Connie's lover Mellors, of course, contrasts sharply with her husband, Clifford Chatterley, a wealthy landowner and industrialist who was terribly wounded in World War I and is now paralyzed "from the hips down." Clifford's paralysis not only symbolizes the lack of sexuality in the marriage, it also mirrors the emotional paralysis in Connie's life. Exactly at the point where Connie feels most "meaningless," and just as Clifford announces that the "real secret of marriage" is not sex but commitment, Mellors is introduced into the novel. Lawrence has Mellors say "to himself" as he "went into her," "I stand for the touch of bodily awareness between human beings, and the touch of tenderness. And it is a battle against the money, and the machine, and the insentient ideal monkeyishness of the world."[8] (He is quite fluent in his private thoughts during intercourse, apparently.)

Connie's choice of sexual passion with Mellors over traditional marriage, money, estate, privilege, and gendered virtue is comparable to Catherine's preference for Heathcliff over her husband, Edgar, in Emily Brontë's *Wuthering Heights*, where Heathcliff stands for all that is dark and instinctual. But it is also utterly different, since in *Wuthering Heights* those dark and primal impulses are also potentially (and potently) destructive, antisocial, and violent. To put it another way, we might say that Lawrence wants to rewrite Emily Brontë. In *Lady Chatterley's Lover*, Connie's choice is a rejection of lifelessness and a regeneration into a truer and more vital selfhood.

Why the Couple Quarrel

Though both Austen and Lawrence forefront the question of class through the medium of the love story, the differences do run deep. Austen is critical of the class system but wants to maintain it; that is to say, she wants to buttress it with better, more humanistic foundations. For Austen, a marriageable girl should not focus on trying to be a lady, but it is a truth universally acknowledged that there *must be* ladies, after all. A Jane Austen novel proposes a new system of signs of superiority that rework fundamental social and religious categories such as duty and obedience, but in doing so are meant to support them. Speaking of the conventional social obstacles, the traditional privileges of class and gender that stood in the way of what she called "the play of spirit" in Austen's life, Virginia Woolf remarked insightfully about Austen, "She believes in them as well as laughs at them."

It isn't too far off to say that Lawrence's working-class hero, who challenges social hierarchies through illicit sex, is the very thing Austen avoids and fears. In *Pride and Prejudice*, when Darcy is offended by Elizabeth's initial rejection of his marriage proposal, he says to her, angrily but not irrationally, "Am I supposed to rejoice in your connexions?" Given the assumptions that we see in Austen's novel, it is very rude to say this aloud, but not really unreasonable to feel it. Austen has made it clear that most of Elizabeth's "connexions" are quite unbearably vulgar, after all. Lawrence, however, rejoices in his gamekeeper's social class (though it's carefully noted that Mellors reads extensively, not unlike Lawrence himself), while Connie's husband appears to be an upper-class ass (though sometimes so clueless as to be pathetic and even sympathetic).

Then, too, whatever would Austen have made of this loving declaration of Lawrence's hero to the heroine: "Tha'rt real, tha art! Tha'rt real, even a bit of a bitch. Here tha shits an' here tha pisses; an' I lay my hand on 'em both an' like thee for it" (240)?

Love Blooms

Comparing these authors of tales about love shows not only the radical contrast between Austen's society and Lawrence's but, more specifically, what was going to happen to love in the twentieth century and beyond. Austen sculpted the iconic fictional girl-in-love for the next two hundred years, while Lawrence smashed it, yet oddly, their methods are parallel: both enlist the love story as a way to carry the burden of their social and moral critiques of a world on the cusp of a revolution in manner and morals. Jane Austen laments the loss of traditional values in a modernizing society, and is therefore suspicious of romance as the sexual, self-interested element of desire that detracts from "true" love; D. H. Lawrence decries the alienation in modern relationships, and so rejects romance because he associates it with our contemporary "sex in the head," a rejection of the body.

Tellingly, Lawrence is careful to avoid the common use of the word "love," and the affair between Connie and Mellors is surprisingly lacking in teary or mushy emotionalism. He finds modern romance, like modern casual sex, self-consciously fashionable and pretentious, as opposed to the truth of what in his *Psychoanalysis and the Unconscious* (1921) he calls "blood-consciousness," or the "natural riches of desire." Because he sees love in popular media as mere "sentiment," as opposed to "real" love, which encompasses both fleshly passion and emotion, he avoids conventional romance altogether as tainted. The authority of feeling in *Lady Chatterley's Lover* requires that it refuse to rest on given social practices and language, that it be grounded in the material reality of bodily desire and connection. A novelist, Lawrence insisted in his essay "Morality and the Novel," should truthfully portray the "oscillating, unestablished balance between two people," not interfere with their relations by adding "sweetness."[9]

In Austen's defense, however, her "sweetness" is not sentimentality, however much readers sentimentalize her. Austen, like Lawrence, does not make much use of the conventional language of feeling and often finds its pretenses delightfully absurd. Her novel *Sense and Sensibility* parodies the trendy value of sentimental rhetoric in her time, for example. Rather, Austen's intention is to examine how character development shapes love and how, in turn, love shapes character development. As in all of Austen's novels, the characters must understand themselves before they earn the privilege of loving, but they also learn *through* love who they are in a deeper sense than their social identities can provide them. While Austen heroines are (more or less) physically attractive, they use their wits first to overcome their problems. Though Austen is often cited as the template for mass-produced romance, love is not something that happens magically, as in Harlequin romances. We see why a heroine deserves to be loved rather than being told she is.

In *Persuasion*, as so often in Austen's work, "prudence" (often the wisdom of going by the rules of the privileged class) comes up against the egalitarian progressive ethos of meritocracy, identified with "romance" and its transformative capacities and possibilities. The heroine's traditional solution to a classic problem of the novel, the conflict between categories one may also call "community" and "individual," is mutual love with a worthy man. Through this legitimation of her personal feeling, the heroine's worth is recognized, her social status established, and her economic future as middle-class or better secured.

In *Lady Chatterley*, the relations between Connie Chatterley and Oliver Mellors are certainly idealized, but they are not moralized, or even resolved in the old way. The reader feels a new turn has been taken in the depiction of human relations in the novel, a turn that is distinctly modern in its new vision of class relations and in its willingness to challenge the state of modern culture. Lawrence saw himself as a poet of *real* feeling, which he identifies with the working-class hero in *Lady Chatterley's Lover*. In fact, Lawrence has Connie think about how "the novel, properly handled," can "reveal the most secret places of life: for it is in the *passional* secret places of life, above all, that the tide of sensitive awareness needs to ebb and flow, cleansing and freshening" (108). Aside from the sentimental or conventional, Lawrence once observed, "We have no language for the feelings."[10]

To some in the reading public, D. H. Lawrence's "language of feeling" was vulgar pornography; to others, he was an apostle of sexual liberation. It is interesting and ironic to note, therefore, that the early working title of *Lady Chatterley's Lover* was *Tenderness*. Lawrence was indignant and disgusted by the public misunderstanding of his intentions, for he loathed casual sex or promiscuity, but he was also not an advocate of what he called "modern" romantic love. "Love is chiefly bunk," he wrote in 1925 to his friend Dorothy Brett, "an over-exaggeration of the spiritual and individualistic and analytic side. . . . If ever you can marry a man feeling *kindly* towards him, and knowing he feels kindly to you, do it, and throw love after."

Certainly the early title suggests that Lawrence meant his final novel to be a story of real tenderness, but he also intended to write about a different sort of love affair than can be found in literary history. Unlike in the European novel, which is rich in tales of adultery (as in *The Red and the Black*, *Madame Bovary*, and *Anna Karenina*), romantic love in the nineteenth-century British novel either tends to lead to marriage or is destroyed because of illegitimate sexual activity. But in Lawrence's last novel something new is going on, a new look at the cultural values by which we live: Lawrence's characters are healed by their forbidden sexual love, rather than destroyed by it.

Marriage: Cold Feet

Confidence in marriage as a solution to problems of class and gender is an obvious wedge between our couple. The central role of the courtship plot for Jane Austen is just what D. H. Lawrence despised; Austen has faith in the institution of marriage, and Lawrence wants to shatter its rigidified conventions.

In Austen's novels, not only is the love story legitimized by the social quest for marriage, but the selection of a mate is a test of personal worth and character—it matters what people think and how the couple will live on their income. Yet marriage itself is not really "romantic" in an Austen novel: her depictions of mutual avowals of love or of the proposal scene, the highlights of both the traditional courtship novel and the modern category romance, are either absent or given short shrift.[11] She mostly isn't interested. Marianne, one of the heroines of *Sense and Sensibility*, marries happily at its conclusion with "no sentiment superior to strong esteem and lively friendship" for her future husband. The language of romance is generally avoided when it comes to the point in an Austen novel: "If I loved you less, I might be able to talk about it more," says Knightley when he proposes to Emma in the novel that bears her name, a rationale that may appear to the modern reader as convenient evasion; for Emma's part, we are told, "She could really say nothing."

In fact, it is questionable whether Austen herself desired or even admired marriage: "Oh what a loss it will be when you are married," she wrote to her favorite niece, Fanny. "You are too agreeable in your single state, too agreeable as a Niece. I shall hate you when your delicious play of Mind is all settled down into conjugal & maternal affections" (letter of February 20, 1817). There are remarkably few successful marriages in her novels, not counting the hero and heroine's marriage, which rarely gets more than a skimpy paragraph or two at the end. Austen doesn't *describe* marriage as often as she *prescribes* it.

In *Persuasion*, the hero's relatives the Crofts, who are a rare happy couple in Austen's works, cheerfully admit they married without knowing each other well. Their mutual devotion is based on companionship and "open, easy and decided" manners, which is to say neither cultivated nor proud but rather frank and honest. Mrs. Croft, Captain Wentworth's sister, castigates her brother because he speaks as if women "were all fine ladies, instead of rational creatures [who don't] expect to be in smooth water all our days" (60). The point is that Mrs. Croft was a woman willing to exert herself and bear discomfort as a captain's wife living aboard a ship rather than aim for the social status of the privileged fine lady.[12] The Crofts admit they decided to marry quickly, she for his character (meaning virtue) and he for her beauty. "And what were we to wait for besides?" they say, emphasizing the naturalness implied by the simplicity of it. The Crofts' contented marriage is not really "romantic" in the modern sense; their union is more like a happy combination and rational balance of pleasant attraction, good sense, and good character.

As for Lawrence's view, we can turn to the moment in *Lady Chatterley's Lover* when Connie has a liberating sense of ditching a marriage, and with it a whole social system that has lost its reason for being: planning to leave Clifford at last, she is thrilled to "feel bonds snap" (252). Institutions that Austen believed in wholly no longer work in Lawrence's novels. For Jane Austen, a good marriage is the end of the novel and the beginning of an ideal, an emblem of the way we ought to live now. For D. H. Lawrence, neither love nor marriage provides an easy answer, but especially not marriage: the struggle between lovers goes on with or without marriage (as did his own), and the struggle itself, rather than a condition to be resolved, embodies the richness of the passionate life.

A NEW KIND OF LOVING

In spite of radical differences surrounding sex and marriage, what weds our pair, Jane Austen and D. H. Lawrence, is that love and sex, by their presence or absence, carry the burden of a vision of how we ought to be. *Persuasion* and *Lady Chatterley's Lover* are both novels of love whose plots about the ups and downs (in Austen's case) and ins and outs (in Lawrence's) of love affairs are intertwined with important social commentary and moral problem solving. In the end the love stories in these novels present competing forms of value, including above all the relative value (and price) of romantic, passionate, or sexual feeling in its modern setting.

In *Persuasion*, the heroine, Anne Elliot, must choose between her desire for her lover and the traditional order of moral rules that govern a woman's life, including respect for and obedience to authority, represented by Lady Russell. The debate about feeling and reason as the source of moral values in the Enlightenment (mid- to late eighteenth century) and the Romantic era (late eighteenth through the early nineteenth century in Britain), were current and pressing in Austen's time.[13] At some points Austen seems to favor the primacy of emotions, since the novel validates Anne's early intuitions about Captain Wentworth's value, but then Anne ultimately affirms the supremacy of prudence and rational wisdom in Lady Russell's advice not to marry him. Feeling and reason are not depicted as easy to define and separate, much less choose between; in the end her hero and heroine must partake of both. In this ongoing social dialogue, Austen was not so much a groundbreaker as a seeker after principles that could ground us in tradition while upholding humane values in daily life and personal relationships.

As *Persuasion* brings the lovers together in its final chapters, their reunion is said to be better than their first courtship because it is "fixed in knowledge of each other's character, truth and attachment"—in other words, like the marriage of the Crofts, in realism rather than runaway emotion, which makes them "more justified in acting" (215). Wentworth has had to overcome his resentment at his beloved's dutiful obedience to the social view of prudence, while Anne has had to learn to value the truth of her own feelings. Anne and her lover overcome the split between mind and heart by splitting the difference in their views.

Startlingly to a modern reader, though, Anne then tells Wentworth that she was "right in submitting" to Lady Russell *even though her advice was wrong*. This is because it's especially a woman's duty to submit to authority. So Anne—and Austen—come down squarely on the traditional side after all, trusting in providence to make it all come out right, the "event" (consequence), she says, deciding the rightness of judgment. The lovers have their way in getting Anne's family's approval for their marriage, based on "maturity" and "right" feeling—but also, not incidentally, on their "independence of fortune." Rather than posed in opposition as in the beginning, the confluence of love and suitable social and economic capital is Anne's reward at last, a template for the conclusion of romance in the centuries following.

Persuasion is on its surface yet another "voyage of discovery," the story of a woman fully arriving as an adult through marriage: by the novel's conclusion, Anne Elliot has acquired competence in the psychology of love and mastery of its fit into the moral and social worlds. In this context, what does the title *Persuasion* mean? Lady Russell gives both good and bad advice in her early act of persuasion: good in that it is based on tenderness and authority, bad in that it is motivated by class pride rather than true feeling. But this seems to raise the question: How, then, does one know what "true" feeling is (presumably as opposed to egoistic feeling)? How does this help us to conciliate modernity with tradition, to reconcile the authority of individual desire with the authority of systems, to classify the classifiers? It is a radically modern question—as Captain Wentworth is a modern hero and the heroine's marriage will be a modern marriage—and the question itself is left unresolved to a surprising degree.

Those who are attracted to Jane Austen because of their longing for the stability of class and clarity of old-fashioned values in picturesque English villages overlook this most profound theme in her writing. Celebrated for simplicity, quaintness, and old-fashioned certainties, Austen in her last novel turns out to be complicated, thorny, and, most of all, anxiously uncertain about the world developing around her.

D. H. Lawrence, writing a hundred years later, asks many of the same questions as Austen but is perhaps more sure of the answer. In a way *Lady Chatterley's Lover* is the quintessential modern novel because it is grounded in disgust with tradition. Like Austen's Anne Elliot, Lawrence's heroine, Connie Chatterley, also learns how to read morality and society through the comparison of two men, this time her husband and her lover. But in *Lady Chatterley's Lover* in particular, Lawrence wanted to do something pointedly different. For better or worse, his treatment of the fictional theme of transgressive "tenderness" became fraught with the burden of a new meaning he wanted to place on it, a kind of morality of love free of conventions and religious prohibitions. This rebellion is not simply one of individual freedom; Lawrence embedded in *Lady Chatterley's Lover* the meanings of sexual love and class conflict in a kind of war against our "civilization" as he had come to understand that term. His story is intended to give us a vision of a new morality based on the natural potentials of free individuals, a hero and heroine who loose themselves from traditions that, for Lawrence, freeze us and separate us from ourselves and one another.

Lawrence wanted to substitute a different mode of employing plot and character than that of the romances that had become conventional since Austen. Further, he saw the novel as a kind of weapon against a peculiarly modern development: the social alienation from our bodies and the pleasures of the senses that he viewed as the direct result of a soulless industrialism, the spirit of the principles of possessiveness and commercialism. Because Lawrence believed that we in modern society have lost our way in the great rush to wealth, social status, and ambition, giving up the pleasures of the body and of the natural world, he wanted to restore the passion that he saw as our birthright.

In spite of the treatment of gender in his fiction that has infuriated some feminist critics, Lawrence was by no means interested in the conservative project of returning to Victorian ways of thinking.[14] He complained that *both* men and women rely more and more on what he called "mechanized" civilization. This phrase does not only refer to commercialism in economic life or technology in industrial life; it refers as well to the way we treat our bodies. Sex, he argued, was no longer sexy. Instead, in the new "liberated" age of promiscuity and casual encounters, sexuality is less and less connected to who we really are and has become more and more a kind of performance that we "flaunt" (to use his word). The dead values of past customs and doctrines and the alienating effects of egoistic ambition are aligned against the spontaneous, deeply human life of feeling, for which sexual feeling stands as a trope.

Many critics and readers reacted with disgust and condemnation, to say the least, at the language and details of sexual description in his last novel. Outside the secret world of pornography, no book had described eroticism in such explicit terms, and Lawrence was vilified by critics who called the work obscene and immoral. To his fury, *Lady Chatterley's Lover* was banned in both Britain and the United States. After his death some critics mounted a defense of Lawrence as a serious and revolutionary artist, and after Penguin Books challenged the ban by publishing an unexpurgated edition of the novel in 1960, the laws of obscenity were themselves challenged in a landmark case. In his lifetime, however,

Lawrence was less interested in setting legal precedents than in revising the meaning of sexuality in Western culture. "I always labour at the same thing—to make the sex-relation valid and precious, instead of shameful," he wrote, " . . . beautiful and tender and frail as the naked self is" (letter of April 12, 1927).

Sexual passion stands for what Lawrence liked to call the "blood-consciousness," the life of the senses, in opposition to the spirit of acquisition, with its abandonment of all that is most human for money and material goods, its privileging of calculation over spontaneous feeling, its substitution of efficiency for honest labor, its admiration of possession over connection. Connie's feelings for and experience with Mellors are not simply about her self-development or his; for Lawrence, shared sexuality is salutary precisely because it brings us out of ourselves at the same time that its pleasure fulfills and strengthens us. Conversely, Lawrence associates the greedy, willful modern self with self-centeredness, isolation, and what he termed "self-consciousness," a dangerous separation from our own lived humanity.

D. H. Lawrence's narratives often refuse the plot development and "happy ending" that make the traditional novel, including all of Jane Austen's, so satisfying to read. We are not given any certainty at the conclusion of *Lady Chatterley's Lover* that Connie Chatterley and her lover will have a "real" marriage of passion or find a community to nurture that passion. We know that they have rejected coldness and indifference, including what Lawrence called "cold-hearted fucking," for kindness and warmth, but also that they must exist in a world hostile to what they live for, as Lawrence himself felt he did. He does not allow us to imagine a certain future for the couple that is a projection of what they feel at the moment the narrative concludes.

Instead, Lawrence dreams of "a new life among us," as he wrote to Lady Ottoline Morrell on February 1, 1915, "a life in which the only riches is integrity of character. So that each one may fulfill his own nature and deep desires to the utmost, but wherein the ultimate satisfaction and joy is in the completeness of us all as one. . . . And this shall be the new hope: that there shall be a life wherein the struggle shall not be for money or for power, but for individual freedom and common effort towards good. . . . It is communism based, not on poverty but on riches, not on humility but on pride, not on sacrifice but upon complete fulfillment in the flesh of all strong desire."

Though *Persuasion* has the "happily ever after" we expect, the lovers, Anne Elliot and Captain Wentworth, must similarly live in a society whose values do not resemble their own, just as at the end of *Lady Chatterley's Lover*. Austen carefully details the reactions of Anne's kin to her marriage, and it is an occasion of a "lively pain" to her that those connected to her lack "respectability, harmony and goodwill." Anne and Captain Wentworth have found felicity in each other and will be exemplars to their friends and children. But when Connie wishes, as lovers so often do, that "the rest of the world [would] disappear" and she could simply live with (and live simply with) Mellors, he bluntly replies, "It won't disappear." Lawrence knew the world could not so easily be remade.

Our own milieu is urban rather than the rural village life of Austen's time, marked by geographical mobility rather than stable lifelong family and social ties, and by a general breakdown of tradition and authority rather than unquestioning respect for them. Yet Austen is still surprisingly relevant because so much has *not* changed. Her most discerning readers love her less because of empire waistlines and antiquated manners than for her shrewd and brilliantly funny insight into the comically troubled quest for money, status, social approval, and, of course, love. In an odd and counterintuitive way, Lawrence took up that beacon and ran forward with it when he gave us his portraits of the riches of the deepest and most human of all strong desires, a love that is unashamedly sexual at its core.

As in life, (imaginary) love in fiction isn't as simple as it seems. In the end, what unites the wildly contrastive authors of *Persuasion* and *Lady Chatterley's Lover* is that both use the reader's psychological response to the love story of two individuals to illuminate a complex perception of social crisis and renewal. This is their bond. I hope that by the end of this chapter, as in the last chapter of any good romance, our prospective pair, Austen and Lawrence, appear to be on the road to a successful match.

Too much poetic license, you might say. You may as well dream of Lady Chatterley hooking up with Wentworth, or Anne Elliot running off with Mellors. The imagination reels. Still, if the best couples are made up of strong individualists who are complementary, I like to think of Austen and Lawrence waltzing off together in some heaven where great novelists go. Would they have even liked each other if they had met at a fantasy dinner party? She might very well have bored him; he almost certainly would have appalled her. But we all know that's how some marriages are.

2

WHY CHARLOTTE BRONTË DESPISED JANE AUSTEN

(and What That Tells Us about the Modern Meaning of Love)

> Why do you like Miss Austen so very much? I am puzzled on that point.
> —Charlotte Brontë, letter of January 12, 1848

It's a fascinating oddity of literary history that the great Victorian novelist of romantic love, Charlotte Brontë, despised that other great British chronicler of love, Jane Austen, and could not quite comprehend why Austen was valued so highly by critics in Brontë's time. This seems counterintuitive: after all, both appear regularly at the top of lists of favorites compiled by readers, especially female readers, who love classic novels and all things romantic.

Brontë's view of Austen startled me when I first read of it. Until I learned this, I had grouped the two together as if they had a natural affinity. After all, both were of primary importance in the British literary tradition as major female novelists; both were influential in inventing the romantic novel as a modern genre; and both wrote love stories that engaged issues of money, class, and social prestige. But, in Charlotte Brontë's view, their similarities were not as significant as their differences. Moreover, for Brontë, the disparity between them was essential, speaking to the very nature of their literary purposes.

As it happens, Charlotte Brontë's perception of Jane Austen not only reveals much about Brontë herself but also highlights an important change in the evolving definition of romantic love in Western culture. Furthermore, this change foreshadows both D. H. Lawrence and our contemporary understanding of that malleable term "love," a shift in meaning to which, I would say, Charlotte Brontë herself substantially contributed.

We know about Brontë's opinion of Austen chiefly from her correspondence in 1848 with the respected critic George Henry Lewes, later the companion of another great Victorian novelist, George Eliot. When he wrote to give Brontë comments and advice, she took his critique of her novel very seriously. *Jane Eyre* had received a good review from Lewes, but he wanted to underline a fault in the novel, the moments of melodrama in it that he called "suited to the circulating library" (*not* a compliment), and he held out Austen as a model of calm and balanced wisdom achieved through a more naturalistic style. When Lewes praised Austen, whom Brontë had neglected to read, she went to some trouble to obtain Austen's masterpiece, *Pride and Prejudice.*

In Brontë's own words to Lewes, "I got the book and studied it. And what did I find? An accurate daguerreotyped portrait of a common-place face; a carefully fenced, highly cultivated garden, with neat borders and delicate flowers—but no glance of a bright vivid physiognomy—no open country—no fresh air—no blue hill—no bonny beck. I should hardly like to live with her ladies and gentlemen in their elegant but confined houses. These observations will probably irritate you, but I shall run the risk."[1]

For Brontë, something essential was lacking, an element she later called "what throbs fast, full, though hidden, what the blood rushes through." This, of course, is the heart. Brontë resented Lewes's praise of Jane Austen's fiction because she interpreted his admiration for Austen as a requirement that an author, to be worthy of esteem, must eliminate the life beneath the surface, the full-blooded life of experience, including the dark experience of passionate love, while privileging the carefully worked appearance of social arrangements she saw in Austen. "The Passions are perfectly unknown to her," Brontë concluded in a letter of 1850. In effect, Brontë was accusing Austen of being superficial, not truthful, about passion, in spite of Austen's growing reputation as a social realist.[2]

Brontë's scathing evaluation of Austen has a particular irony in view of the popular filmed version of *Pride and Prejudice* (2005), starring the beautiful Keira Knightley as Elizabeth Bennet. The irony I refer to lies in the way the film revises and sells the original love story of Augustan balance and harmony as a romanticized version of the original: one prominent television ad screamed, "Romance hasn't looked this sexy in years!" In the *New Yorker*, the reviewer Anthony Lane put it this way: "What has happened is perfectly clear: Jane Austen has been Brontëfied."[3] Lane was no doubt referring to the quality of wildness that repelled some of the contemporary critics of *Jane Eyre* and *Wuthering Heights*. But what exactly does that imply about what Charlotte Brontë, and the Brontës in general, have contributed to our own definition of love and romance? And is that modern idea the same as the meaning of romantic love to Charlotte Brontë?

The answer to the latter question, I would say, is not quite. But what I will claim for Charlotte Brontë is that she very deliberately altered the term "love" as it was understood in her time, and particularly as it relates to women, in a way that has influenced our society far beyond her own modest expectations and, perhaps, beyond her intentions.

BRONTËFICATION

How did we, the modern audience, come to align with the "Brontëfied" view, to the point where a film based on an Austen novel has to be tarted up with it? By the end of the eighteenth century, when Mary Wollstonecraft and Jane Austen were writing, the term "romance" was still generally associated with fantasized expectations having little to do with real life. "Love," wrote Wollstonecraft in 1792, "such as the glowing pen of genius has traced, exists not on earth, or only resides in those exalted, fervid imaginations that have sketched such dangerous pictures. Dangerous, because they not only afford a plausible excuse to the voluptuary, who disguises sheer sensuality under a sentimental veil, but as they spread affection, and take from the dignity of virtue."[4]

At the same time, in the late eighteenth century, there was an increasing acceptance in the middle class of marriage based on individual choice. A marriage of mutual attraction and affection was commonly known as the "love-match," to distinguish it from the pragmatic exchange of women's attractiveness and domestic labor for the man's economic provision and social power that was the usual configuration of matrimony.

Both Wollstonecraft and Austen favored marrying for love, rather than for money and social prestige, but their definition of love is *opposed* to "romantic love," as Wollstonecraft defines it above. Though Wollstonecraft was a social radical and Jane Austen was conservative in many ways, both devalued "romantic" views of love as flighty, inimical to the importance of rationality and judgment, companionship, sensible affection, education and culture, and admiration for good character in marriage. In Austen's *Pride and Prejudice*, the union of Lydia and Wickham begins in selfish lust, and the marriage of Elizabeth's friend Charlotte to the odious Mr. Collins exposes the limitations of the purely pragmatic marriage with no real affection at all. In between these representations stands a relatively new concept of love, one that is defined by a growth into mature self-development, as well as sober recognition of and esteem for the other. In the view of both Wollstonecraft and Austen, mutual respect and valuing of character enabled women to achieve greater dignity and worth in the social arrangement of courtship and marriage that still ultimately determined their lives.

The Romantic era, as it appeared in Britain in the late eighteenth and early nineteenth centuries following its philosophical and literary origins in Europe, provided an important alternative definition of romance within Austen's time, entangling romantic love once again with sexual desire, intense and all-consuming feeling, and longing for a transcendent ideal, as the great German writer Johann Wolfgang von Goethe had illustrated in the wildly popular tale *The Sorrows of Young Werther*. Admirers of the medieval, the Romantics once again restored to love a deep sense of mystery and the near-religious experience of the sublime, including an admiration for rule-breaking in passion. Romanticism raised the value of emotion for its own sake, the deeper and more extreme the better, explored through plumbing psychological depth and expressed through dreams and fantasy. As opposed to the moderation, balance, and calm of rational affection, the sorrow and alienation of unrequited or forbidden love symbolized the rejection of stultifying convention for the sake of primal emotion. Young Werther, for example, commits suicide at the end of Goethe's novel for love of an unattainable married woman, an act made to bear a great burden of meaning about the nature of the universe itself.

Jane Austen's own ambivalence about this new and rebellious movement is embodied in the characters of Marianne in *Sense and Sensibility* and Captain Benwick in *Persuasion*. The latter, a potential match for the heroine, sighs, reads verses aloud all day, and cultivates "a melancholy air" under the influence of Romantic poetry, a practice both the author and her heroine obviously find amusingly self-dramatizing and pretentious. By contrast, we know that Charlotte Brontë was an avid reader of the British Romantic poets, including the half-adored, half-dreaded Byron, an icon of masculine wildness and sexual experience. It is not difficult to trace much of Brontë's imagery, especially in *Jane Eyre*, to the Romantics' sense of innate sympathy between man and nature, their high valuation of imagination, and their admiration for liberty and equality rather than authoritarianism. It is generally agreed that the Brontës were not only interested in and influenced by the Romantic movement but represent a continuation of it in revised form.

We can see how this contributes to the shape of *Jane Eyre*, the novel that has, perhaps more than others by Charlotte Brontë or any other author, especially defined romantic love through a paradigmatic story that has lasted into our contemporary age. That is, as the film of *Pride and Prejudice* and its reviews imply, we have come to accept the Romantic idea of feeling charged with sexual passion as the very basis for romantic love, but we do not stop there. Instead, we have united this view of romance, as Charlotte Brontë does, with the domestic virtues, affectionate intimacy and support, and suitability of temperament that Austen identified as the proper basis for marriage. This improbable union of romantic passion and marital relationship is now the dominant paradigm, the very one that Western women, and increasingly non-Western women, have come to expect as their birthright. Thus the necessity for revising Austen, for Brontëfying her: in order to sell widely, the Hollywood version must be the Brontëfied vision of romantic love, not the Austenian vision, which is less appealing, if not incomprehensible, to a modern mass audience.

CONVENTIONS AND ANTI-CONVENTIONS

It is a testament to the enduring appeal of *Jane Eyre* that the novel has had so many imitators. In fact, it is safe to say that many popular romances from Brontë's time to our own have adapted the tale of an orphaned, friendless, penniless—but intelligent, spirited, and virtuous—girl who is rewarded for her struggles by marriage to a man who will give her a new life, the one she deserves. In one way we can see Jane Eyre's tale as the extension of the much older story of Cinderella, whose inner virtue and beauty are acknowledged by a prince after a period of hard luck. But *Jane Eyre* combined the orphan theme with the attraction of another very old tale, that of Beauty and the Beast, in which the Prince Charming figure is initially anything but charming and represents a threatening element that must be tamed and domesticated so that social life is restored to its proper order. The thrilling element of this narrative and its many imitators (including Harlequin novels) is that while the hero is gruff to the point of rudeness on occasion, and unromantic to the heroine when she meets him, all of this conceals a tremendous capacity for love and tenderness when unlocked by the right woman. He also may have a mysterious past, a dark secret in his soul, and other features of the Romantic (Byronic) persona.

This configuration of traits has been repeated so many times as to become a formula for a certain kind of romance, especially popular in mass media such as movies, where the hero is lost, misunderstood, seemingly arrogant, and possibly a playboy (formerly known as a "rake"). The canonical modern story, still popular in rom-coms today, begins with a man who is like a boy—goofy, adventurous, rule-breaking—meeting a strong yet sweet, dignified, and desirable woman, who domesticates him through love (think of the movie *The 40-Year-Old Virgin*). In the fantasy, when the man is "caught" by love, *real* love, his "commitment problems" are over, and he is awakened to the inevitability and superiority of permanent monogamy. Having acquired this sure sign of adulthood, he has now arrived as a full member of society.

Jane Eyre was not a typical heroine for her time, however: though her emotional isolation as an orphan is a common feature of both fairy tales and many classic novels, her physical smallness and plain features, as well as her sarcasm, outspokenness, and strong will, set her sharply apart from the sweet and adorable girls often found in Victorian fiction, or from the heroines of Austen's novels, for that matter. We know that Charlotte Brontë insisted over her sisters' objections that her heroine must not be beautiful, as convention required for romance; according to her biographer Elizabeth Gaskell, she told Emily and Anne confidently, "I will prove to you that you are wrong; I will show you a heroine a plain and as small as myself, who shall be as interesting as any of yours."⁵

From this you might infer that Brontë was a feminist and that her view of love would take into consideration the brand-new ideas of women's equality and women's rights that were discussed at great length in the magazines and journals she read. Brontë probably was reacting to the pervasive popular literary depictions of courtship, of which Coventry Patmore's widely read narrative poem "The Angel in the House" (1854) is a particularly good example. Patmore's poem was so well known that the title came to stand for the very idea of woman's domestic role in Victorian culture; the phrase was used by Virginia Woolf when she famously wrote, "In those days every house had its Angel," who was "immensely charming," "utterly unselfish," "sacrificed herself daily," "never had a mind or wish of her own," and, above all, was "pure."⁶ Woolf expressed a strong desire to "kill" her, and when we read the Patmore poem, it is easy to see why. Here is the description of the beloved in "The Angel in the House": "Her disposition is devout/ Her countenance angelical/ . . . She grows/ More infantine, auroral, mild,/ And still the more she lives and knows/ The lovelier she's express'd a child."

The pervasive medium of magazine fiction featured a parade of virtuous, modest, sweet, demure, and submissive girls very much like this, always depicted as beautiful in exactly the same virtuous, modest, sweet, and demure way, who won the hearts of gallant, handsome, well-placed young men. While Rochester is not the young, good-looking, elegant, and well-mannered hero of these fictions, still less is Jane Eyre, though much younger than he, anything like the lovely, genial, angelic, and genteel maiden of popular Victorian culture.

Why did subverting the literary convention appeal so much to Brontë that she would take this risk of alienating her would-be publishers and readers with an "unlovable" heroine? It is all too easy to assign a biographical motive based on Charlotte Brontë's self-doubt about her own womanly charms, but Jane's lack of beauty and status are integral to Brontë's vision of romance. In *Jane Eyre*, Brontë dramatically reveals the power structure that placed little value on children, the poor, and women (especially unattractive women) in Victorian society: Jane suffers from being all three, a poor and plain female child at the beginning, a poor and plain female adult almost to the end. It seems fair, then, to view this rebellious gesture, Brontë's insistence on a heroine who is far from a beauty, as her comment on Victorian notions of romance. This startling choice marks her critique of romantic love as defined in her society, an idealized mask for a social game in which female loveliness is exchanged for the attention of men and the reward of marriage, with its conferral of economic security and prestige on the woman.

Instead, Brontë substitutes an alternative view of romance that is derived from the Romantics. In fact, she insists on it: romantic love entails intense feeling, uncontrollable longing even in the face of almost certain rejection, and, going beyond the Romantics themselves, strong erotic desire in women as well as in men. In the famous proposal scene of *Jane Eyre* (detailed in a way it never is in Austen's novels), when Jane thinks she will be forced to leave the man whom she loves apparently without return, she "sobbed convulsively, for I could repress what I endured no longer. . . . The vehemence of emotion, stirred by grief and love within me, was claiming mastery and struggling for full sway, and asserting a right to predominate—to overcome, live, rise, and reign at last: yes, and to speak."[7] She then tells Rochester how much she loves him, an act of assertion that was conventionally viewed as horrifyingly immodest in women and (therefore) unfeminine. The first-person narration of these rebellious words bestows more weight and intensity on this unconventional act. Jane is said to have a "right" to behave in this wild, impulsive, and improper way because Brontë is underlining the necessity of passion when it is "right" feeling, both in general but very much including for women.

Jane is out of bounds, not just in her plainness of appearance, dress, and manner, but also in her insistence on the validity of her own emotions entirely contrary to the passivity and calm required of respectable females. Brontë appears to affirm nature and feeling as important values when she sets Jane's naturalness of speech and manner, emblems of the worth of her mind and heart, against the artificiality and hollowness of the snobbish "ladies" such as Blanche, her supposed rival for Rochester's affections, who are Jane's social betters.

When Rochester chooses Jane in spite of the social stigma against marrying "down," romantic love appears subversive of the social order, defined through a harmony of minds, a deep understanding of one another, and the superiority of merit over conventional categories of bloodlines, class, and power. It is not difficult to see why *Jane Eyre* is best remembered as a romance at the expense of other important themes in the novel: the depth, spontaneity, and integrity of Jane's romantic desire are continually contrasted with the superficiality and egoism of Celine, Rochester's former lover, of Blanche, Jane's supposed rival, and even of little Adele, Rochester's ward: females who rely on charm and display for their keep, trading on their looks and femininity to please and flatter men.

Nature, emotion, and the "right" to their expression overmaster reason and the strictures of gender roles in Jane's daring declaration of love to Rochester: "Do you think I am an automaton?—a machine without feelings? And can bear to have my morsel of bread snatched from my lips, and my drop of living water dashed from my cup? . . . You think wrong!—I have as much soul as you,— and full as much heart! And if God had gifted me with some beauty, and much wealth, I should have made it as hard for you to leave me, as it is now for me to leave you" (296).

It is impossible to think of Jane Austen writing such a speech. But *Jane Eyre* is not so simple, and its values not so easily derived from this most famous "romantic" part of the book alone (a similar shift of emphasis is often noted in the

interpretations and adaptations of Emily Brontë's *Wuthering Heights*, not coincidentally). As soon as Jane and Rochester are engaged to be married, the tone of
the narrative changes again. The next phase of the novel reveals, with some comic
alarm but also growing unease, Rochester's possessiveness and desire for Jane's
dependence on him; "I mean shortly to claim you," he tells her, "your thoughts,
conversation, and company—for life" (310). To Jane's dismay he wants to lavish
gifts on her as though she were a lady (or Cinderella), calling her a fairy and an
angel. Jane's increasing anxiety is reflected in literal dreams foreshadowing disas-
ter, as well as her statement to Rochester, "You, sir, are the most phantom-like of
all; you are a mere dream" (325).

Brontë associates this dreamlike state of about-to-be fulfilled romance, which
inevitably recalls her own renounced visionary dreams in girlhood, with a sexuality that is heightened and uncontrolled. When Rochester looks lovingly at
Jane, she notices his face is "ardent and flushed" (326). In other words, Brontë
is all on the side of romantic love when Jane thinks her desire is one-sided and
secret, but the author does an about-face when it comes down to living out the
desire itself. The unregulated passion that Rochester demonstrates is not only
antisocial, romantically inimical to living by the real rules of the world, but also
irreligious. As Jane says during her courtship, "My future husband was becoming
to me my whole world; and more than the world: almost my hope of heaven. He
stood between me and every thought of religion. . . . I could not, in those days,
see God for his creature: of whom I had made an idol" (320).

It's worth noting here that popular advice books in the Victorian age, often
aimed at women, attempted to enforce the necessity to look to worthiness of
character in marriage choice *as opposed to* matters of feeling. As one midcen-
tury clergyman, Daniel Wise, intoned: "There are ideas, *romantic*, impassioned,
immodest, derived from impure novels and impurer fancies, which you must
prayerfully exclude from the chambers of your soul. . . . Learn that your affections are under your own control; that pure affection is founded upon esteem. . . .
Restrain your affections, therefore, with vigor." This may sound like a version of
eighteenth-century rational love, but there is a great difference. Because Victorian society was more explicitly concerned with religious matters than was the
freethinker Mary Wollstonecraft, or than Jane Austen for that matter, this emphasis on conduct and character as the basis for love in marriage was steeped in
the language of Christian spirituality: "Marriage, properly viewed," this author
writes, "is a union of kindred minds, a blending of two souls in mutual, holy affection. Its physical aspects, pure and necessary as they are, are its lowest and
least to be desired ones; indeed, they derive all their sanctity from the spiritual
affinity existing between the parties."[8]

Thus mainstream advice literature emphasized the distinction between passionate love, whose basis is essentially sinful and selfish lust, and romantic love
as the spiritualization of desire, ennobling the lovers through serving God's

purposes in holy matrimony. This may be viewed as a descendant of Dante's idea in *La Vita Nuova*, though not so extreme, since the body and sexual relations are folded into the legitimizing arena of marriage, something Dante seems not to consider at all.

SUBVERTING REBELLION

If romance was initially Brontë's form of rebellion against social norms of courtship and marriage, *Jane Eyre* writes its own critique of the rebellion itself in the next part of the novel, as Jane the narrator looks back at Jane the character in love. For Charlotte Brontë is also a moralist, a sincere and devout Christian moralist. This is hardly surprising given that Charlotte, along with her famous siblings, Emily and Anne, authors of *Wuthering Heights* and *The Tenant of Wildfell Hall* respectively, was raised in an intellectual but impoverished family headed by an Anglican clergyman of strong Evangelical bent. For Charlotte Brontë, romantic love and sexual passion, self-interest, self-will, and pleasure were important areas of conflict from an early age. Desire was always situated for her in the framework of the Christian devaluation of the body, the sinfulness of earthly pleasures, and the necessity of self-denial, especially for women.

On the one hand, Brontë was deeply immersed in Evangelical Christian ideology and felt unworthy. Here is an excerpt from a letter of 1837: "If Christian perfection be necessary to salvation, I shall never be saved; my heart is a very hot-bed for sinful thoughts. . . . I go on constantly seeking my own pleasure, pursuing the gratification of my own desires." In another letter to a close friend, she confesses her "evil wandering thoughts" and her "corrupt heart, cold to the spirit and warm to the flesh." She hopes for "the pleasant life which we might lead together, strengthening each other in that power of self-denial, that hallowed and glowing devotion which the past saints of God often attained to."[9]

Charlotte remained devout all her life, and this drive to spiritual self-denial was always at odds with her strong urge to put her own ambitions, interests, and emotional longings first. These desires were lived out on a level of secrecy, therefore, from the beginning. From her earliest years, Charlotte, like all the remarkable young Brontës, lived much of her free time in a fantasy world of melodrama of her own imagining. The many miniature books that the Brontë children produced, chronicling imaginary wars, heroes, and love affairs with wild imagination in an astoundingly microscopic handwriting, for their own private enjoyment, were almost certainly never shown to outsiders.

Some of these private fictions have come down to us, and it is fascinating to see the form that Charlotte's early fantasies take, especially those written in her teens and twenties. The love stories are distinctly not about Christian self-denial; on the contrary, they are about the overwhelming desire of a beautiful woman for a dominating, even brutal man of outsized passions, a character she called

Zamorna. In the story "Mina Laury," for example, she wrote that Mina adored Zamorna so much that she "lost the power of . . . discerning the difference between right and wrong. . . . Strong-minded beyond her sex—active, energetic, accomplished in all other points of view—here she was as weak as a child—she lost her identity—her very way of life was swallowed up in that of another." Mina accepts her lover's embrace "as a slave ought to take the caress of a Sultan. . . . She had but one idea—Zamorna, Zamorna."[10]

It is interesting to see that in letters to friends as an adult, Brontë was explicitly critical and distrustful of romantic passion, and especially of the way its power left women in a state of heightened emotional dependency: "As to intense passion," she wrote, "I am convinced that is no desirable feeling. In the first place, it seldom or never meets with a requital; and in the second place, if it did, the feeling would be only temporary; it would last the honeymoon, and then, perhaps, give place to disgust, or indifference, worse than disgust. Certainly this would be the case on the man's part, and on the woman's—God help her if she is left to love passionately and alone."[11]

Under the pressure of necessity, then, Brontë produced a narrative framework in which "wild" desires are displaced onto the story of a lustful and intemperate character, Bertha, as the elements of *conventional* romance are critiqued and disposed of in the subplot of the triumph of Jane over her rival, Blanche Ingram. She anchors the romantic elements in a plot through which Jane is allowed to manifest and prove a spiritual love for Rochester by rejecting the choice of immoral passion. From the beginning of their love relation, Rochester has looked to Jane to "save" him, calling her his "angel." In this we can see the strong influence of the Victorian view of marital love as spiritualizing, incorporating but also controlling the Romantic view of the essential nature of passion to life.

Just as the tension between Jane's and Rochester's views of love and marriage seems irreconcilable, and Jane is in danger of losing her selfhood to the more dominant Rochester, the melodramatic revelation of Rochester's hidden wife, Bertha, brings the wedding to a sudden halt. The Gothic plotline of the sequestered mad wife who prevents the legal marriage of Jane and Rochester allows Brontë to present the competing claims of an alternate system of values to romance and pleasure, values she identifies as Christian, traditional, and moral. The outsized and physically strong Bertha, with her mad avidity for drink and implied tendency to promiscuity (Rochester calls her "intemperate, unchaste . . . gross, impure and depraved"), forefronts the danger of flouting the Christian ethic of self-denial.

At this point, when Jane makes the choice to leave her beloved rather than risk the sin of an illegitimate sexual love, Brontë seems to have definitively chosen sides in the struggle between the two ideas of love, the claims of intense feeling subdued by the universal law invoked by the Victorian sexual system and authorized by God. Yet the novel does not end there, and in the last phase, the character of St. John Rivers reverses the trajectory of the novel toward an unexpected, if notably ambivalent, critique of the Christian rejection of sexual passion as the necessary foundation for love.

In a way, St. John represents the passionless Angel in the House, restraining his feelings as the advice-giving Victorian clergyman had advised. Though attracted to his Christian self-sacrifice and moral vision, ultimately Jane is horrified at his chilly view of sexuality: "As his wife," she says, "always restrained, always checked, forced to keep the fire of my nature continually low, to compel it to burn inwardly and never utter a cry, though the imprisoned flame consumed . . . this would be unendurable" (472). In the end, she emphatically rejects this alternate lover, crying, "I scorn your idea of love, I scorn the counterfeit sentiment you offer" (473). Though Jane is master of her own *actions* when loving Rochester seems immoral, it is fundamental to her romantic vision that passionate feeling itself is uncontrollable, an idea generally disputed in the popular press, but especially in regard to women.

Perhaps more problematic for critics, including feminist critics, is Jane's subsequent discovery that Rochester has lost a hand and an eye in the fire that destroyed the scene of Jane's almost-seduction. When Jane finds Rochester again, she is touched by the "powerlessness of the strong man" and his "avowal of his dependence" (468). Jane's intense desire to "nurse" Rochester in his debilitation may be related to the pervasive Victorian domestic ideal of the wife serving as helpmeet to the husband, a domestic expression of the Christian ideal of service. The Evangelical idea of "women's mission" stressed chastity, daughterly, wifely, and maternal devotion, and, above all, virtuous self-denial as their God-given purpose in life. The dominant idea of women from about the eighteenth century on was that God gave the sexes different capacities, which fitted men to intellectual and public endeavor and women to maternal and wifely duties. This became known as "the doctrine of separate spheres," and its influence in middle-class Victorian Britain (as well as America) was enormous. The true object of female education, then, was the cultivation of compassion and self-abnegation: "the renunciation of self." Some women rejected this notion, but many if not most women accepted and embraced that they had an important place in the world as the "virtuous sex," the caregivers who were spiritually superior to men. As British writer Sarah Lewis wrote in *Woman's Mission* (1839), though men are better suited to achieve in intellectual and political fields, "the moral world is ours."

The author of *Jane Eyre* might well appear to be an enthusiast for women's equality. After all, Jane seems like the quintessential rebel, passionately outspoken for her own rights and those of the downtrodden in general. But here is Brontë writing to Mrs. Gaskell, the Victorian author and later her first biographer, on the subject of an article she had read in the liberal *Westminster Review* on the emancipation of women: "I think the writer forgets there is such a thing as self-sacrificing love and disinterested devotion. When I first read the paper, I thought it was the work of . . . a

woman who longed for power, and had never felt affection. To many women, affection is sweet, and power conquered indifferent."[12]

When Jane rejects St. John's invitation to join him in a pragmatic marriage
as a missionary, she says she does not "love [her] servitude" to him (461), but
Brontë's implication is that servitude in romantic love, if equal and mutual, allows for the integrity of the independent soul. In her "new servitude" (to recall
her words when pining for new experience early on [102]), Jane is rewarded with
a wishful fantasy that spiritual love in marriage can be made to reconcile the
great rift in traditional and modern values—Christian self-denial versus modern individualism, "rules and systems" versus romantic feeling—that has been so
trenchantly expressed in the novel.

In the trajectory of Jane's story, the character Jane Eyre is a kind of antihero-
ine of conventional romantic love, unattractive, humble, unfashionable, and out-
wardly charmless, while the novel *Jane Eyre* is the very type of a certain kind of
romance going back to Samuel Richardson's *Pamela* of 1740 (arguably the first
true novel in the English language) and still found in popular romances today:
the tale of a poor, spirited, but unappreciated heroine whose worth is finally recognized by her lover, a man of dignity, wealth, and social status in a position to
give her a home in love. As in many eighteenth- and nineteenth-century novels,
virtue and inner worth are ultimately rewarded by a rise in (economic) fortune,
either through inheritance or marriage (in *Jane Eyre*, both). In *Pamela*, Fanny
Burney's *Evelina*, and most of Austen's novels, resistance to ingrained values of
authority and social hierarchy seems contradicted at the end by the reward of the
happy ending of romance (the subtitle of *Pamela* is *Virtue Rewarded*), while the
novel's proposed substitution of merit for blood superiority of rank is undercut
by the absorption of the heroine into a superior social class as the just deserts of
merit after all.

This explains some of the ambivalence that critics, including feminist critics,
have struggled with in understanding Brontë's work (less so in her last novel, *Villette*, which provides no such ending but is far less often read). On one hand,
the romantic narrative of Jane and Rochester entails the political stance that she
is a heroine worthy of his love, as well as the strong assertion of the legitimacy
of erotic feeling for women, the recognition that human love is vital to life and
should not be repressed. But though love is claimed as a human right, a need,
as opposed to St. John's more-than-human ideal of self-abnegation celebrated at
the conclusion, the whole nature of romantic love in *Jane Eyre* is finally redefined
away from melodrama and romance in the childhood sense. As such, it is removed from the passion of Brontë's "dream" life, including the creative dreaming
of her schooldays, which she called in her journal "that burning clime where we
have sojourned too long." Instead romance is re-visioned as the selfless devotion
of marital love, taking care of the other, which takes primacy over uncontrollable
eroticism. This version of love merges with the Christian concept of saving the

soul from sin and thus can be seen as right reward for virtue, as well as socially and psychologically coming into one's own.

The divine justice that punishes Rochester and rewards Jane offers proof of a Christian benevolent universe, makes God's love and will consonant with the desires of the person of integrity, and serves to redistribute the power balance between the lovers. "Some say it was a just judgment on him," says a character of Rochester's injuries (496). Nature itself in the supernatural scene when Jane hears Rochester's call from afar seems aligned with both Romantic and Christian ideals. We may see Rochester's maiming as the fulfillment of Christ's words in the Sermon on the Mount on the sin of adultery, as paraphrased by Jane when she resolves to renounce her own temptation to illegitimate passion: "You shall yourself pluck out your right eye; yourself cut off your right hand; your heart shall be the victim; and you, the priest, to transfix it" (347).

By the time the novel concludes, both Bertha, the intemperate exotic, an icon of selfish and unrestrained sensuality and madness, whose symbol is destructive fire, and, at the opposite pole, St. John with his "ice kiss," who renounces personal happiness, have been extirpated from the text. These two extremes are found wanting as models for Jane, who must find a way to accommodate feeling and desire within a Christian framework. Charlotte Brontë was fascinated with relations of power; powerlessness and estrangement, a sense of displacement from being at home, are the conditions for falling in love, especially for women in her novels. However, sexual love itself is represented as both liberatory and oppressive. Jane Eyre becomes ensnared in helpless love for her master, for example, but she also masters her dominating employer, then goes on to master her own feelings, including anger and desire.

Here we can see why *Jane Eyre* continues to be both a central text in the Western literary canon and a durable fantasy in the popular public imagination. Jane Eyre as heroine is best remembered for the strong will that bravely questions expected roles for women and asserts a woman's right to love and pleasure. Lacking in bodily self, small, thin, and plain, the heroine is nevertheless spirited and tenacious in deprivation. Though Brontë's solution to a Romantic problem is Victorian and traditional, *Jane Eyre* is a unique contribution to the modern view of romantic love and the problem of sexual desire for women, a radical attempt to endorse as well as conservatively regulate female passion.

THE MEANING OF ROMANCE

The meaning of romance to Charlotte Brontë, then, is a complex one, braiding disparate and even contradictory elements of her personal psychology, her private imaginative life, her religious belief, her reading of popular and Romantic literature, and her rebellion against convention. Why, one might ask, did Brontë put so much effort, as her character Jane directs so much energy, into altering the usual definition of romantic love, especially in view of the way it left the author vulnerable to harsh criticism? Again, some offer a psychological explanation regarding her wish to conciliate opposing elements in conflict: her hope to legitimize her personal passions in a romance along with her fearful consciousness of their prohibition. Certainly her own passionate nature caused her anxiety and self-denigration, not to say suffering, when she fell in love with her married teacher. But psychoanalytic analyses of long-dead people are never adequate; one of Brontë's concerns is social, a rebellious desire to protest the keeping down of women, including their sexual repression, without sacrificing her moral concern that this sensual element of love be sanctified in the eyes of God.

In the end, *Jane Eyre* constructs love as the answer to women's emptiness and powerlessness but also deconstructs it. Brontë's critique of romantic desire is grounded in Christian morality, but a fear of the loss of feminine power seems equally powerful. In a way *Jane Eyre* is feminist far ahead of its time in its radical assertion of women's right to pleasure in their emotional and sexual lives, a theme that did not emerge in the women's movement with any force until much later on in the twentieth century. This is the "right" that the character Jane Eyre asserts in the scene of romantic disclosure with Rochester, and it is this scene rather than Jane's religious rhetoric that is always included in modern theater and film adaptations.

Brontë's enduring relevance to our day is the way in which she anticipated modern views of women's capacity and women's desires as legitimate and equal to men's. Though Brontë was ambivalent and equivocal about sexual and moral issues surrounding women's equality and freedom, she raised questions about them provocatively and fearlessly in her novel, risking the scorn and ridicule that some critics did indeed demonstrate. The plot of *Jane Eyre* clearly proceeds from assumptions about sexual behavior and the impossibility of divorce that do not hold up as well today. Yet the moral questions it asks us to think about are very relevant to our society, namely, how much we owe to ourselves as opposed to the claims of others, how far we must go in conforming to the rules, conventions, and laws of society when they appear unreasonable to us, and the place of individual desire and feeling in the moral society.

Jane Austen's heroines need their men—there is no real life without them (unlike in Austen's own life). But Charlotte Brontë shows Rochester completely lost without Jane; he needs her more than she needs him to be happy and productive. I have proposed that *Jane Eyre* is both a high romance and also an anti-romance, rejecting the conventions of femininity in the social paradigm of courtship as well as the destructive immorality and selfishness of illegitimate passion that women have to control in themselves and their lovers. It is this self-contradiction that fuels the fire of Brontë's criticism of Austen, whom she readily (and not altogether fairly) associates with only one side of an issue that Brontë wished to have both ways.

The difference that Charlotte Brontë perceived between her own work and Jane Austen's turns out to be important, not only because it helps us understand the Victorian definition of romantic love, but perhaps even more, our own. Brontë's peculiar mix of conservatism (her rejection of passion not legitimized by Christian values) with distinctly modern elements (a woman's right to passionate feeling) has strongly affected contemporary views of romance. When we comprehend why Brontë was contemptuous of Austen, with the latter's emphasis on social respectability and propriety and insistence on the social control of strong feeling, we can better appreciate major shifts in the history of love between the Victorian and modern eras, and particularly how these shifts evolved with new understandings of women's nature.

To conclude, I would like to go back to a consideration of the effect of Brontëan romance on the 2005 film version of *Pride and Prejudice*. I have said that Charlotte Brontë, along with her sister Emily, has influenced our contemporary ideas of romantic love so that we now expect uninhibited feeling, intense passion, and the drama of strong emotion to define romance, integrated with pragmatic compatibility, psychological intimacy, and marriage.[13] But though the 2005 film of *Pride and Prejudice* is, in the coinage of the *New Yorker* reviewer, Brontëfied, it is also modern in a very particular way that directly opposes and undermines one of Brontë's purposes. That is, in the Austen novel, the heroine, Elizabeth Bennet, is not the most beautiful girl in the town, the room, or even her family, though very attractive. Instead the filmed version features an actress who frequently attracts the epithet "gorgeous," with the result that in the movie the heroine outshines her sister Jane, who is the beauty of the family in the novel. What does this (small?) alteration tell us about the way we see romantic love now?

I would say that our celebrity culture, in which a movie can't sell itself to an audience unless it gives star billing to a young, fabulously beautiful actress with sexy looks, embodies the regressive element in the conventional way of looking at women that Charlotte Brontë herself consciously tried to protest through "plain" heroines like Jane Eyre, as well as Lucy Snowe of *Villette*. In the now-conventional popular ideology of romance, we remember and celebrate Brontë's cutting-edge attempt to make female desire meaningful in Victorian romance, but we couldn't care less about her stated intention to question and revise the system of value that makes women worthy of love only as long as they are the Victorian equivalent of movie stars. This, I would suggest, is the greatest irony of all in considering how Brontë defined romantic love through her critique of Jane Austen.

3

THE TRUE AND REAL THING

Victorian and Modern Magazine Cultures of Romance

> Love, in particular, will not endure any historical scrutiny.
> —Robert Louis Stevenson, "On Falling in Love," *Cornhill*, 1877

Our stereotypes of the Victorian age lead us to expect certain sharp distinctions between nineteenth- and twenty-first-century views on the nature of love, gender roles, sex, and morality: namely, that Victorian women were corseted prudes, culture was genteel and moralistic, and love grew in the context of sweet, mannered, Austenish courtship. As with many stereotypes, some of this is partly true, enough so that immersing oneself in the Anglo-Victorian world of magazine love, as I did, can seem like landing on an unexplored planet: one only wonders how so much could have changed so radically in such a relatively short time, historically speaking.

But from a different perspective, the opposite seems just as true: more than one might have thought, the relationship of gender to romance in our time and theirs remains startlingly similar, withstanding our own new ideas such as feminism, the sexual revolution, and the post-Freudian emphasis on psychological well-being. While sexuality and gender have been radically transformed in Western culture since the turn of the twentieth century, some of our assumptions about romantic relations have proven nearly impervious to alteration.

THE MEANING OF LOVE

What is "real" love? That's an easy question, according to the wisdom guru Deepak Chopra. Writing in a column for *O Magazine* (2010), Chopra responded to an inquiry from one Roger, a sincere single male who had "doubts about marriage" because "I see couples that do not love each other and decide to live together for other reasons than love itself. When I fall in love and I feel the other person does not feel the same way about me, I keep telling myself that it is an emotion I should not identify with. . . . How can a woman and a man be in real love?"

Chopra's reply, called "How to Feel Real Love," frames these worries as "coming down to one question: Can I trust every infatuation I fall into?" His reply to Roger (but really to his own question, which is not quite what Roger asked) is simple but spiced with the gusto of perfect confidence: "The answer is no," he states flatly. Infatuation is a "giddy beginning" with "runaway emotions," but it doesn't last. *Real* love is proceeding to the "next stage," he says, which turns out to be the first of successive "deeper stages of connection" with someone who responds to you in the same way. Whereas infatuation "takes place on a cloud," *real* love is "down to earth," and about the "mundane business of figuring out how to relate . . . sharing one closet, deciding who will live in what house and remembering to get skim milk instead of whole." Chopra identifies Roger's "problem" on the basis of these assumptions: Roger is "addicted to infatuation" and therefore "resist[s] moving on to the more realistic phases of love." His diagnosis is that Roger suffers from the pathology of being "stuck in adolescence." Chopra is just as sure about the cure: 'Your present need isn't for Miss Right. It's for a bit of growing up."[1]

Deepak Chopra didn't invent this idea, of course. I call this the "stages theory" of romantic love, and we can see it emerging in magazines more than a century ago as the chief ideology of Anglo-American romance. Nearly all my students, like most of modern culture, seem to agree on this idea: If we have romantic feelings for someone but they don't lead to an enduring relationship, they aren't "real"; if they do, they were the first immature stage of what is *real love*. The new twist in the twentieth century and beyond is the language of psychology, not yet available to the Victorians: the right love is mature, whereas Roger's "infatuation" shows that he is "stuck" in adolescence. This is the sign of a developmental pathology, but one easily fixable even for an "addict" like Roger—that is, if he listens to the magazine's advice guru and grows up by redefining what love is.

What many scholars know often comes as a shock to my students: this isn't at all a universal belief and wasn't always the accepted definition of romantic love even in Western culture. It's fascinating to see this widely held contemporary idea in the early phase of its development in the nineteenth century, when the modern concept of romantic love was still forming. Before Shakespeare's time, love was often associated in literature with drama and passion but not necessarily associated with courtship. As the importance grew of "home" as a "haven in the heartless world" of urban capitalism, to borrow the historian Christopher Lasch's term, love became increasingly tied to marriage. By the nineteenth century, most romantic narratives, classic and popular alike, plant the flag for love as a contested but valued expectation in a successful marriage, foreshadowing its supposed universalization in the twentieth century.[2]

I say a "contested" expectation because in the Victorian public press, the very nature, forms, and rules of romance in its modern sense were still very much in flux and therefore under intense debate. At the same time that the topic of love grew enormously popular in fiction, producing many of the Victorian novels we still read and many more that we don't, it also sprang to new life in newspapers and magazines aimed at the same growing middle-class audience.[3] There love was presented just as it is in today's *O Magazine* or *Cosmo* or *Glamour*, as a problem to be solved, an occasion for instruction, advice, and amusement. The culture of love in our own contemporary mass media is something we often take for granted; it is so pervasive as to seem natural and obvious. But this was apparently a fresh topic of discussion to the Victorians, who often commented on love's newly ubiquitous presence, as in this typical pronouncement: "We are glutted with fictions [that have] one absorbing interest, that of love" ("Imaginary Love," *Once a Week*, 1868).

Interestingly, unlike today, when romance is an omnipresent topic in women's magazines but not in men's, in the Victorian age love was discussed and defined in high-toned intellectual and literary journals as well as in low-quality penny newspapers, and articles about its nature were frequently written by men. Well-known authors, such as Robert Louis Stevenson, Grant Allen, and Washington Irving, contributed their opinions on the subject, clearly an important one. It seems to have been assumed that both sexes would be interested in thinking about this newly fascinating topic and exploring the feelings and problems associated with it.

Article after article had some variation of "Love" in its title and waxed eloquently on the topic in idealized language the modern magazine reader simply would not stand still for: "Had we a pen plucked from the pinion of Cupid, and dipped in the nectar of the gods, we should fail in describing what love is" ("Lucubrations on Love," *Bradshaw's*, 1842).

In the nineteenth century, both in Britain and America, we can see a struggle between the old and new forms of "love," as its meaning is asserted, argued, and negotiated in the press, in generalizations about "human nature" or "women's nature" and debates about the universality of romantic love. Far from the stereotype of courtly gentlemen and delicate ladies, romantic love had no uniform value in the Victorian age; we can see assertions in these articles that grow out of old assumptions about gender and religious morality, but also resistance to and negotiation around these same ideas.

We may read, for example, that love happens to everyone and is universal . . .

"It's human nature to love even among savages." ("Falling in Love," *Cornhill*, 1861)

"No one escapes from this passion. . . . We must all, being men and women, fall in love." ("Courtship," *Saturday Evening Post*, 1872)

. . . and also that few people actually love.

"Liking is not loving and there is reason to believe that few actually love." ("Courting," *London Reader*, 1876)

"A good many people never fall in love at all." ("Falling in Love," *Bow Bells*, 1882)

Similarly, we might hear love described with rapturous melodrama ("Oh! Love! Thou greatest passion of the human breast—mysterious arbiter of fate below!" ["Lucubrations on Love," *Bradshaw's*, 1842]) and elsewhere condemned as a trifling modern fashion ("The ancient Greek and the modern Puritan should agree in pronouncing the love babble of romance to be ridiculously out of place" ["Imaginary Love," *Once a Week*, 1868]); that it is inimical to marriage, and elsewhere necessary to marriage; that girls are too romantic on the one hand but not as romantic as they used to be on the other; that a woman always knows "instinctively" if a man loves her, along with earnest warnings that men are predatory and women easily fooled by displays of affection; that women need to learn how to get husbands, but also that it is unfeminine to focus on getting a husband.

Sometimes a new strain of opinion, such as the value of a young woman's freedom to love a man of her choice, represents a resistance to conservative ideologies about patriarchal authority. But as we shall see, just as often "true love" itself may be strongly asserted as a conservative solution to an emerging cultural development, such as changing gender roles or the ongoing democratization of romance.[4]

In contrast to Deepak Chopra's confidence about the definition of "real" love, the nineteenth-century press shows deep conflict, apparently fascinating to the Victorian public, about the essential nature of love itself: Is it instinctual or voluntary? Is it under our control, or is it what one writer called a "master passion" that cannot be constrained by choice? The question of the relationship between love and will was everywhere in the Victorian press.

"The important point we have to consider is, how far our affections are in our power—whether falling love is proper, is inevitable, or is always mere fancy." ("Falling in Love," *Cornhill*, 1861).

If love is an appetite, it followed to the Victorians that it must be governed ("Govern the appetites, or they will become tyrants" ["A Warning," *Woman's Exponent*, 1873]), but this requires an act of reason and will.

Love's influence admitted, its nature known, we may all of us make up our minds not to oppose it, but to control it. ("Courtship," *Saturday Evening Post*, 1872)

Is love under our control? Can we love, or refrain from loving, at our will? . . . I say, Don't fall in love. Be very cautious, and keep your heart. ("Falling in Love," *Saturday Evening Post*, 1861)

The most dominant anxiety in the nineteenth-century press is that love is a desire for gratification, a strong and universal instinct that overrides judgment—analogous to, if not rooted in, sexual desire and other egoistic longings. In this view romance is said to lead to no good except pleasure, which was hardly to the Victorians a good in itself.[5] Romantic feeling is often depicted as the very opposite of a moral affection: "To 'fall' in love is indeed a descent from all that is noble, from all that is lovely, and of good report" ("Morality: Falling in Love," *Youth's Companion*, 1833).

The system of courtship that emphasizes romance is seen throughout the nineteenth century as sowing dangerous discontent when the reality of marriage begins, particularly for women:

"In the romantic courting-days the lovemaking is fresh and sweet and all-engrossing. . . . Marriage is the dropping of the curtain. . . . The attentions cannot continue. Nor is it desirable that they should. Yet in getting them for a time, women are taught to expect them forever. This arrangement is cruel to women. It is like the practice of first spoiling children, and then punishing them for being spoiled." ("Before and After Marriage," *London Journal*, 1871)

"A young man so weak and so much the slave of passion, as to 'fall in love' to desperation, is not a fit young man to take the reins of government over a wife and children." ("Falling in Love," *Examiner*, 1872)

The topic's ubiquity illustrates the contradictions inherent in a recent evolution, the changeover from a premodern definition of love as passion and blind devotion to the more recent revaluation of marriage as more equally companionate and personally satisfying, requiring a concept of love nearly the opposite to passion in its values and traits: "Not only does this theory of loving at will . . . serve to regulate the chief joy of life at first, but it both creates the bond, and secures it from rupture in the future" ("Falling in Love," *Cornhill*, 1861).

If love is a passion beyond the conscious will (think of Woody Allen's quoting Pascal as his rationale for his romantic relationship with the young daughter of his girlfriend Mia Farrow: "The heart has reasons that reason cannot know"), how does that square with choosing the best partner for lifelong companionship?

"The man about to select a wife . . . in nine cases out of ten becomes sentimental and affectionate before he has reckoned up in a cool and sensible way the value of the woman he desires to wed." ("Choosing a Wife," *London Review*, 1868)

Often a theme becomes obsessive in popular media as a way of managing the tension between conflicting ideologies, clashes that are embedded in a field of wider values. Romantic desire, for example, was enmeshed with the broader conflict between the wider conservative value of duty, requiring self-sacrifice to an authority greater than oneself, and the new middle-class individualism, which endorsed the value of one's unique feelings.[6] Defining love as yearning, adoration, and irresistible desire (as Alfred Lord Tennyson did, using a medieval setting) engaged the Romantic strain that valued strong feeling as the most human of qualities, foreshadowing our own post-Freudian emphasis on sexual feeling. Yet this definition was at odds with the equally strong and growing mandate to remake daily marital relations on more equal terms through shared affection and esteem.

Many Victorian articles hope to educate women about the virtues of marrying for love over money, describing heroines who find bright visions of pure happiness in love-matches so that "poverty is naught," faithful young women who refuse rich men's offers and stay loyal for twenty years to the man they love until they are able to marry ("Love and Constancy in Woman," *New York Illustrated Magazine of Literature and Art*, 1846), or a "shabbily-dressed, tired-looking woman" who is "cheery" because she married for love ("Woman's Love," *Saturday Evening Post*, 1849). As late as 1903, the *Woman's Life* article "Do Women Marry More for Love than Money?" scolds that while women like to think they prioritize love over money, "this is a practical age in which we live, and the present-day girl, while recognizing the value of love, is apt to look first at a man's worldly possessions." By the modern period, the old conflict of love and money as motives for marriage (*pace* Jane Austen and just about everyone else who wrote about love) is one battle that romance won, though in reality modern young men and women still overwhelmingly choose mates from their own class.

Similarly, the conventional way of controlling the dangers of romance is advocating traditional deference to parental authority: "In this everyday world of ours [as opposed to novels], where one is made unhappy in the affairs of love or matrimony by the coercion of parents or guardians, ten become miserable for life by following their own fancies" (*Godey's Lady's Book*, 1839).

But by the Victorian era, the authority and even influence of parents had been eroding for generations, if not centuries. Love itself was increasingly becoming democratized along with marriage; young people's personal decisions were less and less subject to the choices or even veto power of relatives, as we saw in Jane Austen's *Persuasion*. The role of the media, then, was to teach young men and women "how to fall in love wisely," educating them in the kind of love suitable for marriage: "Love requires reading and general culture to give it grace and sweetness; it requires self-restraint, self-respect, and education" ("Love in the Abstract," *London Review*, 1867). Falling in love "wisely and well" ("Courtship," *Saturday Evening Post*, 1872), rather than being ruled by passion or loving against obstacles, allows romantic love to be combined with older pragmatic marriage, as in Austen's novels. The explosion of advice and wisdom in writing on the subject in the Victorian era, in both fiction and nonfiction, and in both high and low culture, took the place of a quickly eroding family authority in both love and marriage.

A brilliant cultural solution, then, to the tensions and contradictions of reconciling love and marriage began to emerge: a compromise that co-opted the appeal of the traditional rhetoric of "romance" as helpless passion but smoothed its risky—and risqué—edge (as in the famous adulterous knightly epics) to match social developments in the formation of the modern family. "True" love became a glorious feeling distinct from romance because it was meshed with the righteous values of domesticity. If love could be reconceptualized as voluntary, then one could choose to fall in true love with the right person: "First of all, we must get rid of the idea that love cannot be directed. We believe that it can" ("Falling in Love," *Saturday Evening Post*, 1861).

The new definition of "true love" in the Victorian press harmonized well with popular religious orthodoxies through the idea of love as a spiritual force, making it compatible with traditional morality, as it is in the genre of Christian romance today:

"[When] a very worthy fellow—I don't say necessarily handsome—but a man, a noble fellow, a Christian, offers to you his heart, his hand, his home; then set your heart upon him, and love him with all your soul." ("Falling in Love," *Cornhill*, 1861)

"You will love the man whose principles are high and noble, whose soul and body are pure in the sight of God." ("Love, Courtship and Marriage," *Young Woman's Journal*, 1890).

This "right person" might be one chosen for you by God or fate but was at the same time conveniently "suitable," in the old Austenian sense of occupying a desirable class position and possessing the proper character and stability for domesticity. Victorian "true" love, like Deepak Chopra's "real" love, required suitability but, unlike the modern version, was less about compatibility of personality than about "a deep esteem" ("Love and Matrimony," *American Phrenological Journal*, 1857): "The essence of love is kindness; and indeed it may be best defined as passionate kindness" ("On Falling in Love," *Cornhill*, 1877). Thus the so-called love-match allowed you to have your pleasure while eating the wholesome meal of traditional marital values too.

LOVE AS WORK

Ironically, given the widespread spiritualization of romance, the primary means by which love conquered was its rationalization in the Victorian age, that is, literally making it accessible by—and subject to—rationality, an up-to-date aspect of modernizing society. Love began to be treated as a task to be accomplished by those who were preparing themselves for marriage wisely and well. One could learn how to love romantically, in other words, rather than be swept away by potentially selfish, out-of-control, or downright dangerous feelings inimical to the preservation of marriage.

The *London Reader* ran "How to Inspire Love" for women in 1882, concluding that "beauty depends principally on the mind"; the article provides tips on the right female facial expressions (soft, sweet, placid) where cosmetic products would reign today. In America, *Woman's Life* (1896) advised "How to Know if a Man Loves You" ("He will get her, as far as he can, the best of everything, and no other girl on the whole earth will have the slightest charm for him"). The *Young Woman's Journal* told female readers exactly how far to go and the consequences of overindulgence, just as magazines do today:

> "He may assist her in donning wraps and overshoes when leaving a ballroom, but he should never touch her face, pat her on the shoulder, nor stroke her hair. Such things argue, not respect and kindness, but disrespect and unkindness." ("Love, Courtship and Marriage," *Young Woman's Journal*, 1890)

Thus the pursuit and management of love was beginning to be treated as a kind of life occupation, more akin to work than to the older idea of passion.[7]

"REAL LOVE" IN MODERN MAGAZINES

Of course, the rules for romantic courtship in Victorian magazines were mainly derived from Christian morality and social sanctions against premarital sex, precepts that do not much appear in contemporary magazines. Modern articles such as "Could He Be the One?" now invite the reader to use "psychological studies" to get results in romance. The modern reliance on the "science" of love as a selling point nevertheless springs from the late-Victorian application of rules, systems, and rational advice to love and marriage. Then as now, science was part of that rationalizing technique, the power of knowledge harnessed for better living:

> "The rules we have laid down, in connection with such a knowledge of physiology, phrenology, and physiognomy . . . will enable any sensible young man or young woman to judge who are and who are not adapted to them." ("Some Selections from Wedlock," American Phrenological Journal, 1869)

If we compare our own take on love in contemporary magazines with the Victorians', we see enormous differences, of course, but we may also observe how these very differences grew out of the compromises that Victorian ideology made. First, romance has become close to or synonymous with "true love" rather than distinct from and inferior to it; as we saw in Chopra's column, "romance" no longer implies a flighty or self-centered desire threatening to a marriage, and "real" love is now the romance of an enduring and stable relationship. Then, too, the nineteenth-century worry about whether romance is necessary or inimical to marriage, like the ubiquitous Victorian tension between marrying for love or for money, has all but disappeared. Instead, the glaring contrast between the Victorian and modern is that what we now mean by "romance" is relationship love that completely incorporates sexual passion and is assumed to be (at least in potential, if not in actuality) a part of courtship, that is, the road to marriage. "You need chemistry for a relationship to work," says "How Not to Marry the Wrong Guy." "Don't forget this primal truth: there needs to be a sizzle" (*Cosmopolitan*, October 2010).

Since the nineteenth century, the high-minded spiritualization of love has mostly fallen as flat on our ears as the Victorian notion that constant self-denial is the best guide to life. Modern love includes the old idea of passion ("Let the heart take over"), because increasingly in the post-Freudian twentieth century and beyond, sex is considered necessary to a successful life. The pervasive Victorian suspicion of romance as passion has been replaced (and resolved) by the love-in-stages theory, that passion naturally transforms into a love that enables a stable relationship if it's "real," an idea that is widely and unquestioningly accepted.

For example, this is from Judith Orloff, one of the many, many modern self-help authors whose work pervades the commercial publishing market and purports to distinguish "real love" from mere "lust" for the reader who can't tell the difference: "Being in love doesn't exclude lust. In fact, lust can lead to love. However, real love, not based on idealization or projection, requires time to get to know each other. Here are some signs to watch for to differentiate pure lust from love." One sign of lust the reader needs to note is that "you want to leave soon after sex rather than cuddling or breakfast the next morning," whereas an important "sign of love" is that "he or she motivates you to be a better person."[8]

Because sex is now seen as essential to love, the problem is no longer the Victorian conflict between "selfish" romance and "true" companionate (marital) love, but how to tell "infatuation" that isn't based on intimacy and doesn't lead to an enduring relationship from "real" love (Chopra will tell you)—or how to distinguish "lust" from the self-development that marks off "real love" (Orloff will tell you). On the other hand, since the stages theory incorporates both, one must therefore know when to pursue passion and when one is "settling"—thus all the articles along the lines of "The Love Timeline: Figuring Out If He's 'the

One' " (*Glamour.com*, September 18, 2009). Some contemporary articles trace the history of a love affair from first attraction to commitment to marriage in order to demonstrate the paradigm of stages, so you will know "exactly where your relationship is going," as one puts it. *Glamour.com*'s "The Seven Levels of Love" (November 1, 2006) begins with superficial Infatuation, proceeds to Free-fallin', demonstrates Getting Emotionally Naked, and then assures you (Call It ESP) that "being so mentally in sync feels sexy too," lest you worry that you've traded in sexuality for intimacy. Level Seven, called As Good as It Gets, combines a wife who is "so damn hot at 40" with emotional "connection," the favorite word of modern love ideology.

Whereas in the nineteenth century romance could still be condemned as egoistic and therefore open to immorality, we now love the ego and its "needs," reconceptualized as healthy self-love, commonly called self-esteem. As some historians and sociologists have noted, we are immersed in a medicalized language for feelings and behaviors ("functional/dysfunctional") that used to be the weighty province of the moral life, so that they belong instead to the category of the unhealthy.[9] Morality has become maturity, as we saw in Deepak Chopra's approach; what was "wrong" in a moral sense to the Victorians, what God, your family, and morality enjoin against, has become "wrong for you," and to be a "better person" is to be successful in fulfilling one's desires and goals.

Flirting, for example, which appears in the Victorian magazines as a punishable offense to the weighty business of love, is in modern magazines encouraged as youthful play, because our attitudes toward leisure and the pursuit of pleasure have changed enormously. Except in very conservative groups, "love" in our present society is now both recreation and serious enterprise, a universal entitlement that somehow also has to be worked at when it's time to get down to business.

The task, then, as well as the appeal, of the modern woman's magazine is to invite the reader's trust as a source of sympathy, advice, direction, and, not least, motivation to "work at" getting and maintaining a relationship rather than simply pursue desire. Contemporary magazines would not dream of waxing eloquent about the beauties of love in the abstract ("To love is to live in a world of the heart's own creation, whose forms and colours are as brilliant as they are deceptive and unreal" ["Love," *London Reader*, 1882]) because no one has to be sold on romance any longer; rather, they openly ply how-to instruction in becoming what one critic calls "informed consumers of romance" in a weirdly monotonal, ironic, and flirty-cute girlfriend style: "Heading to the beach to meet hot guys? It's a great pickup spot as long as you make the right moves. The Hot Guy Panel tells you what to avoid!" (*Seventeen.com*, 2011). It's as if love were something like buying a car as an "informed consumer," to use the critic Kirsten Firminger's phrase, and then learning how to get tune-ups to make it "last."[10] The magazines' selling point is to educate the audience in the stages theory—the importance of sexuality and passion as leading to and sustaining the love that is the "real" or "successful" relationship—so that the reader believes she can "have it all."

In contemporary writing, the paradox of the modern stages theory is rarely questioned: how exactly does it happen that a relationship beginning in passion, now presumed (unlike in the Victorian era) to be connected to involuntary sexual attraction, morphs into a partnership whose characteristics must be dictated by what is needed to maintain it for life, while still constantly stimulating the passion that initiated it? Though tension and anxiety over this contradiction is everywhere in modern magazines, the obvious unlikelihood of this combination is rarely acknowledged openly.

To the contrary, somehow love can be both mysterious in one contemporary article, "just known" in another ("I do think it's possible to fall in love and know you want to spend the rest of your life with a guy in a short amount of time" ["The Love Timeline: Figuring Out if He's 'the One,' " Smitten blog, Glamour.com, September 18, 2009]) and elsewhere a solvable problem, in which a savvy consumer can be taught to micromanage behaviors and feelings to get and maintain love ("The Art of the Ultimatum: Three Times When It Might Pay to Nudge Him a Bit," Cosmopolitan.com, "Will He Ever Marry You?" screen 7.).

WOMEN AS LOVE

Though the ideology of love in the Victorian age was often discussed as general wisdom for both sexes, a portion of this advice, instruction, and entertainment was (as it is much more today) specifically aimed at women. Romantic love was women's "business," and love of all kinds was explicitly named their chief motive in fulfilling the self-denying nurturing and helping role they were best suited for.

Yet simultaneously in the press, Victorian women were frequently chastised for lack of contentment where they should be self-sacrificing and passive, which indicates that some restlessness was brewing beneath the bonnets. In hindsight, we can see that the evolution of romantic love in its modern form was a rampart against new social changes that were to overrun the Victorian system eventually, beginning with increasingly sharp deviations from conventions about marriage and proceeding to new challenges to traditional gender roles from early in the twentieth century to the present day.

As expectations and opportunities for men and women expanded throughout the nineteenth century, love took on a sharp gender distinction. Victorian women increasingly assumed a special place in public media as the sex that is capable of, and therefore responsible for, refining men through their love. They were also presumed to have been put on earth for recognizing and maintaining the right sort of love, and for carrying out the mandates of religion and social life by means of love. And conversely, love was more and more defined as the sort of ideal feeling associated with women's God-given "nature":[11] "To love is woman's mission. Love whom? The good only? Certainly not. What! Would you have a woman love the wayward, the repulsive, the unamiable, the wicked? Most assuredly" ("Woman's Mission," *Godey's Lady's Book*, 1849).

By contrast, we might expect our modern magazines to encourage a more equal view of the entitlements of both sexes in romance—for example, in terms of mutual fidelity, involvement, and self-sacrifice. But ironically, contemporary magazines, like other popular media in our society, are often more sharply distinguished by gendered audience than their Victorian equivalents. Magazines for women now tend to highlight fitness, health, leisure, self-adornment, self-actualization, play, and emotional fulfillment through love and committed sex, while those for men emphasize adventure, sports, play, gadgets for purchase, and sexual fulfillment through uncommitted sex.[12] Furthermore, all these topics in modern women's magazines often appear solely in relation to romance (beauty and adornment to attract men, being fit and toned as a component of attractiveness to men, and so on), while in men's publications, other pursuits and experiences, such as being buff, owning the latest technology, or having physical adventures, are valued in themselves.

While so much of Victorian culture might appear antiquated and foreign to us, especially in the realm of sexuality, our modern focus on the female as the icon of love became an unquestioned presumption to a new degree in the nineteenth century. Article after article in both Victorian Britain and America was titled "Women and Love," or "Woman's Love," "Women's Tenderness and Love," "The Strength of Women's Love," and so on, whereas there were relatively few titled "Men's Love." Almost all such articles appearing in general-interest publications and addressing an audience presumed to be male as well as female, like the high-toned meditation "The Philosophy of Woman's Love" (1840), claim that men's nature is not made for love, though in time of courtship, men are persuaded into marriage by romance as a temporary state.

After reading through more than a hundred of these articles, most of which say almost exactly the same thing, I couldn't help wondering if the press was protesting too much. Why does the public need the incessant repetition of this message about love and gender? Here are the oft-repeated declarations about "woman's love" (as distinct from man's):

Women are made for love.

> "The one focus of woman's character, is her love. The one mainspring of woman's power, is her love. The one crown of her charms, the one bond of her entire nature, is her love." ("Love and Constancy in Woman," *New York Illustrated Magazine of Literature and Art*, 1846)

> "Woman must love with all her soul or she ceases to be a woman."
> ("Women Must Love," *American Phrenological Journal*, 1865)

Men are naturally ambitious and self-interested.

> "Man is the creature of interest and ambition." (Washington Irving, "Woman's Love," *Godey's*, 1852)

> "A man is a creature created for work.... He can perfectly well do without love." ("Is Love a Necessity for Women?" *Woman's Life*, 1904)

While women's love is purer because it is spiritual . . .

> "Woman's love is truly holy and sublime." ("Woman's Love," *Atkinson's Saturday Evening Post*, 1838)

> "Those fine feelings of which the pure heart of woman is susceptible [are] the fountain from which piety and ardent affections gush." ("Woman," *Literary Inquirer*, 1834)

. . . men are more "passionate."

> "If he be properly organized, he is a more passionate—less spiritual— lover than woman." ("Women Must Love," *American Phrenological Journal*, 1865)

Since romantic love is based more on pleasure than is "true" love, which is related to Christian virtues, piety, chastity, and self-sacrifice, woman's love is directly related to and derived from religion and morality. For this reason they are "missionaries of love":

> "If she would reform a faulty or depraved husband, she must *love* him into reformation." ("Woman's Love," *American Phrenological Journal*, 1846)

Women's love endures through all trials and obstacles.

> "To bear on unceasing; unchangeable to endure all change, to speak hope amid hopelessness to wear a smiling brow and aching heart; this woman's task—this is woman's love." (*The Amaranth*, 1847)

> "It is a holy, deep, devoted passion—once gains its admission into true woman's breast, it lingers there for ever . . . for without it her bosom would be a dreary void, and her existence a blank.... Loves she you once, she loves you eternally." ("Love and Constancy in Woman," *New York Illustrated Magazine of Literature and Art*, 1846)

Women's angelic love for men is an extension of maternal self-denial; it is particularly suited to sickness and the deathbed.

> "Woman's love shines forth in its native, heavenly purity . . . when the spirit is stricken to the earth by misery, sickness or poverty." ("Woman's Love," *Rural Repository*, 1843)

> "In sickness there is no hand like a woman's hand, no heart like a woman's heart. . . . Night after night she tends him, like a creature sent from a higher world." (*Boston Cultivator*, 1847)

However, since women are particularly prone to love and devotion, they are in great danger of heartbreak, according to the magazines.

> "If a woman's character has one defect, it is that extreme confidence, that blindness with which she devotes herself to the object of her love." (*Corsair*, 1840)

> "Men are not always what they seem/ And love, though fair enough in a dream/ Is another word for woe." ("The Maiden's Heart," *Once a Week*, 1866)

Magazines were particularly fond of the "true" anecdote, often beginning, "We know a woman who . . . ," describing women who pitifully but admirably stick by their alcoholic and abusive husbands, or become "raging maniacs" because of a man's abandonment.

> "Weeks and month passed away, and Amanda was a raging maniac! Oh, what a lesson to thoughtless and unprincipled young men, *to trifle not with woman's love!*" ("Trifle Not with Woman's Love," *Ladies Garland*, 1849, emphasis in original)

Some of these anecdotes were distinctly lurid, such as the tale of a wife who searches all over the American West for her husband, only to find him at last—in bed with his new wife and child (*National Police Gazette*, 1867). As in Victorian novels and poetry (like Tennyson's), there is a pervasive fascination with heartbroken women: "A woman never bargains or barters hearts, and so, commonly, gets the worst of the exchange" ("Men for Friendship and Women for Love," *Round Table*, 1866).

Because of the danger to vulnerable women, it's important to know the nature of romantic love at the beginning; thus clues must be read, signs interpreted.

> "Ladies, beware of wolves who come to you in sheep's clothing. . . . It is not worth while to barter your peace of mind . . . for the sake of receiving attentions from a set of worthless, heartless scamps." ("A Warning," *Woman's Exponent*, 1873)

So strongly was all this ideology about women asserted, so confident was the tone of these assumptions, that one might be surprised to see that this ideology also contains its contradiction: Victorian women were also quite often condemned for egoism and superficiality, sometimes in the same article in which they were praised for their self-sacrifice and depth of character.

> "How eager is simple, vain woman to believe them [men] . . . because they can scatter a little gold dust upon the surface of that hollow mine of selfishness within their [women's] bosom." ("Women in Love," New Yorker, 1839)

> "If the female mind were not happily impervious to logic, we might demonstrate, even to its satisfaction, that the history of the sex presents no single instance of a famous friendship." ("Men for Friendship and Women for Love," Round Table, 1866)

We are told that young girls often imagine they are in love because they want to be admired, petted, and praised by a man ("True Love and Love of Love," Bow Bells, 1871) or feel a "flutter of pleased vanity" ("Love, Courtship and Marriage," Young Woman's Journal, 1890). Women were also frequently scolded for materialism in marriage. In 1860, the magazine Once a Week claimed that men were marrying less frequently because they didn't want to support women's growing demands for an upper-middle class household ("Starving Gentility").

Sometimes the same "womanly" trait is viewed as evidence of women's piety and goodness and her worldliness and weakness at different times. Take, for example, passive reserve, considered all at once a trait inherent in women, a religious trait, and a prescription for women in romance. In general throughout the Victorian era, women were restrained from showing feeling or being assertive in their relations with their suitors. A good woman loves only when loved ("Woman never ought to love until she at least thinks she is loved" ["Falling in Love," Cornhill, 1861]); moveover, "the more she betrays her feelings, the more she repels and disgusts him" ("How to Know if a Man Loves You," Woman's Life, 1896). Yet elsewhere the supposed innate passivity of femininity is a sign of her narcissism compared to men: "A man's love is purely love of her; hers begins, for the most part, by love of being loved" ("Falling in Love," London Journal, 1894). The combination of breathless, extravagant idealization and unapologetic, blatant contempt is head-spinning.

RESISTANCE, DOUBT, AND THE DEVELOPMENT OF MODERN "ROMANTIC" LOVE

There is one indication of why there seems to have been such single-minded Victorian insistence on what was presumed to be (and loudly declared to be) perfectly natural, universal, and obvious to one and all in the relationship of love and gender. Here and there we can see a small but growing crosscurrent of sub-versive ideas about women in the very midst of all this repeated wisdom.

In an American article of 1846, for example, Mrs. S. T. Martyn resists the idea that love and marriage are essential to women:

> "[There are] false maxims and dangerous sentiments everywhere preva-lent in reference to [women's] interests, capabilities, and duties. . . . Is it true that love constitutes 'the essence of a woman's being,' that, without which, 'she has no life'?" ("Love and Marriage," *Ladies' Wreath*, 1846)

Few in the popular press were willing to ask that critical question. More typi-cal is "Women's Thoughts about Women: Growing Old," which warns grimly that single women will be terribly lonely in old age:

> "It is a condition to which a single woman must make her mind, that the close of her days will be more or less solitary. . . . Extreme loneliness . . . is the saddest of the inevitable results of her lot." ("Woman's Thoughts about Women: Growing Old," *Friends' Intelligencer,* 1859)

The more the ideology of women's purity in love was asserted in order to make the marriage based upon love succeed, however, the less it seemed to be working. In 1873, an anonymous British article stated the usual, that "the possession and ex-ercise of this love that we want more of is woman's greatest and crowning right. In it lies her greatest power: without it, she becomes a cipher on the face of the earth," but tellingly adds, "albeit she may have gained the point of female suffrage and a place in all the learned and unlearned professions" ("Woman's Love," *Tinsley's*, 1873). The defensiveness is hard to miss, running up a standard of protest against the coming battle.

At the turn of the twentieth century, along with greater access between men and women, the idea that women uphold the temple of pure, unselfish love was already showing strain in the many public complaints that women were growing more bold in love:

> "There was a time called in books 'good old times' when it must have been an exception, and not the rule, for a girl to have a bona fide love affair, not arranged by her parents or guardians. Now in what we will call the 'bad new times,' young men and women meet pretty often, and they are not looked after too much." ("About Falling in Love," *London Journal*, 1893)

In 1904, the confident assertion by innumerable articles that love is an essen-tial component of women's nature is replaced with the same idea as a question: "Is Love a Necessity for Women?" Here is the author's answer:

> "A large number of women these days aim rather at distinction, ambi-tion spurs them on; they are not content to settle down; they clamour

for excitement; they want amusement. . . . They have, in a word, revolted against the old, homely, and be it said, correct rule, that matrimony, following on love, was the be all and end all of life, so far as woman is concerned. . . . I pity her. . . . The woman who never loves or never has love offered her, may be called one of life's most decided failures." ("Is Love a Necessity for Women? An Important Question Answered," *Woman's Life*, 1904)

We see the sharp reaction to women pulling away from traditional roles here, and therefore the more strident insistence that women entering men's arena will be miserable. Yet only seventy years later, *Cosmo's* famous editor, Helen Gurley Brown, proclaimed that women can "have it all": leisure, ambition, and of course sex.

An American article of the early twentieth century has a college professor lecture his male students: "Heaven help the man who marries a college-bred woman," because "there is altogether too much domestic discord in the world," as "the result of the wife having too much sense." The female author points out that there are great advantages to intelligent women being educated. Though "it undoubtedly lessens a girl's chances in getting married," an educated wife makes a better "housekeeper and manager," and the "beauty of her mind and soul" can charm her husband into old age. But the conclusion is firm:

> "If I had a daughter I should let her looks decide the college question for her. If she was ugly and unattractive, I would move heaven and earth to give her something to provide her with the way of making a living for herself. If she was a dimpled darling, on the contrary, I would know that matrimony and not the higher mathematics was her predestined career, and I should be careful not to circumvent nature by making her a blue stocking." (Dorothea Dix, "College-Bred Wives," *Current Literature*, 1905)

We often hear about the influence of the media over the minds of consumers; rather, what we see here seems to indicate the converse, that these popular magazines are sensitive to the cultural and economic changes around them, asserting sometimes progressive, sometimes defensively conservative messages in response to rapidly fluctuating values.

POSTSCRIPT: "LOVE OF LOVE" AND THE MODERN FEMALE MAGAZINE READER

"If you want to marry, do not court or try to attract the attention of a gentleman," said *Bow Bells* in 1868, while in August 2011 *Seventeen* magazine offered "Sneaky Ways to Ask HIM Out (without actually asking)." What, then, has changed and what has remained the same in the modern magazines aimed at women, compared to their Victorian counterparts?

One obvious difference between modern and Victorian magazines is that those in our own time have adopted (and adapted) the language of feminism. The theme is played over and over that young women are and should be independent earners, brave and adventurous fun-lovers who have strong "self-esteem" and who are (at least in theory) in charge of their own desires and spending on their pleasures. Contemporary magazines harness romance to leisure (fun) and consumption; fashion, shopping, adventure and beauty all harmonize with romance to form a perfect "lifestyle."[13] One might say that romance is essential to the picture of the marriageable middle-class young woman's cool life, while at the same time, the magazine-promoted lifestyle has become constitutive of what romance is.

> "On date two, you did drinks, dinner, and an end-of-the-night lip-lock. What do you tell your BFF the next day?" (*Cosmopolitan*, December 2010)

> "Today, do your own thing—go for a run in the park, catch up on gossip magazines at Starbucks—and keep your eye out for guys. . . . Going at it alone makes you seem extra-confident—and guys can't resist!" (*Seventeen*, August 2011)

Women are more than ever presumed to read in order to be educated in romance: "A high IQ doesn't translate into romance-savvy," warns *Glamour* magazine's Sex and Love Issue (November 2009), which promises to teach the reader "romantic moves" (such as the answer to that ultimate question, "Should you pee with the door open?"). "The Law of Attraction Begins with the Law of Subtraction," cries *Oprah.com* (October 22, 2009). Whereas an article of 1896 admitted that "it is difficult to tell when a man really loves" ("How to Know if a Man Loves you," *Woman's Life*, 1896), *Cosmo* will readily provide "4 Signs a Guy's into You," break down "What His Texts Really Mean," or use his "spending habits" to tell if he wants "A One-Night Stand or Something More" (*Cosmopolitan.com*, 2011).

The most glaring distinction between the world of Victorian magazines and our own, of course, is not so much the easily assumed equality of the sexes but the openness in the realm of sexuality.[14] Overlapping feminist and sexual revolutions have combined to make explicit details and instruction about sexuality an expectation of the female reader, in ways that would (yes) make the Victorians faint. There is little talk in American mainstream magazines about women's love being more "spiritual" or heroically self-sacrificing, or women as angels, fallen or otherwise: "My girlfriend looks sweet and innocent, but I love that she has one dirty mind" is a typical quotation ("What Guys Want in a Serious Girlfriend," *Cosmopolitan*, September 2008).

Rather, sex is a primary selling point in both *Cosmo* and *Glamour*, where sexual techniques offered in articles ("The Sex Thing I Do Best," "Make Him Burn with Pleasure," or "How to Touch a Naked Man: 16 Naughty Strokes That Will

Send Him Over the Edge") are often called "romantic moves." Women are told that "it's fine to be proud of our sex appeal and share the brilliant moves we've developed in bed," because it's time to "stop that double standard" ("The Sex Thing I Do Best," *Glamour*, October 2009). What feminist could disagree with the desire to erase the double standard, since it was feminism that applied the concept to women's sexuality in the first place?

On the other hand, though sex is presumed of prime importance, sexuality plays different roles in men's and women's love lives in the contemporary magazines. In modern magazines, sex is necessary to courtship, but it's women who must be careful to distinguish between, as *Cosmo* puts it, "Sexy vs. Skanky." It's hard to imagine what a Victorian audience would make of this question from *Cosmo*'s online advice column, "How can I tell a guy that I'm a virgin and not freak him out?" The answer, however, rings of traditional gender stereotypes: "He hears you're a 26-year-old virgin, and he thinks responsibility, commitment." A different world, yes, but *plus ça change*?

Then, too, in a manly modern men's magazine such as *Maxim*, you will find an article called "Cheat and Don't Get Caught" (March 2010); you're not likely to find its twin in those aimed at women. Conversely, *Cosmopolitan* features "YOUR ORGASM FACE: What He's Thinking When He Sees It" (December 2008), a concern I did not find reflected in a single magazine for men.

In the world of contemporary magazines, male and female are continually said to be equal but men are still identified with sex and women with love, just as in the Victorian era. Because men supposedly don't love as women do, they must be approached with great care. Victorian magazines featured naive girls who needed to know how men's minds work so they could avoid the sexual dangers of romance and the emotional risk of heartbreak; in modern magazines, women are openly informed how to "get" men as they are told to get everything else they want, even if it takes making a hair band out of your thong ("Fun and Fearless: Fun Little Tricks Guys Love," *Cosmopolitan*, October 2009).

The Victorians were monstrously prescriptive about women's behavior, but then modern magazines are also bizarrely directive in their own way. It's clear that women in contemporary magazines are still responsible for maintaining relationships and marriage, though in relationships before marriage they are no longer expected to be passive, but rather, manipulative.

"4 Times He Wants to Be in Charge," *Cosmopolitan*, October 2008 ("Let him feel like a man in these situations.")

"Do This, Not That: Smart Girlfriend Behavior," *Cosmopolitan*, December 2008 (The article advises the female reader uninterested in sports to "watch the game with his friends" but not behave like a guy.)

There are numerous articles on this subject of How I Got Him To (move in with me/buy the right present for my birthday/show me off). For example, one young woman offers, "When my boyfriend and I started dating, he was kind of skittish about telling people we were in a relationship"; her solution was to wear a "slinky black dress," at which point he proudly claimed her (*Cosmopolitan*, November 2008).

Though women are no longer told that their lives are "incomplete" or that they will have "lived in vain" if they don't find love and marry ("Is Love a Necessity for Women?" *Woman's Life*, 1904) it's clear that contemporary women who lack the right kind of love are understood to be deficient in personal and social identity. How far have we really come from 1846, when a Victorian author could say that love is the "one focus of woman's character" ("Woman's Love," *American Phrenological Journal*, 1846) or that without love, a woman's life "would be a dreary void, and her existence a blank" ("Love and Constancy in Woman," *New York Illustrated Magazine of Literature and Art*, 1846)? Because the topic of finding or "getting" love, as though it were a consumer item, is now more than ever obsessively treated and dissected, with a tone of what we might call anxious expectancy, a young girl must be romantically super-desirable, or at least willing to be taught how to be, or she is rendered completely invisible. And so in contemporary magazines, all women are either looking for love, or already in love, or troubled by love and looking for an easy fix, in more than one sense of the word.

Looking back at nineteenth-century Anglo-American magazines, we can see an astonishingly rapid expansion and transformation of romance into its modern form. Rather than "love" being a fixture in personal life across time, the subject of love and romance appears as a set of theories about emotions in an era of changing gender relationships and a parallel debate about women's value. Victorian culture presented "love" as a way for both sexes to have exalted meaning preceding marriage, but it especially seems to have functioned as part of a campaign to have women believe in their own power and status in an established (though far from stable), restrictive gender role system. Today we see the results of the process of modernization in contemporary magazines, where women are portrayed as self-supporting, sexually liberated, assertive, and empowered— to do what, exactly? To make romantic relationships happen, if only covertly, and to make them work . . . or else.

Much has changed in the world of popular magazines, and much has not, but the multiple meanings of "love" produced by the Victorian popular press have apparently devolved into this eloquent contemporary cry of female nostalgia for traditional courtly romance: "I deserve to be spoiled! I want to be appreciated. It's the chivalry thing" ("Seven Things You Didn't Know about Carrie [Underwood] . . . Until Now," *Cosmopolitan*, July 2008).

4

VICTORIAN DESIRES AND MODERN ROMANCES

Pocahontas on a Bridge in Madison County

> I gave my family my life.
> —Francesca in *The Bridges of Madison County*, Robert Waller, 1992

When scholars have studied contemporary romances, they have often viewed them as an opportunity to examine the conservative, if not regressive, view of gender in our society. More recently, they have been celebrated as implicitly feminist and subversive. But these are not the only ways to look at the modern popular story of love. Even more interesting and useful is to see how conservative views can be united with progressive ideas, or sometimes disguised in seemingly modern forms, and to ask who benefits from that odd union.

As a case study, I would like to compare two enormously popular romances with wide distribution in the same decade: the hugely successful novel by Robert Waller, *The Bridges of Madison County* (1992), which remained on the *New York Times* best-seller list for three years, and the Disney animated children's film *Pocahontas* (1995), based on a legendary American heroine. Their audiences were very different: *Bridges* was aimed at romance-loving women, but particularly older women like its heroine, while *Pocahontas* appeals to children of all ages, as they say, but was particularly designed for and marketed to very young girls.

The Bridges of Madison County, the novel and the 1995 film of the same name directed by Clint Eastwood, concerns a repressed middle-aged housewife who has a brief romantic encounter with a passing photographer, or what Amazon. com calls "an experience of uncommon truth and stunning beauty that will haunt them forever." The figure of Pocahontas, of course, is an icon of American culture who does seem to have been haunting all of us forever. Waller's novel is a "romantic classic" of the 1990s; *Pocahontas* draws on historical narrative, centuries old. The plot, characters, and settings of these two appear to have nothing in common.

What connects them, however, is their direct ancestry in a very old story about women that was still being told over and over, under the cover of contemporary issues and views: a story about female desire, where it may be directed, and when it is imperative that it remain unfulfilled. For example, that best-selling Victorian arbiter of female taste and morality Sarah Stickney Ellis, writing in one of her many manuals on the subject of proper womanhood, rhetorically asked, "For what is she [Woman] the most valued, admired and beloved?" promptly answering herself, "For her disinterested kindness. Look at all the heroines, whether of romance or reality—at all the female characters that are held up to universal admiration—at all who have gone down to honored graves, amongst the tears and the lamentations of their survivors. Have these been the learned, the accomplished women? No, or if they have, they have also been women who were dignified with moral greatness" (*The Women of England*, 1839).

And how do women best achieve "moral greatness"? By pursuing a goal "unconnected with their own personal exaltation and enjoyment," said Ellis, related only to "some beloved object, whose suffering was their sorrow, whose good their gain." In a word: self-denial, for loved ones or for the larger good.

How, then, has our idea of female desire changed over time (or not), and how does this supposed change appear so that it may be enjoyed by a modern mass audience? The story of female desire denied and therefore ennobled is a traditional one in the genre of the novel, but after the Second Wave of feminism and the social transformation in attitudes and practices concerning sexuality in the sixties and seventies, one would expect a change in popular narratives preoccupied with female passion. You would think that novels and movies would treat this subject with far more frankness and openness, a greater range of possible endings, and, not least, a more progressive social agenda.[1]

Instead, these two contemporary stories astonishingly remind me of nothing so much as the high Victorian novel, in which passion is always at war with duty. As in Victoriana, female desire is presented as so dangerous to a stable moral, social, and familial order that it must be contained by conversion to domesticity or utterly renounced in some way. Think of Jane Eyre's marriage to the crippled would-be adulterer Rochester, or Catherine Earnshaw's death before she dare consummate her forbidden love for Heathcliff. Pleasure, in those Victorian narratives, is always (though not without some ambivalence) suspected as a threat to the moral good, as one would expect in an age permeated by conservative Christian values under modern pressures.

The Victorian novel of which I am most reminded, however, is George Eliot's *Mill on the Floss* of 1860, in which the heroine, Maggie Tulliver, makes the mistake of falling passionately in love with a man engaged to her cousin and redeems herself for it only by drowning while attempting to save people during a flood. (Yes, Victorian heroines died like flies if they did not wind up safely married, and poor Maggie did not even have a night of sex to show for her loss of literary life.)

Now, in comparing Maggie's fictional destiny with the modern treatment of Pocahontas or with Waller's heroine, Francesca, we can easily see the difference contemporary culture makes to the treatment of women and sexuality. Maggie Tulliver's overweening desire for her would-be lover is seen as a tragic flaw, while Pocahontas's dalliance with the fictional John Smith and Francesca's inability to resist adultery with her roving photographer are treated as both natural and understandable. The dead giveaway is that the male movie roles are played by those 1990s icons of female desire Mel Gibson and Clint Eastwood, respectively, whereas George Eliot has a far more ironic view of her heroine's lover: for example, the narrator tells us that he partly pursues Maggie because he would enjoy "see[ing] such a creature [as Maggie] subdued by love." Perhaps the modern heroines are allowed their desire because the men they love are so heroic, or the men they desire are now heroic because contemporary culture endorses sexual love.

Nevertheless, certain unmistakable structural similarities between our Victorian example and the modern romances leap to mind. Just like Maggie, both Disney's Pocahontas and Waller's Francesca are described as dark, wild, and exotic (a very old Anglo code for passionate). George Eliot's Maggie Tulliver stands out from her peers by virtue of her "gypsy" looks and impulsive ways; Francesca is Italian by birth, and therefore marked as an alien in her husband's Iowa community, while Pocahontas is a native and consequently allied with the earth, woodland creatures, unrestrained physical activity, and all-around unspoiled primitive innocence.

However, though simmering with unrealized sexual and emotional needs, these heroines are also markedly self-denying. All three ultimately sacrifice love itself to the interests of the males in their families who seek to dominate them: Maggie Tulliver's fool of a brother, Francesca's dull but virtuous husband, and Pocahontas's traditionally authoritarian father, the chief of their Native American tribe. Though their superiority of character to all these males—brother, husband, or father—is established early in each story, these heroines ultimately choose duty to family (for the primitive figure, Pocahontas, her "people" is the extended family of her tribe) over pleasure; that is, in all three texts, desire and duty are treated as inimical opposites, the poles around which a woman's life must revolve. The woman's task is to discipline or transform unruly romantic and sexual feeling into noble submission.

What interests me, though, is not just the similarities of structure but that contemporary romance has added certain fascinating pseudo-feminist twists to the Victorian story of self-denial that both accommodate and subvert present-day feminist (and other politically progressive) demands. Disney, for example, incorporates into the story not only the rebellious, "spirited" heroine with quasi-feminist implications but also a child's version of the Rousseauian natural man, plus modern ecological green movements and multiculturalism in general, all projected through the idealization of the Native American's relation to nature. That's an impressive menu of goals. Waller presents a different buffet of righteous appeals: the resistance to a kind of "Main Street" narrow provincialism and stifling Puritanism in general, an awareness of the double standard in judging a woman's reputation, and a New Ageish self-help celebration of a woman's opening up to sensual pleasure as a "feminist" adventure of self-development, a kind of *Lady Chatterley for Dummies.*

Yet I would maintain that these worthy issues of modernity are merely the sugarcoating to make the medicine of tradition go down: behind these screens, the agendas are strikingly Victorian. The method is the same: hidden assumptions are built into the forms of narrative so that it always appears to be about something else than it is. That is, our eyes are kept on the noble heroism of the feminine (what Sarah Ellis in *Women of England* called the "influence" of women's "moral greatness"), whereas the true emotional center of the narrative is the inviolable sanctity of the family or community to which the female must surrender. In both Pocahontas and *Bridges*, the woman's heroism consists almost entirely of the power to direct the men to do the right thing. Specifically, she is able to tell the hero about the necessity of sacrificing *her* "personal" needs for *their* good, or that of the family/tribe, thereby enacting women's highest calling.

THE BRIDGES OF MADISON COUNTY: FEMALE DESIRE AND THE FAMILY

One novel feature of *Bridges* is the hero's and heroine's ages—midfortyish in her case, fiftyish in his, suggesting that the appeal is to an older audience with whom the traditional theme of self-denial reverberates. *Bridges* presents its love story as if far more is at stake than a fling in the cornfields, not *Brief Encounter on the Prairie* but a tale of mystical and elemental wisdom. In this it resembles *Pocahontas*, as we shall see, which represents itself as only in part a story about true and impossible love.

Robert Kincaid, our hero in *Bridges*, is not just a lover but a professional photographer. As the novel is told partly from his point of view, we luckily get to hear all his meditations on his profession and on the subject of art, which is to say on life in general. Francesca, his married lover who in her unadulterated (pardon the pun) admiration stands in for us as his adoring audience, is absolutely enthralled by his tidbits of wisdom: "For Robert Kincaid, this was everyday talk. For her it was the stuff of literature. People in Madison County didn't talk this way, about these things. . . . Not about art and dreams."[2] Robert, you can see, is identified with "art" and "dreams"—which in turn vaguely stand in for all aspiration that is buried under the need for "safety and comfort." So insistent is this theme of general salvation through imagination and ambition that we easily fail to notice that Francesca herself, intelligent, cultured, and (once again) "spirited," has no aspirations of her own, before, during, or after her affair.

Sexual love, of course, represents the missing stage on Francesca's journey to spiritual uplift, or rather sexual love in the form of the woman's recognition and worship of male sexuality. In the scenes of early mutual seduction we see this titillating recognition displaced onto an object passed between them: Robert offers her a cigarette, and she "surprised herself and took [it]. What am I doing? she thought. She had smoked years ago but gave it up under the steady thump of criticism from [her husband]" (39). She then feels "the warmth of his hand and the tiny hairs along the back of it" for the first time. So the drama is presented as a conflict between indulging the self or its opposite, repression of selfhood— "giving things up," as she had been pressured to give up smoking, which, like adultery, is a habit not really good for you. Fulfilling needs is an expression of and recovery of identity, a very contemporary notion if there ever was one.

We know what's going on when we hear about her married sex life: "Richard [her husband] was interested in sex only occasionally, every couple of months. . . . She was more of a business partner to him. Some of her appreciated that. But rustling yet within her was another person who wanted to . . . be taken, carried away, and peeled back by a force she could sense, but never articulate, even dimly within her mind" (80–81).

A woman has to be "taken by force," it is implied, not by crude brute physical force but by some external principle of masculinity that "articulates," makes manifest, a submerged feminine part of herself. And Robert Kincaid is the man to do it: sensitive and artistic, yet a self-described cowboy, a true New Age warrior: "He had a certain plunging aggressiveness to him, but he seemed to be able to control it, turn it on and then let go of it when he wanted. And that's what had both confused and attracted her—incredibly intensity, but controlled, metered, arrowlike intensity that was mixed with warmth and no hint of meanness" (122). Hard yet soft, we might note, wild yet controlled, arty yet down to earth, aggressive yet warm—wow! "You're so powerful it's frightening," Francesca confesses while they make love, and he doesn't disagree (126).

Understandably, Francesca is "worried" by all that controlled power that could lead God knows where and make her do . . . we know what. But she makes her decision to plunge in anyway, and at this point, the novel seems to come down strongly on the modern side of self-gratification, risk-taking, experience, and adventure as values for women: "She was worried, but something in her had taken hold, something to do with risk. Whatever the cost, she was going" (94).

His sensitivity (artistic nature) is set up as the worthy opponent to the safe-and-stifling, thus showing her the way women can be like men. All well and good, if trite and poorly written.

Then Francesca has her revelation, just in time: she puts her irredeemably boring, unaffectionate husband and barely sketched children first, voting with her feet to end the affair, as they say, "forever." But what about risk, spontaneity, adventure, art, dreams, and power, all of which Francesca now knows she wants and which the novel has bent over backward to endorse as life-affirming modern values? Robert Kincaid is disconsolate, but she is determined, so he obediently skips off to continue his adventurously lonely life of artistic cowboyhood, while she sadly but wisely resumes her plain cooking and virtuous ennui.

What happened here? In this type of narrative, the submerged part of women's lives is transmuted into the "romance," which is morally and aesthetically elevated as high-minded and beautiful (that is, they are not just having it off), but then our heroine has to fall back into a secure domestic relationship—the very one originally seen and implicitly condemned as safe but stifling. Francesca and the reader are consoled for the loss of stimulation and ambition by the aura around self-sacrifice as nobly tragic, the renunciation of passion perfumed with exemplary virtue. What is truly at stake, however, is revealed in Francesca's posthumous letter to her children, when she says, "If it hadn't been for Robert Kincaid, I'm not sure I could have stayed on the farm all these years" (182). So the romance is the shot in the arm that enables her to face a dreary but righteous woman's life, perhaps a life like those of real women who don't have cowboys conveniently arriving at their doorsteps.

DISNEY'S *POCAHONTAS*: INNOCENT ROMANCE VERSUS "MY PEOPLE"

The Disney film of the traditional legend of Pocahontas represents a case of quite another story, wildly different yet oddly similar, constructed out of the enduring ruin of culture's myths about women and passion, this time aimed at little girls. Almost nothing besides the names and setting has been preserved of the actual history of Pocahontas's relations with the Jamestown colony in Disney's film, as in the popular story of Pocahontas the Indian Princess in general. The rest is propaganda, stereotyping, and hype. At best the main idea of the story, that Pocahontas saved John Smith's life, is a dubious legend. In fact, historians agree upon very little about her, as sources of evidence are mainly limited to memoirs by the colonists themselves, and these are hardly without bias or romanticization of the colonial enterprise.

Unsurprisingly, the Disney movie repackages the legend primarily as a coming-of-age story about an "Indian princess" in love. The cross-cultural "romance" is

both titillating and also neatly disposed of at the end when Pocahontas is conveniently made to choose duty to her people over following her lover across the
Atlantic. End of cross-cultural romance. Absolutely none of this has any basis
in history, or is even suggested by the original legend. In fact, the story as it had
evolved by the nineteenth century had a different theme: namely, that some
"good" Indians, as opposed to the vast majority of "bad" and "wild" ones, could
aid in the colonization of America (the Squanto legend about Thanksgiving has
the same theme). Rather, as the American Indian Historical Society's *Textbooks
and the American Indian* (1970) puts it, Pocahontas and Squanto "were not heroes to their race; they were informers upon their own people, and helped the
invaders in their efforts to grab lands."³

Disney movies that feature heroines are generally geared toward romantic love, but as far as can be determined, Pocahontas was probably as young as
twelve years old when she knew John Smith; she was subsequently forcibly captured by colonists, and finally while still a teenager married another colonist who
later died fighting her own people. If she did save John Smith's life, and it isn't
certain that she did, it is not at all clear what her motivation was, and there is no
indication whatsoever that it was romantic love. Yet in the movie, not only does
Pocahontas have the curves and cleavage of an Indian Princess Barbie, but the
middle-aged John Smith morphs into Mel Gibson, cute and boyish as all get-out.
Nothing in the way of actual sexuality takes place onscreen, of course, but the
love affair is presented through codes that make the romantic goings-on clear to
the preteen audience.

Significantly, Disney downplays the colonial-patriotic theme of resisting Indian treachery and sells Pocahontas herself as a proto-feminist heroine, a strong
woman of color, which weirdly gives her a special meaning in ways the eighteenth
and nineteenth centuries certainly did not value. The threatening wildness of
natives as they appear in white patriotic legends is deftly reshaped as the rebel-
liousness of youth, adorably rendered as Pocahontas with a full and sulky lip. She
is determined to see the right thing done by resisting her well-intentioned but
stubborn and less cosmopolitan father, like the Little Mermaid before her. So her
rebellious streak is associated with the sort of passionate and "spirited" heroine
who has come to be a feature of a certain kind of (supposedly feminist) romance,
including the briefly rebellious Francesca in *Bridges*.

Meanwhile, the theme of wildness that formed a border between native aggression and the civilized Euro-American rational technology of war in the earlier versions of the legend has been transformed. The former contemptuous view
of Indians as primitive is swapped out for an idealization of Native American respect for and preservation of the wilderness, in opposition to a colonial greed
wryly depicted as exploitative. Why can't we all just get along? the Disney movie
seems to ask, throwing treats to every possible liberal cause—feminism, ecology,
multicultural understanding, maybe even affirmative action—while making the

multimillion-dollar profits for its parent company, money that is implicitly as innocuously American as turkey and corn (in both senses of that latter word).

SELF-DENIAL AND PSEUDO-FEMINISM

Oddly, even though *The Bridges of Madison County* is about adult sexual love while *Pocahontas* presents no sex onscreen, *Bridges*, like the Disney movie, also hooks its theme of forbidden passion into the unspoiled primitivism of the American wilderness and the restrained warrior mentality of its hero, the American almost-cowboy. Like Pocahontas, Robert Kincaid can't be domesticated or tamed because he too belongs to the earth, to the past, to a level of integrity few of us can achieve—and therefore is capable and deserving of a love more innocent and enduring than we ordinary folk can actually experience.

Both movie and book rely on our admiration of the heroine's renunciation of romance as a kind of ennobling deprivation. The heroes and heroines must not be allowed to experience romance for too long, to preserve that all-important quality of being sealed off from how the world really works. These characters are better than the world, this implies, though underneath, the narrative relies on our secretly recognizing ourselves in their stories. The world had better listen up, because they teach what is really important. But what is that, exactly?

While both these works of contemporary popular culture emphasize the heroine as the supposed center of moral values, restraining the wildness they both claim to rate so highly, unlike Victorian texts, which at least had the virtue of consistency, modern pop culture wants it every which way. Thus the greater part of each narrative dwells on the very un-Victorian acknowledgment of the pleasure of romantic love as the highest good, reflecting the expectations of late twentieth-century markets. You can have it all, these stories say, by just ignoring the contradictions.

First, a concession is made to feminism and other modern ideas: both Waller's and Disney's romances appear to reverse traditional conventions about the Other, the dark female and/or native, in that adultery is not condemned and the heroine is not punished by the community in *Bridges*, while the natives are idealized, not stigmatized, in Pocahontas. Presenting each heroine as innocent and brave, and each hero as masculine yet not physically aggressive, distracts us from the covert satisfaction the narrative offers in celebrating male power. And then each story can conclude in a way that preserves a structure of male dominance sans its unpleasant odor of privilege and brute control: Francesca's decision to sacrifice her life-transforming desire in the name of the family, and the victory of the colonists over the native territories that follows the establishment of Jamestown in the Pocahontas story.

Sarah Stickney Ellis would hardly have admired either the adultery celebrated in *Bridges* or the contrarian spirit of the disobedient Pocahontas, but she would have recognized and approved the heroines' sacrifice of sexual love, their "own personal exaltation and enjoyment," as she put it, for the sake of family or community.

Everyone goes home wistful but happy: the bridges of Madison County symbolize the values of family and land that arch over the concerns of rebellious female impulse, and we can all whistle while we work at making peace with troublesome groups like women and dark peoples, by co-opting them into romantic scenarios that better belong in Disneyworld. Meanwhile, Disney and Waller surely whistled all the way to the bank.

5

FOR THE LOVE OF MERMAIDS, BEASTS, AND VAMPIRES (AND GHOSTS, ROBOTS, MONSTERS, WITCHES, AND ALIENS)

Romancing the Other

> There are the lover and the beloved, but these two come from different countries.
> —Carson McCullers, *Ballad of the Sad Café*, 1951

Who is lovable and who is not? What sort of person *deserves* love, and why? Many stories turn on the matter of *whom* we may love, which is often another way of asking what *kind* of love is forbidden or out of bounds. When love stories address these important questions, what they answer gives us a yardstick for how we readers measure up. In the weave of their narratives are instructions as to how to locate ourselves within the social order, where we fit or how we stand out against the framework of society. Either way, these tales are expressions of value, inevitably our own worth measured against others.

Comparison is suggested by difference, and it's the nature of stories themselves to organize the world by focusing our gaze on a stated or implied asymmetry or aberration—one that often narrows down to Us (normal, ordinary, human) and Him/Her/It as Other, as if all shades and nuances are dissolved in the distinction. To play along, which is to say to enter into the story, we must forget the arbitrariness of the dividing line. Just as almost any two phenomena can appear to have a family resemblance, nearly anything can appear to us as the Other. The world can all too easily be made over into opposites and oppositions—alien and familiar, East and West, animal and human, black and white, or masculinity and femininity—if we invent and believe in the categories. And categories may be subdivided into warring factions: some women are treated as Other to other women, as is the heroine of *The Scarlet Letter*.[1]

For this reason it's often the boundary between subject and Other that is meaningful: the limit where Otherness begins, and the reason it's a boundary at all. It usually turns out that the boundary of Otherness is what is left over when we have established what is "normal." Stories about love for the Other have no singular function: they may seek to affirm that limit, undermine it, or evade the question by seeming to erase the border of difference. Flirting with dissolving the boundary by merging (as a couple) can be subversive or, paradoxically, can affirm the social need for difference (as when the tale of Cinderella celebrates the idea of privilege even while uniting its cross-class lovers). When this difference serves our purposes, it's emphasized; when it serves us to imagine that we are all alike, or all one, it disappears. In the modern era, with its ideal of individual worth, we love the idea that the Other is really just like us under the skin (as in a cross-cultural romance like *West Side Story*).

One way a story of boundaries provides us with meaning is that difference itself may stimulate romantic attraction. Conversely, one way to give meaning to romance is to make Otherness the narrative problem that drives the story. Modern romance ideology takes two opposing sides on likeness, namely that a) opposites attract, and b) we love others because we have so much in common with them. Oddly, no one seems bothered by this conceptual paradox. Furthermore, lovers who are too different may be threatening to social harmony (such as interracial couples until fairly recently), but lovers who are too much alike (for example, of the same sex) can be equally threatening.

A complication of investigating heterosexual Otherness in romance is that gender itself is commonly conceived as the pairing of opposing forces, as in the familiar rhetoric of "the opposite sex" or Mars and Venus.[2] "Hetero," after all, *means* other/different, though not necessarily opposite, and gender itself is a system of social difference. Love stories of the gendered Other often explain and justify the "inherently" different nature of males and females by upholding the concept of sexual complementarity in love, illustrating the theory with successful couplings of super-feminine women and super-masculine men. Heterosexual romances thrive on the idea of the Otherness of the sexes as first an attraction, then a problem, and finally a union or meshing of "opposites."

"TALE AS OLD AS TIME": LOVING A STRANGER/SUPERHERO/ WILD MAN/MONSTER/ENCHANTRESS

From traditional folktale to modern film and fiction, there is a long history of interspecies romance of male or female human with the Other, a nonhuman or unnatural figure who may represent all that humans wish to have or do or, conversely, all that we reject or deny in ourselves. The forms the Otherness of the lover may take have infinite variety: gods and animals, demons and monsters, statues, machines and angels, creatures from Krypton or the devil himself.[3] It's the supposedly essential difference between the lovers in these stories that tells us how to understand being human, though human ideas of gender often stay intact: the Lamia beloved by Lycius in the poem of the same name by John Keats may be a monster, for example, but she is also decidedly female.

Gender as a stable part of metamorphosis is the underpinning of many narratives from the Greeks onward. The beloved begins as human but morphs into something else (Lamia is a woman who has been trapped in a serpent's body), or a nonhuman becomes humanized through love (the story of Pygmalion and his statue). In these cases, gender is preserved: you see, the Beast was a prince to begin with, so he has to be a male when he is Other.

The idea that the story of love between a human and an Other is a "tale as old as time," to quote from the title song of the Disney movie *Beauty and the Beast,* which is to say mythic, primitive, rising up from some communal unconscious, implies that it appeals because it taps into some universal drive or symbolism. And it's true that Otherness has a very broad presence in world mythologies.[4] On the other hand, even when the structure of these tales is similar, as in the many variants of Cinderella around the world, their meanings are entirely malleable by those who tell and receive the stories. For example, the film *Pretty Woman* may be "based on Cinderella," but the meaning is transformed by what the literary theorist Roland Barthes called "a type of social usage which is added to pure matter."[5] As we saw in the transformations of the Pocahontas story, they are as historically specific as they are in some vague and loose way "timeless" and "universal."

Love stories that are meant to appeal to an audience of women tend to focus on the irony that woman is already conceived as the Other and treat this as a problem to be mastered. A woman's Otherness might represent her as, for example, a threat that must be extirpated through death (the bunny-killing seducer played by Glenn Close in the movie *Fatal Attraction*), an exotic fruit to be consumed (the Vietnamese mistress in Graham Greene's *The Quiet American*), or a creature that has to be domesticated (the irascible Jo in Louisa May Alcott's *Little Women*) or rescued (Truman Capote's feckless Holly Golightly in the film version of *Breakfast at Tiffany's*). But because there is no universal meaning of the Other that is not cast in the mold of culture, the gendered Other can be an affirmation of conservative ideology in one text or, alternatively, a critique of the conventions surrounding femininity and masculinity in another.

Heterosexual love stories are a mode of explaining romance as a gender divide; in stories for women, casting the man as the Other who is beloved makes the strange familiar to the female audience, a way of lessening anxieties. Learning to understand the male Other is part of the old romantic formula for "reading" the man in order to survive.[6] For example, a male character may have brute sexual power, but love will render the monster's Byronic intensity sympathetic, as at the end of the movie *King Kong*.[7] Similarly, when woman is the Other, the male may join her realm of beauty and nature, assimilating her Otherness to himself, as in the film *Splash*, where the hero is able to spend the rest of his life underwater with his beloved mermaid through the transformative magic of her kiss. The story *means* differently to the woman who identifies with the heroine who is beloved by the Other, or is oppressed by him, or who is herself seen as Other in a narrative about love.

HOW TO HANDLE DIFFERENCE

Though the perception of Otherness is often a social problem in real life, provoking destructive fear and hatred (racial or sexual difference, for example), as well as attraction (thus the word "exotic" applied to certain celebrities and tourist places), love *as a story* has a way of giving shape to our anxieties and (seemingly) resolving them through our sympathy with characters and the resolution of the ending.

This narrative method takes many forms. Ghosts and witches can be comic in order to reduce the power of their horror, as in the play *Blithe Spirit* or the TV show *Bewitched*, where the "friendly" monster is benignly different. Tragedy, by contrast, may underline the irreconcilability of the difference, focusing our gaze on the inflexibility of the limit by showing us the fatal consequences of violating a taboo, as in *Romeo and Juliet* or the long novelistic tradition of the so-called tragic mulatto. The Other may belong more to nature than society and be idealized for that, like Peter Pan or Tarzan, while the Other who is wild may be feared (the mad wife Bertha in *Jane Eyre*). The abnormality of the Other may be celebrated as superior and serve as a critique of the status quo, of conformity, or of the tedium of everyday life.[8] Or the monster might be a deformed body or soul who is the exception that proves the rule about the normalcy of love (as in *The Hunchback of Notre Dame* or *Wuthering Heights*.)

Here are some ways that stories resolve the problem of antagonistic difference in love by manipulating what it means to be human:

1. *Conversion:* one lover ceases to be Other, as in "The Frog Prince" and many other folk, fairy, and mythic tales.
2. *Complementarity of essential traits:* difference is accepted as "natural," and the union of protagonist and Other is viewed as "interdependence"; for example, in movies featuring a pretty heroine with a nerdy guy, where she loosens up while he becomes domesticated (as in the comedy *Knocked Up*).
3. *Merging:* splitting the difference, lovers become a third thing together. Both may become androgynous, or the fusion of the two might be symbolized by the child of the lover and beloved Other.[9]
4. *Discovery that there was no difference in the first place:* the peasant girl is really a princess all along, as in some folk tales; the boy who is loved by another boy (the homosexual Other) turns out to be a girl in disguise, as in Shakespeare's *Twelfth Night*.
5. *Tragic love that's doomed:* Othello; the TV series *Beauty and the Beast*; Elizabeth McCracken's *The Giant's House: A Romance*.
6. *Escape from the concept of boundary*—as in the movie *Blade Runner*—into an idyll of natural pleasure. If the critic Leslie Fiedler was right in saying that

Huck and Jim represent homoerotic love, we might say they attempt to escape from the boundary of race by taking to the river.

Because stories address the themes that trouble us as individuals and as a society, differences in lovers frequently embody themes of dominance and submission, power and powerlessness.[10] In the last few hundred years, as the rights and privileges of groups other than the white male propertied elite have increased, gender difference has been a problem and an argument for Western society; who should dominate, and why? Since gender began to be less fixed in meaning and women's roles have been particularly in flux, stories of struggle for control between the genders in love abound.

Here are three examples of modern stories based on traditional versions about, respectively, a mermaid, a beast, and a vampire. In their contemporary versions, at least, all are love stories aimed at a mainly female audience. There have been many critical analyses of each of these stories separately, but here I am mainly interested in exploring parallel differences between the traditional and modern versions in order to show how and why they evolved into contemporary love stories. How do these Other lovers take on a meaning that signifies what the audience wants from romance at specific historical times?

DISNEY AND THE ROMANCE OF THE OTHER

The first two of our examples, *The Little Mermaid* and *Beauty and the Beast*, are fairy-tale stories of the conversion of Otherness, one female and one male, renewed in modern form by Disney productions.[11] Many American girls growing up in the 1950s fed their fantasies of adventure and romance on Disney's cartoon movies based on famous fairy tales and children's literature: *Pinocchio, Snow White, Cinderella, Peter Pan, Alice in Wonderland*, and so on. These films were vivid and comforting because they were all alike in some way: they said more about the hopes of the middle class in post–World War II America than about the prose tales on which they were based, and to which they bore only a tangential relation. Disney's Alice was more like Shirley Temple than Lewis Carroll's heroine, Pinocchio and Peter Pan came out for family values and the brave idea that there was really no place like home, despite impulses to the contrary, and Cinderella and Snow White emphasized the magical ability of their cartoon heroines' sweetness to make small, cute, cooperative creatures like dwarfs and mice promote perfect romance. Most of us knew this had nothing to do with what our real life was like, and that was exactly why we loved it.

Like television, Disney movies have changed to accommodate the social upheavals begun in the sixties, and two fairy-tale cartoons, *The Little Mermaid* and *Beauty and the Beast*, are good examples of the direction of this shift toward what the filmmakers would call "realism." In response to the surging wave of feminism in the 1970s, the characters of Disney heroines were given a new emphasis and development in the 1980s and 1990s. Whereas an older version of a heroine like Snow White could be encompassed by two or three adjectives (beautiful, sweet, and given to compulsive domesticity in the presence of a broom), Ariel and Belle, the heroines of *The Little Mermaid* (1989) and *Beauty and the Beast* (1991), respectively, were clearly meant to be detailed portraits of Modern Girls. They are beautiful, yes (the sure marker of this is that the cartoon eyes are literally three times the size of the pert little nose), but independent and outspoken also, and both heroines initially want more than merely to marry a prince.

Both these films deal with the transformation of animal into human as their theme, though each locates the site of transformation in a different gender, namely the mermaid's conversion to female human and the Beast's to male. Disney hardly invented the theme of metamorphosis, but its selection as the common element for the Disney movies of the early 1990s is surely telling. Both *Snow White* (1937) and *Cinderella* (1950), after all, had very different themes, namely the threat of female envy (embodied in stepmothers and stepsisters) and the rewards of female selflessness, nurturing, and domestic drudgery, perfect for their times. Sleeping Beauty, as Simone de Beauvoir pointed out, was the very image of femininity and pure passivity—the girl in the coma, encased in glass. In these older films, the hero is a cardboard prince without character who barely figures in the plot and/or appears mainly at the end, and no other identifications of masculinity really matter. The point is to define and elaborate the heroine's femininity as goodness, so that it can be proven through the courtship and rewarded by the marriage. Courtship as the revelation of male character is unnecessary.

By contrast, the focus in *The Little Mermaid* and *Beauty and the Beast* is on the "spirit" of the heroine herself, but her will, ambition, and activity are turned in only one direction: in each case the difficulty and desire turns out to be a threatening and violent male. In both, machismo is the problem, and the young girl's spirited response to it appears initially as inspiring, which is to say surprisingly progressive.

Disney's *The Little Mermaid* and *Beauty and the Beast* are about female identity in relation to the bestial, a negative image of nature uncontrolled in its power, frighteningly opposed to both human reason and the humanistic freedoms associated with "civilization." "We polish an animal mirror to look at ourselves," says the critic Donna Haraway,[12] and indeed the young girls in the Disney audience are encouraged to measure their own marginality against the deformity, limitations, and anarchic freedoms of the mermaid body of Ariel and the supposedly hideous male beast who imprisons the lovely Belle. The fantasy of Snow White and Cinderella, that of being a princess in disguise, gives way to a contemporary drama about how women can deal with problematic masculinity very directly (if magically). In particular, both these films deal with the theme of men's potentially frightening power to dominate and control women, and the way love reverses that anxiety.

She's Got Legs: Two Versions of the Little Mermaid Story

When my students read Hans Christian Andersen's "The Little Mermaid," published in 1836, they are astonished, even indignant, at the (to them) weird themes in the original story that intersect with the well-known romance between beautiful mermaid and handsome prince.[13] They are familiar, of course, with the Disney film *The Little Mermaid* and the successful Broadway musical it spawned (a word that seems oddly appropriate in this fishy context), neither of which prepares them to encounter the early-Victorian concerns and religious vocabulary of the Andersen story. That Disney slapped on a happy ending is predictable (though Andersen might very well have claimed his as the happier), but the implications of the changes in the story itself go far beyond this. A direct comparison of the two versions illustrates perfectly how the meaning of Otherness alters with the very different—and yet in some telling ways not so different—view of women's nature and their place in society.

Hans Christian Andersen's "The Little Mermaid" (1836) In Andersen's original version of the fairy tale, the Little Mermaid is a "strange child" who is marked by strong desire: "None of the [other mermaid princesses] longed so much to see the earth."[14] So far, so Disney, but not for long. The emphasis is on the beauty of the natural, not on the enviable commodities or socialized behavior of human life as in Disney's film. Andersen's Little Mermaid is a child of nature who despises status: when her grandmother orders "oysters to attach themselves to the tail of the princess to show her high rank," the Little Mermaid says they hurt her and "would have shaken off all this grandeur." What she envies most is the human soul, which "lives forever, lives after the body has turned to dust." Grandmother Mermaid informs her that as a nonhuman she cannot "rise up through the clear, pure air . . . to unknown and glorious regions which we shall never see." However, if she can win a man's pledge of love, "his soul would glide into your body" and she would "know the happiness of that glorious world above the stars." That's not going to happen, though, warns the old lady mermaid, because humans think tails are ugly compared to legs.

Here's where the story focuses on an idea alien to the Disney movie: the Little Mermaid wants that "glorious world" of spiritual afterlife through the immortal soul more than she wants human life. Admirers of Disney's version might note that the longing for a soul no longer plays quite the same role in the movie. In the 1836 story, romantic love is not valued for human happiness on earth so much as it is a conduit to spiritual reward.

As in the Disney film, Andersen's Little Mermaid rescues the beautiful young prince and is more sorrowful than ever with obsessive love, because he doesn't notice. And yes, this Little Mermaid also goes to see the Sea-witch and learns that in order to be loved and get an immortal soul, she has to suffer great pain: her legs and tongue are cut off. The differences between nineteenth- and twentieth-century versions are considerable from here on, however. For one thing, Andersen's Mermaid bears terrible suffering and degradation for her greater goal. Our sea princess joins the prince's "beautiful female slaves" who sing for him, but she is tongueless and dumb, so she dances . . . and bears the pain like sharp knives on her feet "willingly."

And what does she get in return? She "receives his permission to sleep at his door"; he "loves her as he would love a little child," but not romantically, nor does he ever know she saved him. In fact, she sees that there is another pretty maiden he loves and will marry. Nevertheless, since she is a typical Victorian heroine, this makes no difference to her abject devotion: "I will take care of him," she vows, "and love him, and give up my life for his sake." It's clear we're supposed to admire this, not want to send her to a therapist. Here is where my students are simply appalled, even more than by the violent description of tongue and leg cutting: But wait, they moan, isn't love about recognition of the best one? Isn't love mutuality and connection?

With the typical goriness of traditional fairy tales in general and Hans Christian Andersen's in particular, the Little Mermaid's sisters offer a grisly deal that doesn't show up in Disney: if she plunges a knife into the prince's heart, his blood spilling on her feet will make her into a mermaid again and she won't die. Our heroine loves him too much to do the deed, however, so instead she becomes "a daughter of the air" who doesn't have an immortal soul but can procure one. All it takes is serving three hundred years, in the same way she has already "suffered and endured and raised [herself] to the spirit-world by [her] good deeds." Before going off to suffer and do good deeds, she nobly kisses the forehead of her rival, the bride (talk about selflessness), and fans the noble brow of the prince: romantic love is defined as moral, a manifestation of self-abnegating virtue, so jealousy is not permitted.

Andersen's story concludes with the didactic information that when the spirits find "a good child" who deserves the love of his or her parents, their reward is one less year of the three hundred needed for these angel-figures to "float into the kingdom of heaven." But naughty or wicked children make them cry, and every tear adds a day to their three hundred years. Don't look for wicked children in the Disney version.

What is Andersen's tale really about? The theme is characteristically Victorian: the triumph of the moral (self-sacrificing) superiority of women, expressed through self-restraint, submission to a greater good—in other words, the Victorian version of love. The Little Mermaid experiences two conversions: the first enacts essential difference (legs/tail, human/animal), while the second resolves the moral opposition these categories represent. This is accomplished by converting her Otherness to that third thing, a spirit that overcomes the flaws of both animal and human states and renders her pure femininity, which is to say a vessel for caretaking love.

In Andersen's "Little Mermaid," female desire is Otherness, counterbalanced by femininity itself, since true moral femininity opposes the uncontrolled wildness of mermaids and children (especially the wicked ones). Romantic love is equated with religious values: heaven (literal heaven, not the metaphor for ecstatic emotion) is the reward for self-renunciation and the restraint of will in women and children. Andersen's story is typical of Victoriana in that the suffering of romantic love is the occasion or, better, opportunity for the self-sacrifice necessary to rise above the bestial Otherness of the human body. *That* is Andersen's happy ending, not the formation of the couple.

Disney's The Little Mermaid (1989)   While both Andersen's version and Disney's are conversion tales and similar in essential structure, the intersection of gender and romantic love in the two stories is completely different.

If the Victorian idea of women's moral superiority in self-denying love dominates Andersen's "The Little Mermaid," Disney's movie is another kettle of fish altogether. In Disney's version, the power of the father stands in for dominating men. The entire first part of *The Little Mermaid* develops the father-daughter relationship, beginning with the first scene, which features not the heroine but the King of the Sea, Ariel's father. We see him bearing his phallic symbol of power and authority, the magical trident, and the cartoon form emphasizes his hyper-muscularity; he is a sort of aging Arnold Schwarzenegger of the ocean.

We then cut to our independent-but-naive heroine, who is humorously observed busily exploring and misinterpreting the signs of the world above the sea, oblivious to her duties as daughter. This spirit of curiosity and wonder clearly marks her as a kind of rebel-scientist and/or rebel-artist figure, one of Disney's New Women. Her marginality to the world of the expected and known is romanticized, so that her absence from her father's palace can be comically presented as a gentle, absentminded individuality. We see that she is not an undutiful daughter, in other words, but merely a restless soul in pursuit of a humanistic authenticity of identity. The authority of this "human" freedom is then held up against the unreasonable dictatorship of the dominating patriarch of the sea, a kind of Jungian oceanic world of the unconscious. Since we moderns sympathize with youth finding their true identities, Ariel's rebellion justifies her disobedience, reducing the potential of an attack on the hierarchy of gender domination. Just a teenage girl and her overly strict dad, in other words, nothing more serious than that.

Naturally, so to speak, we are all on the side of brave little Ariel cutting loose from her female restrictions, defying Daddy Triton's unreasonable demands and exploring the adventure of the Unknown. Her first song is "Part of Your World," a prayer of envy for the glamour of the human ego, encompassing experience, versatility, competence, and, most of all, freedom, as compared to swimming below in that Jungian sea. Meanwhile, Sebastian, the mediator between father and daughter, who sings reggae-like songs and speaks with a Jamaican accent, advises the father to "show her who's boss" (thus adding the spice of racism to the stew of marginalities). The lines seem clearly drawn between generations, between traditional role restrictions and the ideal of humanistic individual freedom, and between excessive masculine rule and precocious female subversion of male control.

Like many a cartoon ingenue before her, Ariel has the face of a small and innocent girl and the voluptuous torso of a woman, barely encased in a bikini top, though of course her curves end asexually in a tail. When Ariel falls in love and wishes for a transmutation into adult sexual form (symbolized by legs), the father's anger is transmuted also, into an extreme but understandable form of protectiveness against the danger of human sexuality; as Sebastian says, "Human life is a mess," and it is safer under the sea, where one will not be attacked and eaten up by humans or human desire. Thus the daughter's longing to be free becomes a story about growing up into romantic love, which is presented as undermining not only the authority of the father to control her desire but also his power to protect her from the sexuality of other men.

In a scene meant to be frightening, the king invades his daughter's "secret cave" (yes), where she keeps her collection of human artifacts, smashing all her precious possessions with his trident. Ariel responds by making a Faustian bargain to become human with the ugly Sea Witch, Ursula. The latter underlines the contrast between her own malignancy (based on greed, envy, and an unfeminine desire to wrench power from the king) and the violence of the father, now justified because motivated by his well-meaning overprotectiveness against a very real danger to his naive teenage daughter. Somehow the father's domination has been converted to loving paternal vigilance.

As in the Andersen fairy tale, our mermaid-heroine pays a high price for her metamorphosis into leggy womanhood. Though no blood drips, she must surrender her ability to speak, the speaking of her desire, which is to say her very identity. So, oddly, the conditions for being a good daughter to the powerful king and a potential lover to the prince are the same: dumb (in both senses of the word) submission. The prince, however, can still hear her beautiful singing voice, which marked her femininity in relation to her father. I should note that the prince also makes beautiful music, but he pipes it on a flute—phallic symbols always abound in Disney movies—and he is the aestheticized version of masculinity: a flute rather than the huge, lightning-powered trident; gentle, aristocratic, and artistic rather than magical or threatening. He is, in other words, a fellow the heroine can handle, a regular prince, as it were, if she can only capture him by sunset.

But because Ariel is mute, she has to make him fall in love by looks alone while trying to be authentically human, a situation that seems to describe the difficulties of women in romantic love pretty well. These are traditional fantasies loaded with a modern dilemma: growing up into modern sexual freedom, on the one hand, alongside the necessity of growing into traditional femaleness through the focus on sexual and emotional desire.

It is here that the film takes an important and very old narrative turn: if Ariel can pass through the ordeal of "making" the gentle prince fall in love, she will get to eat her fishcake and have it too. The reward held out is a sexuality that is "civilized," proof of worthiness for a female role coded as grown up, freed from the overbearing authority that in Disney movies is only located in parental figures, not in the lover/husband. The passage into romantic love and marriage is presented as the only way girls can break free of paternal authority, overcome the dark temptations of fishy sexual desires, and become fully human. This is a theme straight from traditional narratives aimed at women.

What distinguishes Disney's *The Little Mermaid* as a modern work is that it moves masculine domination to the center of this movie as a problem, rather than take it as a presumption. It also appears to actively oppose it by the heroine's contemporary-seeming spirit of rebellion. But this turns out to be a comic tease: in the final scenes of the movie, the king is rescued by the lover-prince from the evil power of Ursula and blesses his daughter's passage into marriage and humanity. "I guess there's just one problem left," he says ruefully. "How much I'm going to miss her." The modern definition of romance, missing from Andersen's original fairy tale, subsumes the problem of domination into an ingenue-and-her-adoring-rescuer paradigm.

He's Such an Animal: Two Versions of the Story of Beauty and the Beast

De Beaumont's "Beauty and the Beast" (1756) The source of the version of "Beauty and the Beast" most well-known to children is the eighteenth-century tale by Mme. de Beaumont. Once again, the original theme and intention of the traditional story, in which young girls are instructed to be virtuous (mainly meaning obedient and self-abnegating) through an entertaining (but didactic) tale of courtship and marriage, differ from the modern version in subtle ways that reveal how we think about love.

In Mme. de Beaumont's story, Beauty is a wealthy merchant's daughter, the youngest of six beautiful girls. Unlike the others, who are vain and proud of their family's money and status, however, Beauty is unselfish and good. The sisters are a type we modern folk will recognize: they "talk endlessly about . . . beautiful clothes."[15] We know Beauty is virtuous because she works hard at housework when their father loses his fortune; otherwise we know little of her character. Typically of an eighteenth- (and nineteenth-) century heroine, Beauty proves her worth through self-denial: when the father goes to redeem merchandise from a ship that arrived safely, Beauty asks for nothing at all.

We all know about the father's encounter with the "dreadful" Beast, also called a "monster" in the English translation of 1757. What is less familiar is the strong emphasis on money and trade in the story, and not only in merchandise. When

Beauty learns she can exchange her life for her father's, she cries, "I feel fortunate to be able to sacrifice myself for him," and the Beast replies, "The good deed you have done in saving your father's life will not go unrewarded." The idea was to impress a social and Christian bargain onto young girls: be obedient and good and you will be repaid in unexpected ways; the universe is like this.

For our purposes, the most interesting aspect of the eighteenth-century version of the tale is how *anti*-romantic it really is. When Beauty stays too long at her father's, she dreams of the Beast and reasons:

> "Is it his fault if he is so ugly, and has so little sense? He is kind and good, and that is sufficient. Why did I refuse to marry him? I should be happier with the monster than my sisters are with their husbands; it is neither wit, nor a fine person, in a husband, that makes a woman happy, but virtue, sweetness of temper, and complaisance, and Beast has all these valuable qualifications. It is true, I do not feel the tenderness of affection for him, but I find I have the highest gratitude, esteem, and friendship."

You could be reading the latest self-help best seller—say, Lori Gottlieb's *Marry Him: The Case for Settling for Mr. Good Enough* (2010).

Oddly, the Beast in the original tale is not only beastly-looking (and not in the cuddly manner of a stuffed lion, as in the Disney film), it's also hinted that he's dull and stupid ("neither wit nor a fine person"), though it's clear in that Beauty herself has superior qualities of mind (Mme. de Beaumont, the author, was a teacher). Their union is not about compatibility of tastes and interests, as modern coupling is supposed to be. Rather, the character of the Beast is meant to be a direct contrast to the husbands of the wicked sisters, who are unhappy with their choices: "The eldest had married a gentleman, extremely handsome indeed, but so fond of his own person, that he was full of nothing but his own dear self, and neglected his wife. The second had married a man of wit, but he only made use of it to plague and torment everybody, and his wife most of all."[16]

Another motive for Beauty's acceptance of the Beast as her husband would certainly not be found in a modern advice manual: "I will not make him miserable," declares Beauty. "Were I to be so ungrateful I should never forgive myself." The woman's gratitude for the man who loves her and pledges to take care of her for life is often mentioned in Jane Austen's late eighteenth- and early nineteenth-century novels as well, but would hardly fly as a justification for marriage today.

After Beauty agrees to marry him, the Beast metamorphoses and she sees, at her feet, "one of the loveliest princes that eye ever beheld." He turns out to be intelligent as well as gorgeous—as he reasonably explains, the evil fairy who "condemned me to remain in that form until a beautiful girl would consent to marry me" also "barred me from revealing my intelligence." Beastliness is dumb and ugly, not protectively lionlike and brave, as in Disney. Note that the virtue motivating our heroine to decide on marriage for what the author calls "judicious" reasons, having nothing to do with strong erotic attraction or material gain, is rewarded by giving her . . . yes, an extremely good-looking, smart guy who has a castle. If you've read *Pride and Prejudice*, you know this logic isn't confined to popular culture.

As in all versions of the Beauty and the Beast story, the sisters are satisfyingly punished at the end for not properly appreciating the heroine, and the royal couple will live in "perfect happiness"—not, however, because they were in love but because their marriage was, as we are told in Mme. de Beaumont's unambiguous words, "founded on virtue."

What is this story about? Like Andersen's "The Little Mermaid," it is not so much a romance as an intentionally didactic tale aimed at pubescent girls to illustrate the need to put virtue higher than personal feeling. Though love and marriage appear in both as a kind of sauce to make the dry meat go down, ultimately female submission to duty is much more important than romantic love. At just the time (mid-eighteenth century) when the commercial middle class was growing in numbers and status and women were allowed more choice in marriage, the "love story" of Beauty and the Beast presents this particular configuration of women, money, and romance: girls shouldn't indulge their sexual, romantic, or materialistic desires . . . but if they are dutiful and practice self-denial in marriage as in all other aspects of life, they will be rewarded for their virtue by getting everything they want anyway. This is doing love and marriage the "right way."

Disney's Beauty and the Beast (1991) Disney's *Beauty and the Beast*, by contrast, is not about "judicious choices" in marriage at all. Rather, it imagines a potentially violent lover as abnormal and deformed—only to trace the supposed power of women to transform the men who love them from angry and domineering to familiar and comfortable. The film begins with a comically loving depiction of the heroine, Belle, as superior in beauty but marginal to a milieu that does not value her intellectualism: her pert nose is always in a book, and the sign of her difference as an intellectual girl-beauty is that while her hair is traditionally long and lustrous (and her eyes are only twice as large as her nose, unlike Ariel's), a stray lock falls unexpectedly on her forehead. In other words, the film takes a minor detail of the original story, the heroine's superior mind as well as body, and runs with it as a postfeminist adaptation.

Like Ariel (and Jane Eyre and Jo March and Maggie Tulliver and Dorothy, stuck in Kansas), Belle longs for a wider experience: her first song has her wistfully regretting wasting her life in "this poor provincial town," and the deliberate use of Broadway musical devices helps depict the dullness and comic stupidity of the townsfolk who cannot appreciate the cultured Belle. The index of Belle's character is her love for adventure books—her absorption in a world of possibilities closed to her makes her, like Ariel, initially "peculiar," absentminded, unfit for her domestic feminine role.

A new addition to Mme. de Beaumont's tale is Belle's father, who is the fuddled, helpless, inadequate inventor-genius figure, entirely incapable of protecting his daughter from harm, precisely the obverse of the Little Mermaid's dad. His benevolent but unhelpful parental character is underscored by his early encounter with the dreadful forest wolves, malignant beasts with glittering eyes and slathering jaws, who do nothing but hunger for human flesh and should sue Disney for slander.

The male-as-beast/helpless-female-as-human dichotomy is immediately complicated by Belle's father's entrance into the enchanted castle. In this magical space of transformation and infinite possibilities (as opposed to the stifling, dull normality of the "provincial" town), we first see the Beast as an enlarged wolflike shadow, so that the overlap of Beast and wolf, the malignant side of the animal and the natural, are underlined.

The cut from that frightening scene to Belle's cheerful competence in handling Gaston's arrogant marriage proposal is significant: Belle prefers, she says, adventure in the "great wide somewhere" to marrying this fool, with his biceps and remarkable ability to spit. We see the vista that pulls her outward to the world, a colorful panorama of hills that stands for the limitless possibilities for action and experience out in the world. We don't doubt at this point, given the information that we have, that our heroine can and will go out there and do . . . we don't know what, exactly.

But Belle never goes out into the world; as with Jane Eyre or Maggie Tulliver, her Victorian analogues, her longing for a wider experience of life is immediately channeled into the intense rush of danger and pleasure found in romantic love, the world within the confined space of the heart and psyche. Out of selfless love for her father, who needs rescuing, she must enter the enchanted castle of sexuality and encounter the Beast. The struggle ensues, dramatic and fearful at first, gradually yielding to the comic. The Beast, who imprisons her, is threatening and bullying, but as his character is carefully developed, we are led to see that his distemper is lovable and he is just misunderstood; his taming is a matter of education rather than a reshaping of nature.

This is the old story, repeated over and over in modern popular romantic novels and movies. One of the traditional powers of women, much celebrated in eighteenth- and nineteenth-century literature and journalism, is to "settle" the wild man (formerly known as a "rake"), to end his days of loose behavior by a love that reins in his promiscuous sexuality. While the Beast threatens to "break down the door" if she doesn't obey his will (which, in this film for children, means come to dinner rather than submit sexually), the antidote is presented as Belle's "teaching him to be a gentleman" and to groom himself, reforming him with the values of nobility and civilization so that he can court Belle properly. By the second half of the movie he physically comes to resemble a cute St. Bernard or the Cowardly Lion in *The Wizard of Oz* more than a wolf or a monster.

The rest of the film depicts that courtship. Interestingly, books, which appeared initially as a symbol of Belle's superior culture and rejection of superficial, conventionalized female beauty, reappear only in one scene: as a surprise, the Beast gives her an outsized library as an offering of love, a counter in the game of courtship. The world of intellect, so highly valued in the beginning, becomes a product that has an exchange value for romantic love. The Beast himself does not appear to read (perhaps this is an activity for passive women only), but he too is educated when she teaches him table manners. The emphasis is on learning, although secretly the audience comes to appreciate that Belle's happiness depends on neither her book learning nor any other accomplishment but rather on the Beast's ability to learn how to change into a mate worthy of the "naturally" superior Belle.

Belle's transformation from book learner to tamer of wild male beasts leads to her triumph: the Beast, "captured" by love, releases her from captivity to be with her father. The climax of the movie occurs when Belle is granted the power to choose her own life—a power she then uses to return to the Beast of her own free will. The love of Beauty in the fairy tale literally transfigures the threatening Beast, and, to quote Samuel Richardson's Pamela, who was also initially imprisoned by a violent male she fell in love with in the eighteenth-century novel of the same name, the prison "becomes my palace."

The conclusion of the movie pits the vile machismo of Gaston against the good masculinity of the Beast, as the former taunts the latter, "Are you too kind and gentle to fight back?" Apparently not, since the Beast then musters one last round of his violent temper and demolishes Gaston and all the barbaric townsfolk who followed him. Traditional male power, that of the "natural" man, is found to be useful after all, provided that feminine nurture keeps the violent/sexual nature of masculinity under control with "love." Needless to say, when the movie closes, Belle is dancing with the restored prince (who turns out to be as boring as every other prince) and is about to marry him, having apparently forgotten both books and panoramic vision of the world.

Neither film includes a mother of any kind, and I take that as significant: the problem for women, these films seem to say to children, is how to construct a female identity in and around the problem of men. In Disney's *The Little Mermaid*, femininity is at first seen as disfigured and insufficient, then normalized by the reshaping and channeling of the heroine's independent "spirit" so that she is worthy of the love of a man. Belle begins with the competence that the Little Mermaid lacks but uses that ability to rescue and refashion a male who can confer identity on her. In other words, these are two different versions of the same idea. Both of these narratives present romance as an updated solution to old problems, reworked so they address current fears about men and masculinity: what can we do without them?

As models of femininity for their child audiences, and especially for female children, both *The Little Mermaid* and *Beauty and the Beast* are especially insidious in their false appeal to contemporary "liberal" thinking on women. The voguish rhetoric of independent and outspoken femininity in these and similar films helps to heighten the effect of "newness" in their depiction of women and their problems. Traditional fairy-tale plots are combined with devices from a potpourri of sources (such as Broadway musicals, the spirited romantic heroine of the nineteenth century, 1940s "career woman" movies, and older Disney film traditions) to raise anxieties about issues of interest to women—the meaning of female identity, the limits of independence, the desirability of male protection weighed against the threat of domination, how to find and shape a male lover and husband—only to refigure and repress them. No need to rebel, these movies say: Daddy knows best, after all.

DEFANGING THE VAMPIRE: FROM DREAD TO ROMANCE IN TWO VERSIONS OF THE VAMPIRE MYTH

Our last example of romantic Otherness is perhaps the ultimate Other, the vampire, focusing on two best sellers: Bram Stoker's popular late-nineteenth-century *Dracula* and Stephenie Meyer's even more popular early twenty-first-century *Twilight*, where the demon is deformed—and defanged—almost beyond recognition, as the vampire lover is used to work out the complexities of modern gender relations for women.

Bram Stoker's *Dracula* (1897)

"How blessed are some people, whose lives have no fears, no dreads," says Lucy in the nineteenth-century horror classic *Dracula*.[17] Modern women whose lives have plenty of romantic fears and dreads, the vampire lover in contemporary fantasy is for you; Bram Stoker's *Dracula*, however, not so much. Published in 1897, it is clearly a male fantasy. The original Count Dracula is not a young hunk at all but a repulsive old man who crawls like a lizard face-first down the castle wall—far from a sexual or romantic object of desire. He has shockingly red lips, something like the reddened sexual swelling on some female primates, as well as those famous pointed teeth. In another telling detail that is code for his dangerous exoticism, he has a "high aquiline," "beaked" nose as opposed to the English gentlemen who must hunt him down, or even the good Dutch doctor Van Helsing, whose nose is said to be "rather straight." (Apparently the Netherlands is near enough to the U.K. so as not to imply an eastern degeneration.) The count stands for the dangerous appetite of Otherness whose wildness cannot be contained or domesticated and so must be destroyed.

Stoker's complicated story involves a group of stalwart Christian gentlemen and the two young, pure, beautiful English women they love and strive to protect from . . . well, the evil that is Dracula and his minions. "The girls are mine," proclaims Dracula, and the battle lines are drawn on who will possess Lucy and Mina, either the forces of good or Dracula, the Force of Evil. But what exactly is the nature of this evil? What lies at the dark heart of this over-the-top potboiler that has made the late-Victorian best seller still well-known, if not as often read, one hundred years later?[18]

Yes, Dracula famously sucks blood, is a shape-shifter, and lives on in an inhuman state while pursuing an ever wider circle of those he will forcibly convert to Otherness. But the core of the novel's original appeal is encoded in a key word that is repeated an astonishing number of times in the text: voluptuous. Take, for example, the three horrid young women with "voluptuous lips" who live with Dracula in his castle in Transylvania. Our hero, J. Harker, records in his journal that "I felt in my heart a wicked, burning desire that they would kiss me with those red lips" (38). These exotic and erotic women have a "hard laugh," devoid of femininity (39), and they frequently "lick their lips" as they laugh their horrible laugh (54). "There was a deliberate voluptuousness which was both thrilling and repulsive" (41), notes Harker with a shudder, of the women who are "waiting to suck my blood" (51).

It is shooting fish in a barrel to trace the symbols of sexuality in this text. The entire description of these she-monsters is luxuriously carnal, as if naively enacting Freud's later theory of men's doubling of women into whores and beloveds.[19] As the scientific savior of men, the vampire-hunter Dr. Van Helsing later remarks in his fractured English, "Man is weak" when it comes to the "voluptuous mouth present to the kiss" (372). Bad women will suck the healthy life out of men, and because males are inherently so vulnerable to devouring female sexuality, they need good women whose love will restrain them, pure women utterly devoted to their men.[20]

"Voluptuousness" in Stoker's Dracula, as it turns out, is a code for the desire for sexuality for pleasure alone, devoid of romance. As such the quality of "voluptuousness" is expressed in metaphors of disease, infection, pollution, and the devil's curse. The mouth in Dracula is a site of impurity; a Freudian would say it's a displacement of the vagina. This is conveyed not only by sensual kissing and fearful biting but also through an obsession with eating: Dracula and other vampires "cannot flourish without this diet" (240), namely the blood of living things. The disgust of unrestrained appetite is invoked by the character of a lunatic who ingests small living creatures. Now, the word "appetite" was a common one in the nineteenth century, used frequently in Victorian pornography as well, as when the narrator of the famous text The Romance of Lust (1873) repeats that an act of intercourse only "took the edge off my carnal appetite."

Though a master plotter, Dracula is said to have a "child-brain" (304) because sexuality is coded as primitive, like Dracula's foreign nose, just as it is "selfish" and criminal (the count is said to be "a criminal type") (343). It's amusing how blatant the coded sexuality is, as when Mina recounts that Dracula "seized my neck and pressed my mouth to the wound, so that I must either suffocate or swallow some of the—Oh my God! My God! what have I done?" Recalling this shameful moment, she then "began to rub her lips as though to cleanse them from pollution" (289). It is women, of course, who are most titillatingly subject to the stain of impure sexuality.

If we cannot resist our own "voluptuousness," we are (here literally) inhuman, a message common in the Victorian age. Dracula's command "When my brain says 'Come!' to you, you shall cross land or sea to do my bidding" (289) represents the loss of control over sexual desire that all humans, but especially women, must fear. And so the suspense of the plot centers on the quasi-medical, quasi-military adventure quest to rescue the two ladies' purity from the fate literally worse than death, namely un-death, where women sink into the dark shadow-version of their own nature. Once converted to Otherness by Dracula, Mina will be, Dracula says, "my companion and my helper" (289), as women are meant to be to men in any case, though not evil ones.

The two heroines are Lucy, the embodiment of Victorian traditional womanhood, sweet and passive, and Mina, who is more interesting because she is intelligent and brave. Why these two women in particular? Lucy is the iconic Victorian woman-as-victim, whose story can end in only two ways: rescue or tragedy. After Lucy, described as normally "angelic" and childlike, has been infected, her nature flips and turns "voluptuous" (again!) as, breathing heavily, she tries to kiss her fiancé (161).

But Mina is a different type of woman, one more associated with the growing trend of the fin-de-siècle New Woman, assertive, sturdy, and clever.[21] In fact, she jokes early on that she and Lucy have been eating so well that "I believe we should have shocked the 'New Woman' with our appetites" (91). When Lucy "breathes softly" in her innocent sleep, Mina wonders aloud whether the "New Women" writers will "someday start an idea that men and women should be allowed to see each other asleep before proposing or accepting. But I suppose the New Woman won't condescend in future to accept; she will do the proposing herself" (92). By contrast, at one point Lucy is proposed to three times in one day.

It's important to note that Mina is not actually a New Woman, and her references to the idea are always ironic and lighthearted. Though some of her traits— her courage, her readiness to undertake adventure and even take charge—are by Victorian standards almost manlike, in fact she is only brave out of womanly love and care of others, which is in fact a deeply Victorian belief: "They had told me to go to bed and sleep," she narrates, "as if a woman can sleep when those she loves are in danger!" (244). While she has a "man's brain," according to Dr. Van Helsing, she also, he adds pointedly, possesses "a woman's heart" (236). And when she is praised, it's as the perfect feminine: "That sweet, sweet, good, good woman in all the radiant beauty of her youth" who pits "her loving kindness against our grim hate; her tender faith against all our fears and doubting." Over and over, it's emphasized that Mina, in spite of hints about her mannishness, is associated with "purity," "love," and "tenderness," the woman's essential and eternal nature (310).

Once unleashed on the world, the desire Dracula represents goes wild and unchecked, spreading like a virus through the hyperactivity of "that so wicked mouth" (215). When Our Christian Gang try to affirm what has happened to Lucy, they must unscrew her coffin, an act that feels to her lover like shamefully "stripping off her clothing in her sleep" (197). The remedy for Lucy's undead, horridly "voluptuous smile" is to cut off the head (with its voluptuous lips) and stuff the "unclean" mouth with garlic. Famously, they also "drive a stake through the body" (201). Penetrating "voluptuous wantonness" through the heart turns her pure again: the heart, center of woman's love, successfully opposes the body (211).

It's Mina, the more articulate and intelligent of the women, who states the real problem: when Dracula appears before her and tries to take her, she finds herself paralyzed. "Strangely enough," she narrates, "I did not want to hinder him. I suppose it is a part of the horrible curse" (288). Ultimately, the secret heart of darkness in *Dracula* is not sexuality; it's that women are beginning to seem cursed with their own desires rather than restraining desire, as nineteenth-century heroines were supposed to do. In late-Victorian Britain, when women were pushing the boundaries that had stood firm for centuries in education, professional work, and the vote, the heroine must find a way to resist those new enticements. In my reading, it isn't enough to say that mouths and stakes and blood stand in for sexuality, but rather that uncontrolled sexuality itself stands for a larger social revolution in rights and gender, expressed through metaphors of violence that will reach the heart of the audience.

No wonder Mina is more complicated and has a more active role to play in the novel than Lucy: it is Mina who has the ability to be the real Other to the conventional Victorian woman. But in praising her yet again, lest we miss the point, Dr. Van Helsing notes that Mina is "true, so sweet, so noble, so little an egoist" in "this age [which is] so sceptical and selfish." In other words, she is the perfect New Woman who is actually the same old woman, "one of God's women, fashioned by His own hand to show us men and *other women* that there is a heaven where we can enter" [my emphasis] (188). That heaven, you can be sure, is not the society of any future liberated woman; rather, it's a place where long-entrenched categories can be preserved and new ideas like the potential for women who are bright, assertive, and sexual can be co-opted. We might say that in *Dracula*, a stake is driven through any incipient women's rights and modern desire itself with some old-fashioned Victorian feminine love, an idea much endangered at the very end of the nineteenth century.

Stephenie Meyers's *Twilight* (2005)

One hundred years later, the venerable masculine vampire genre, with its focus on terror, death, and hate for Otherness, was to be transformed by the phenomenally successful *Twilight* series of novels by Stephenie Meyers into a kinder, gentler, feminized romantic story that emphasizes undying (pun intended) love, maternal caring, and take-no-prisoners protection of the beloved woman. In *Twilight*, the powerful male object of women's accumulated "fears and dreads" is now on *our* side, ready to kiss but not kill us: oh, if only!

Compared to Dracula, the vampire lover in *Twilight* is more toothsome than toothy. If Bram Stoker's version was about the buried life of sexual desire and its relation to traditional and newer forms of femininity, the *Twilight* series is more about female emotional longing for some old-fashioned strong-arm protection by powerful males, of the sort that is no longer quite politically correct in actual men.²² The hetero-hero Edward, who somehow manages to be "dangerous . . . but not bad" (93), is simply another incarnation of the older, conventional version of Byronic lover, whose vampire-ish traits allow for a hyper- (or hyped-up) masculinity that is—you guessed it—conveniently and thrillingly restrained by romantic love. So once again, as in the Victorian texts as well as in both eighteenth- and twentieth-century versions of the Beauty and the Beast story, the woman functions as domestic constraint, the humanizing (here, literally) force.

This isn't to say that *Twilight* is not at the same time a contemporary invention; it reeks of current preoccupations, such as coolness and the shopping interests of teenage girls. *Twilight* has more in common with the Disney versions of the Little Mermaid and Beauty and the Beast stories than it does with the original spirit of *Dracula*, which is to say it is far more modern romance than horror. For example, it begins, just as they do, by drawing a portrait of the heroine as naively unaware of her beauty and unspoiled. You remember that the sign of being human in Disney's *The Little Mermaid* was participating in the material culture of "civilization," rather than having a Christian soul as in Andersen's fairy tale. Similarly, the material accoutrements of the castle are visualized in detail (and animated, of course) in the film *Beauty and Beast* but not in the original story by Mme. de Beaumont. In *Twilight* we are frequently told the heroine is above it all. She even drives a beat-up truck, for goodness sake! No Valley Girl or Hollywood ingenue she; she's different, alienated, just a modest extremely beautiful girl who is not materialistic or hung up on status—in other words, just like the heroines of de Beaumont's and Andersen's tales.

As a heroine, Bella (Belle, Beauty) is the caretaker of her loving but inadequate mother (another missing mother) and also cooks for her father . . . but, Cinderella-like, nobody takes care of *her*. She could use protection! And she deserves protection, because she is clearly superior, though she is too humble to know it. Though it's established early and mentioned constantly that she is a great beauty, she narrates defensively that she isn't "tan, sporty, and blond," though she *is* "slender, but soft" (10): the softness is supposedly her nonathleticism, which also is cute clumsiness. (We know this is a sign of her adorably quirky femininity.) As in all pop romance stories, the heroine must have no idea how lovely she is, lest she be vain and use her beauty as power, both marks of the bad woman.

Also, she describes herself in the first person as "ivory-skinned" (Hollywood code for beautiful), but she believes she looks "sallower, unhealthy . . . pallid," which makes her a double of Edward, her future vampire lover. He is also her double in that she "didn't relate well to people, period," and . . . well, let's say he doesn't either. This is an element of popular romance dating back to *Jane Eyre*: the loved woman as fellow outcast, whose value is not recognized by ordinary society because she doesn't conform to its shallow standards. As in so much pop culture, though, the text has it both ways. The heroine is supposedly special in all conventional romance, but here that is flimsily disguised by the teenage rhetoric of self-put-down: "my brainless and embarrassing babbling," "I almost died of humiliation," "I felt ridiculous" (54–59). This is an adolescent version of the heroine's conventional insecurity and self-diminishment, the new equivalent of Victorian feminine modesty: "Of course he wasn't interested in me, I thought angrily. . . . I wasn't *interesting*," Bella narrates (79, original emphasis). Oh sure. *As if.* Jane Eyre thought the same thing about Rochester, but at least she was supposed to be plain. Though our heroine Bella is different and alienated—she keeps her face "pulled back into my hood" as she walks by the other teenagers (14)—it's the right kind of alienation: the kind that mirrors the vampire Edward's dark eyes, shadows ("bruise-like"), and "straight, perfect, angular" (meaning Anglo) features.

Another mark of Bella's Otherness to the teenage female crowd is that Edward can't read her mind because "her mind doesn't work the same way the rest of theirs do" (181). Yet she doesn't appear to be all that different from the rest—we're just told she is, or rather other characters say it, the way some people boast by telling you how others have praised them. The reader senses the importance of the preoccupation for the reader: am I just another girl or really special? Talk about fishing for compliments: when Bella says she's "absolutely ordinary," Edward tells her that this idea results from not understanding how desirable and special she really is: "You didn't hear what every human male in this school was thinking on your first day. . . . You are the opposite of ordinary" (210). How gratifying, though she claims not to believe it. But that is exactly the way modern romance is supposed to function in real life: when you are beloved, you are both comfortingly ordinary and yet thrillingly extraordinary to the one you love at the same time.

Because Bella is exceptional, she is desired by everyone without knowing it: the teenage dream, as the pop singer Katy Perry would say. Eric, a "boy with skin problems and hair black as an oil slick," whom Bella disdains as an "overly helpful, chess club type," is all over her (16). (Apparently that's the wrong kind of marginalization.) Two other boys simultaneously pursue her in short order, but she apparently has no vanity about this at all, providing further proof of our heroine's innate superiority to all around her.

As for our hero, he is "hostile, furious" for no obvious reason, as heroes in romances have so often been, with an "antagonistic stare" so common in Harlequin novels.[23] His eyes go "coal black" when he expresses these dark feelings that appear to be unreasonable, but soon we learn what it means when he clenches his fist. It's all because of Bella, of course. He is so overwhelmed by deep and instant attraction that he has to restrain his desire forcibly, "his forearm surprisingly hard and muscular beneath his light skin" (24).

Naturally, as in all romances, the heroine herself has no clue at all why he behaves this way: "It was impossible that this stranger could take such a sudden, intense dislike to me" (27). The romance *reader* always knows the real (flatteringly romantic) reason for the hero's inexplicable hostility before the heroine does. Imagine the message this gives the teenage female reader: that man who is ignoring or avoiding you (as Darcy did), or is downright rude or antagonistic to you (as Rochester was), is likely to be fighting off his irresistible attraction to you. Sigh, gulp.

Oddly, though Edward's strength makes him super-masculine, he also has some stereotypically feminine features: besides the pale skin of the Victorian lady and the designer clothes of the modern glamour girl, he also possesses an unusual ability to talk intimately. Really, he is outstandingly empathetic and insightful: "You're suffering," he quickly discerns as Bella sulks (49). None of these were necessary features of Victorian heroes, but Edward's type reaches back to the classic Byronic emotional vulnerability (Rochester again), expressed by a "tortured" demeanor and "agonized eyes" (273). Painfully sensitive underneath, the Byronic hero always loves the wrong woman, so he can never be truly domesticated, though when he lifts those agonized eyes to hers, he reveals the key information: that she is "the most important thing to me ever," as Edward comes to realize (273).

As a matter of fact, Edward follows the generic template for the pop romance fantasy without a single quirk besides vampirism. At first the two lovers don't make eye contact, so he seems to refuse the psychological intimacy that might lead to romance, as women fear men will do. This opening represents the dangerous doubleness of men to the romantic woman: after ungovernable anger, he is inexplicably "friendly, open," and smiling. How in the world do you read men? The best-selling answer in this case: by going to another world. For example, at one point early on, Bella worries that "he almost sounded mad" and concludes with bewilderment that "he was definitely mad" (75). Why the bad temper here? It turns out it's because she suggested that he had regretted saving her from an oncoming car. This is a contrived reason if there ever was one, but what's important is to display the masculinity of anger, which is sexy but safe when it is directed at the heroine because (though she is always too naive and humble to recognize it) he is only mad at her because he cares so much.

As in nearly all pop romances since Richardson's *Pamela*, our heroine is spirited (in the eighteenth-century *Pamela*, that was called "pert"). Bella is independent, willful, and brave (she's "fascinated but not afraid" of Edward [93]), but, also like Pamela, she also faints and blushes easily. Her courage and dash are not opposed to dependence; on the contrary, her "spirited" qualities are what get her into trouble, requiring Edward to put himself bodily between her and an approaching evil. Similarly, when Bella shows independence ("I am perfectly capable of driving myself home!" she fumes [104], as many a Harlequin heroine has before her), Edward is bossy and commanding in response, forcefully taking charge: "Get in, Bella." She momentarily bridles against that (as do the Harlequin heroines), but his ability to dominate when necessary is clearly important to his allure. *Twilight* is as obsessed with the word "power" as *Dracula* was obsessed with the "voluptuous": the "full power of his burning gold eyes" makes her "nod helplessly" in assent, for example (108).

In line with conventional romantic heroines, Bella's feminist "spirit" mainly manifests itself in adolescent glaring and snapping, not decision-making. When she is frosty to Edward, he "laughs at her, his eyes warm" (173); you see, he thinks she's cute, even though (again!) she supposedly doesn't know it. Cute, of course, is the allowable way for women to be funny, and the man who chuckles warmly at the adorable antics of his kittenish woman who is being clumsy, silly, or sweetly illogical is a feature of many modern date movies as well (though seldom found in Jane Austen).

The vampire's supernatural strength and potential for violence lend a titillating air to the same old theme of male aggression and its relationship to romance. Edward is dangerous to others when the occasion calls for it (and you can be sure the plot calls for it) but "furious" with the girl he loves only on behalf of her safety, something like the response of a parent whose toddler wanders into traffic. In other words, his fury is there to demonstrate the degree of her value for him, which is the true source of the pleasure of reading. Edward often talks to Bella as if she were a child: "Finally, a rational response!" he murmured. "I was beginning to think you had no sense of self-preservation at all" (328). As in Disney's *Beauty and the Beast*, male dominance, control, anger, and aggression are all rendered understandable, in fact *valuable*, in the context of love. For example, when Edward spies on her every night, Bella says she should feel "outrage" but instead is "flattered" (292). In another scene, he rescues her when she is surrounded by a gang of men; it seems he's been hovering over her like a helicopter parent. Bella wonders "if it should bother me that he was following me; instead I felt a strange surge of pleasure" (174). Stalking is love in a different form.

The Victorian view that dominance is alluring because it's really just male protection is countered by a popular modern insurance policy: the heroine controls the controller with her feminine desirability. When Edward says "I put myself in your power" (272) or Bella calls him her "perpetual savior" (166), the conventions of knight and lady are invoked in a peculiarly modern mash-up: you can have the magic of teenage love, rescue fantasy, courtly romance, and even pop religion, all in one. Elsewhere Edward is called "archangel" and "godlike," a "Greek god." The demon/Satan/villain/dark god really is "good" underneath, and when he's good, he's *very* good, as in perfectly yummy.

Soon Edward can't leave Bella at all: "It makes me . . . anxious . . . to be away from you" (188), he tells her. What in real life would be grounds for intense psychotherapy is normal for the nonhuman. On the other hand, as a vampire he himself is dangerous to her, so there's an irony for you. "I could kill you quite easily," he observes, "simply by accident" (310). Fortunately, romance takes the bite out of the danger.

Now, Bella too is obsessed and "can't leave him": "It really seemed like my life was *about* him," she cries (251, original emphasis). Fortunately, the feeling is mutual: "You are my life now," he says "simply" (314). If the woman is psychologically dependent on the man, she had better be the only thing in his life, especially because pretty much nothing else matters in her fictional world. In one bizarre scene, Edward sits watching her while she sleeps, then rocks her in a rocking chair, carries her around, and actually sits her up in a chair while telling her she is the center of his world, like a new mommy obsessed with her helpless infant. Later, when he rescues her from a predatory male, he "soothes" her: " 'You can sleep, sweetheart, I'll carry you.' And I was in his arms, cradled against his chest" (457). All this infantalization, of course, is an eroticized expression of his romantic caring.

Sexuality in Stoker's *Dracula* was deliciously weird because it was channeled into the symbolism of penetration through biting, sucking, and infecting, as a late nineteenth-century means to present the corruption of bodily desire. In our own time, where sexuality is sure to be less repressed for the audience, the plot of *Twilight* keeps it weird in an entirely different way. The whole point of this first novel of the series, it seems, is to keep the lovers apart as long as nonhumanly possible, so Edward can't even kiss Bella. Instead we get a lot of eroticized, gentle, nongenital touching, culminating eventually in no-tongue kissing— a preadolescent's idea of romantic initiation. We are told that neither has ever had sex, as though it were the fifties; why, one wonders, especially in view of the sexual involvement of the pair in the subsequent novels of the series? Perhaps it's because Bella invokes the classic virgin of the Harlequin novel of decades ago, while Edward's virginity marks her specialness to him (he was saving it for her for *ever so long*). He is continually monitoring himself to see if "he is in control of his need" (282), and like a fifties virgin, she "had to be good; I didn't want to make this harder for him" (308).

Yet since the novel wants to work both sides of the street, the representation of sexual desire has to be part of the story's appeal. The compromise, once more, is that Bella is so innocent she has no idea she is seductive; we only know about her sexual irresistibility from the endless compliments that are given her. "No one should look so tempting," Edward murmurs straight out of a Harlequin Temptation romance. "It's not fair" (319). To which she ingenuously replies, "Tempting how?" Uh-huh. In another scene, when Bella innocently "lean[s] closer," triggering overwhelming desire in Edward, it causes him to leap back like an Evangelical Christian caught in a strip bar. He is "very sorry" that he is aroused, but he is "only human," wink wink. His ability to rape or kill her is part of the thrill: "As if you could outrun me," he tells her, "as if you could fight me off" (264). But, like a Victorian gentleman, he also vows, "I can control myself," and is "on his best behavior." In fact, Edward, as Bella notes, speaks "in the gentle cadences of an earlier century," gesturing toward the courtly self-restraint of the old-fashioned Austen hero.

What is this all about? As with Beauty and Beast, the vampire romance fantasy is that women *need* masculine force, a power that is channeled for their good if the man loves you romantically. A superhero is the other side of a villain when the lover is nonhuman: Edward insists that if he killed to save "a young girl" from rape, that wouldn't be bad (270). He later explains that when he first met Bella, "I so very nearly took you then," referencing the threat of rape. But when he "leaps at" her, crashing her into the sofa and knocking it into the wall, "all the while, his arms formed an iron cage of protection around me—I was barely jostled" (345). Instead, he will fight *for* her, a much more satisfying fantasy.

We've seen that male dominance and aggression are nothing to be afraid of if love is "real," which is to say the story is a romance, and serve as proof of the intensity of the lover's need. At the core of the fantasy is the displacement of aggressive behavior or callous sex (meaning for pleasure only) by female emotional power onto romantic sexuality. Behind this modern story is women's fear of being used and manipulated through emotional dependence on men, symbolized in the vampire lover's "hypnotic eyes" and the "magnetic force of his personality" (139). Vampire love in *Twilight* is the occasion for the transforming and redeeming power of woman's desire, which will surely be fulfilled if she is desirable (beautiful and special) herself. Edward's inability to control himself is symbolic of her ultimate romantic dominance over him.

The real danger, you see, is the cold, predatory male who is drawn to the heroine's irresistible charms as a hunter, rather than a lover bonded by emotion. In the final action-drama of the novel, the evil vampire James comes after Bella in particular: "If you didn't smell so appallingly luscious, he might not have bothered," says Edward (397). Romantic love is the safety net against being hurt by this "user" sex, still very much a preoccupation of women even in the contemporary world of equal sexual rights. But of course this insurance only applies if you are all the lover lives for, if you are so special that no one can ever replace you, and how are you going to know that if you are an actual ordinary girl?

All pop romances give you the secret code, the signals the female audience must look for. For example, when a waitress flirts with Edward, he has eyes only for Bella: "He didn't look away from me. . . . I suppressed a smile" (177). Okay, so that's how you know. If he pays attention to you, all the rest doesn't matter: he can be as "dangerous" as anything, but he isn't "bad."

LOVE WITH THE PROPER OTHER

Bella tells Edward near the conclusion of *Twilight* that "a man and woman have to be somewhat equal," which she explains means, recalling the last lines of the classic romance movie *Pretty Woman*, that they "have to save each other equally" (473–474). This very modern equality (or somewhat equality) consists, as it does in *Pretty Woman*, in an exchange: she has saved him, presumably from loneliness, much as Jane Eyre saved Rochester, while in return, like Rochester, he will elevate her in value and "never let anything hurt her" (486).

In the end, the woman's risking life and limb (or in the case of the Little Mermaid, amputating a tail) is nothing compared to the satisfaction of making a good bargain. Whereas the traditional texts (the original "Beauty and the Beast," Andersen's "The Little Mermaid," Stoker's *Dracula*) rewarded women for being virtuous, modern romance is a deal: legs for love in the Disney's *The Little Mermaid*, emotional rehabilitation of the beastly male in return for the lifestyle of a princess in the movie *Beauty and the Beast*, and male protection in exchange for never being lonely again in *Twilight* (and I mean *never*, in the case of a vampire).

What, then, do our three traditional and modern popular romances of interspecies love have in common? One way to look at romances between human and nonhuman is to see them as a form of miscegenation, a pejorative term that historically implied the corruption of "purity" in race through marrying Otherness. Just as the purpose of the concept of "miscegenation" was to serve the interests of white economic and social domination, these romantic stories of love with the Other confirm the purity of traditional gender roles—*whether the Other is male or female*—even while appearing to be about overcoming difference.

My argument has been that the meanings of romance with the Other always converge with changing ideas about power relations in society. In our time, we are squeezed between traditional social values of gender and newer understandings of feminism and sexuality that are incorporated into the story in order to defang them. As the critic Cora Kaplan has said, rather than simply affirm or disconfirm norms of femininity, fantasy displays the "contradictory and ambiguous place" of women.[24]

The love stories between a human and an Other discussed here work the margins of those traditional rules around gender that have been violated, like Dracula's victims, and are still undergoing metamorphosis. The wild female from nature who sacrifices her body for the love of the human male, the woman's love for the godlike male who is "super"/superior, the adoration of the manlike creature for the human female and his protection of her: these are all fantasies about how to deal with—or evade—the modern complications of femininity, masculinity, and romance in our brave new world. In the end, the meaning of love in these stories has altered, while gender codes have stayed much the same. It's safer that way.

6

WOMEN WHO LOVE TOO MUCH . . . OR NOT ENOUGH . . . OR THE WRONG WAY

The Tragedy and Comedy of Romantic Love in Modern Movies

> I remember feeling a desire . . . that was hard and pure, that contained me and could not be contained, and I remember making that bargain that people always make—anything for this thing.
> —Dave in "The Age of Grief," Jane Smiley, 1987

In the Victorian era, angels were in, and "in" meant in print in full force. There were angelic young heroines in novels, such as those by Charles Dickens, who were at once the reward for the hero's pluck and compensation for his undeserved trouble. In essays and articles in newspapers and magazines all over Britain and America, the inherently loving nature of woman was extolled, her inborn gift for self-denial celebrated. The association was so well known that Virginia Woolf declared, in a famous act of literary execution, that the Angel in the House had to be done away with in order for modern literature to be born.

Female goodness, in the form of family devotion, caring for the sick, or public charity, was a theme that harmonized well with Christian ideals of service and brotherly love. In Elizabeth Stuart Phelps's short story "The Angel over the Right Shoulder" (1852), angels materialize in the nick of time in the epiphanic dream of a restless, harassed wife and mother, inspiring her to do her duty and give up the two hours a day she had tried to carve out for her own intellectual pursuits. (Apparently the author herself was not as self-sacrificing as her character, since she was a published writer who chose to work at her craft with several children at home.) When it came to loving, romantically or maternally, the angelic woman simply could never love enough, even if it killed her in body or soul. The question of the day was "Is there an Angel in this House?"

In fact, women who were good as gold in Victorian texts, from Little Nell in Dickens's *The Old Curiosity Shop* to Beth in Alcott's *Little Women*, were frequently hurt or died for the delectation of the audience, whose tears spread the warmth of sentimental sympathy for a condition that was vaunted as noble: the (self-) sacrifice of the innocent. It's not difficult to conclude that those tears were meant to obviate the pressure for change in the status of women; their moist abundance smoothed over the rough edges of odd paradoxes like strong, "spirited," yet ultimately conservative heroines in popular novels. Behind the many proclamations of woman's constitutionally superior moral nature was the opposite conviction: that a woman is better suited for self-denial because she has a lesser, and therefore more expendable, self than the hero. As we saw, Hans Christian Andersen's brave and independent Little Mermaid in the fairy tale of the same name is not romantically loved by her prince, but she does get to renounce her humanity and become a "spirit," a kind of angel who rewards good children and reminds naughty ones of their unpleasant fate.

Critics almost from the beginnings of feminism objected, claiming that the nobility of the "wounded angel" masqueraded as a universal character of womanhood when in reality the idea of self-sacrifice served the social organization of gender at a particular moment in history. By the twentieth century, so much had changed that many women not only wanted rooms of their own but were revealed to have sensual desires of their own as well. Yet in the 1960s, when women's movements were gearing up for a new and stronger push toward the social equality of gender, conservative thought could still pull on a particularly resilient, tensile thread woven deeply into the fabric of society: the allure of the selfless female whose loving nature makes it possible for fragile romantic relationships to endure. The "good" woman was no longer semidivine, as in the Victorian age, but had morphed into a girlfriend or wife making a pragmatic decision about keeping a romantic relationship going. *Cosmopolitan* magazine's advice in 1969, "Don't become a man in skirts. Don't fight. Don't argue. You are the stronger sex. . . . It is enough that you *are* . . . that you are there . . . quiet . . . unshakable . . . always ready to give. That is your strength," was the great-great-granddaughter of Sarah Stickney Ellis's exhortation in 1839, "What man is there in existence who would not rather his wife should be free from selfishness, than be able to read Virgil without the use of a dictionary?"[1]

But if the cultural concept of women as angels did not entirely disappear after the Victorian era, a new version of the hurt innocent emerged in the later twentieth century: her dark shadow appeared in her place. Since Freud and feminism, we now construct the angel's wound as unhealthy, even masochistic: in the 1980s, the best-selling self-help manual *Women Who Love Too Much* by Robin Norwood focused on those women who loved . . . *too much*, urging them to shore up their well-meaning but pathetic selfhood by working hard to get the loving *right*. This took the form of a feminist revelation based on pop-psychology truth: the nobility of the woman giving more than she got back was simply a cover for the emptiness of not having had her father's unconditional love. Low self-esteem was at the bottom of every romantic problem ("You don't have a man because you feel you don't *deserve* happiness," single women were—and still are—told), rather than the moral choices that guided judgment in the Victorian era, in keeping with the psychotherapeutic ethos of the twentieth century.[2]

Aimed at self-improvement, this well-meaning interpretation borrowed from twelve-step addiction programs was, in my view, still another burden for an audience of women, to whom books on the subject of love were overwhelmingly aimed: if romance does not "work," in other words, lead to an enduring domestic relationship, it's the woman's own fault because she hasn't "worked on herself."[3] Certainly this is an enormous step forward from the Victorian idea that when a woman experiences, as one article of 1835 put it, "misusage and neglect" or "intemperance and debauchery" from men, she ought to exhibit only "meekness and patience [while] she endures his ill treatment" ("Woman's Love," *Albany Bouquet and Literary Spectator*). The problem with the modern pop-psychology perspective for me is that while it helpfully describes the pathological woman's compulsion to repeat romances in which she is in a one-down position emotionally, the frame of self-help tends to elide the social inequality in romantic relations between men and women.

Not coincidentally, from the seventies through the nineties there was a spate of films that focused on a heroine who loves too much. This "masochistic" woman, willing to pay any price for an incomplete, unsatisfying, or doomed love, actually appeared to take pleasure in destroying herself for the sake of love. In 1975, François Truffaut's *The Story of Adele H.* traced the obsessive love and frightening slide into insanity of a young woman who follows a handsome, rejecting man everywhere. Twenty years later, the film *Carrington* (1995) focused on the true story of the female artist known as Carrington, who loved the brilliant, fascinating, and homosexual Bloomsbury author Lytton Strachey her entire adult life. Illustrating the eternal frustration of perversely loving without fulfillment, she chooses to be used as his "pen-wiper" in spite of his sexual rejection of her, setting up the culminating moment of her own suicide at his death.

Both of these were "historical" movies, yet were less about history than about women's obsession with love, one literally self-destructive in mind or body. The heroine's single-minded devotion no longer invites admiration for the loftiness of self-sacrifice for love, but pity for the pathos of a defective soul. We now ask, what is *wrong* with this woman, who is a monster of passion for what she cannot have? A female character pursuing what and whom she wants has become a frightening figure, especially if her passion does not lead to a workable relationship, and the audience is invited to look sorrowfully and wonderingly at her unseemly intensity of desire. Such neurotic (because unrequited) avidity for love can only lead to tragedy and, in the rhetoric of today, is therefore not "real," meaning legitimate, romance. To want "unsuccessfully" in love ("success" meaning a permanent coupling) is to be found wanting.

A heroine's aggressive pursuit of love without an equal return may seem progressive, a reversal of the old-fashioned Victorian angel figure whose hallmark was passive submission to the man's power to choose, a heroine who was elevated by stifling her own needs and desires. I would say, however, that our post-Freudian understanding of "masochistic" female love is a way of reconstructing the traditional category of women as hurt angels, though in a more covert and self-consciously ironic modern form than in Victorian literature. Representations of the loving woman who gives more than she receives serve much the same social purpose as that iconic angel figure of the Victorian era: to idealize the aesthetic value of the woman in love for the cultural reassurance of the audience.[4]

Movies are the modern lingua franca of romance as drama, melodrama, and, of course, one of the most significant of modern cultural forms straight out of Hollywood, the romantic comedy. The spirit of the nineteenth-century wounded angel still hovers over both modern romantic tragedy and comedy, oddly enough. Comedy and tragedy may appear to be opposite in their functions (one makes you laugh, the other makes you cry), but here they are different paths to the same end: eliding difficult issues surrounding women's relations with men, even as the stories encourage identification with women's troubles in love, just as in the nineteenth century.

To test out my theory that comedy and tragedy occupy two sides of the same coin of romantic narrative, enacting a ritual fantasy about the culture's version of the way women should or should not love, let's trace a path through a pair of tragedies of women in love that emerged as critical favorites (and not just aimed at women) in the 1990s and a few popular romantic comedies (aimed much more at women than men) from the 2000s to see what ideas about love they have in common.

The differences in dates and audience are not insignificant. If the scholars James J. Dowd and Nicole R. Pallotta are correct, in the late twentieth century the genre of romantic dramas and tragedies that had flourished until then decreased significantly in proportion to romantic comedies.[5] Their painstaking study of almost two hundred films beginning with the 1930s leads them to the conclusion that romantic movies are currently the most popular they've ever been but that the vast majority of these are now comic. "Today it is the romantic comedy that is the dominant form of the Hollywood love story," they conclude (559). For one thing, while romantic drama needs a significant impediment to work, such as a married lover (*Brief Encounter*) or separation by social class

(*Titanic*), unavailability for marriage is less of a problem in an age of easy divorce, while social barriers have fallen markedly in a democratized social world. The other challenge to drama is what Dowd and Pallotta call "postmodern irony and disbelief": our contemporary inability to take all that drama seriously.

While their study does not dwell on gender issues, we might add that romantic tragedies, such as *The English Patient*, have often appealed as high-quality, original fare to both men and women, while romantic comedies are associated with low female tastes (like romantic novels) as fluffy "chick flicks" or "date movies," defined as those to which women drag reluctant men as the price of their feminine company.

THE TRAGEDIES

Leaving Las Vegas (1995): "This is the house of an angel"

In 1995, Mike Figgis directed a well-received film based on a novel by John O'Brien, about the doomed romance of a Las Vegas prostitute and an alcoholic bent on self-destruction. The prostitute, Sera (Elisabeth Shue, in an award-winning performance), seems to embody Simone de Beauvoir's claim that love is disproportionately more important to women than to men. We see in *Leaving Las Vegas* that Ben, her lover (played by Nicolas Cage), won't give up alcohol for Sera, though it's clear she'd give up anything for him.

As *Leaving Las Vegas* opens, Ben is fired from his job as a writer. Ben is bright, charming, and presumably talented but washed up through his own weakness. He is a sorry loser: literally, as he cries childishly when fired, sobbing pathetically, "I'm sorry!"[6] The early scenes of the movie establish that he's "lost." For example, he drinks an entire bottle in a strip club, showing that even sex doesn't mean anything to him; a prostitute steals his ring; he makes the usual empty promises—lend me money, trust me one more time—and obnoxiously comes on to women who are repulsed by him. Moreover, Ben burns a picture of his wife and child, deliberately choosing to be alienated and free-floating. This is not husband material, or even lover material. Robin Norwood would not approve.

But Sera is no ordinary romantic heroine; she is a prostitute, as we find out when we see her servicing a client before the lovers meet. Talk about abjection: her pimp tracks her down and performs aggressive sex, which she clearly doesn't enjoy, accompanied by the song "My Heart Is Crying" on the soundtrack. This is (still another) woman who has the wrong sex, sex without love, the dark side of the megahit comedy of 1990 featuring a prostitute and her lover/john, *Pretty Woman*.

Then a strange thing happens: we see Sera as she narrates her story (a pure white lily in the background) to an invisible therapist, with whom we are encouraged to identify, as Sera is simultaneously narrating to us. There is a frame around this love affair, a therapeutic context that Robin Norwood would endorse after all. From the beginning, we see an end: Sera is trying to overcome her dysfunction by understanding it. This is a kind of confession, the movie seems to say, appropriately told by the heroine herself, rather than narrated like *Pretty Woman* in the third person as a "fairy tale."

Ben and Sera meet to the soundtrack of the passionate blues song "I'm gonna love you/ Like nobody's loved you/ Come rain or come shine" and head to his motel room. A sense of foretold doom is thick in the air. When Sera offers "anything he wants" (her examples are "fuck my ass" and "come on my face"), Ben appears shocked. He isn't that kind of guy, apparently . . . yet he will humiliate her emotionally in the course of the movie time and time again.

She begins to give him oral sex and Ben stops her, saying, "I want to talk to you a little." Next follows what sociologists warmly call "emotional disclosure": he tells her he wants to drink himself to death. She volunteers to stay and lies beside him with her head on his chest in a lover's posture, as his hand encircles her. These gestures, as any semiologist will tell you, imply the romantic stance, as much as the words that the theorist Roland Barthes called the "lover's discourse."

But we are quickly reminded that Sera is a prostitute when in the next scene her pimp beats her because she didn't make enough money that night. At that low point, Ben asks her on a dinner date. On the soundtrack is "You appeared in all your splendor/ My one and only love." After dinner Sera asks Ben back to her place: "I like you, I trust you," she tells him. When Ben says he's "not much good in the sack," Sera replies it's not about sex, she'll take care of him. So it seems the affair is not about sexual desire for either of them but about neediness of some sort, the hope of filling an emptiness that Norwood would recognize as the problem at the root of too-much loving.

Sera is the woman who loves too much because she is desperate for love, though we don't know why. The only backstory we get is that she was previously abused by a pimp, but otherwise she seems middle-class, pleasant, and ordinary, though of course beautiful. Her problem is narrowed down to her loneliness— she is a prostitute like all women on display, putting on performances to please, dressing up, offering sex in the marketplace. And Ben is only the extreme of the universal oblivious man who wants her but won't or can't change for her, the kind that Norwood would have us dump immediately.

The solution to this problem of being wounded is—surprise—that Sera becomes an angel. And certainly the film works that imagery in a rather heavy-handed manner. At Sera's place, for example, Ben remarks, "This is the house of an angel!" Later, he asks her, "What are you, some sort of angel visiting me from one of my drunken fantasies? You're so good."

When Ben sees and is not repulsed by the scars that Sera has from her past beatings, it seems to mean that he accepts her scarred emotions as well. And he tells her she's "extremely beautiful" when she has wet hair and no makeup, implying that their relationship consists of stripping away artifice to get to the real, not the performance of her profession. Sera says in voice-over: "It happened so quickly. So easy. I felt like I was me, not someone else." Yet she no sooner discovers and displays her "real" self than she is compelled to accept less than she wants in order to hold on to the relationship, as, for example, when she asks to move in with him:

SERA: I want it.
BEN: Right now you're an antidote balancing the liquor.
SERA: I'm tired of being alone.
BEN: You can never, never ask me to stop drinking.

The ideal of their love is the supposed mutual acceptance of distorted lives, yet Ben seems to be the one who has power in the relationship, who directs it and gets what he wants from it. When Sera presents Ben with a silver flask, he says with his signature dark humor, "I'm with the right girl." But nothing is right.

Some of the iconic gestures of romance are there: Ben gives Sera a gift of earrings, and he is jealous (as when she dresses for her work as a prostitute). But at the same time, he begins to break down and degrade her. In one powerful scene, they go to a desert motel and seem loving as the soundtrack plays, you guessed it, "Angel Eyes." Sera pathetically uses liquor to seduce him, undressing to drip alcohol from her bared breasts, mirroring his earlier scene with a bank teller when he said, "If . . . you had bourbon dripping from your breasts and your pussy, and said 'Drink here,' then I could fall in love with you." But this romantic sexuality is interrupted when Ben drunkenly crashes down, breaking a glass table, and they are thrown out of the motel. Ironically, as soon as Sera is "herself" with Ben, she is a social outcast.

It only gets worse, as if Sera is descending the circles of hell: we see her go to work, then cut to her coming home to find him with a whore in her bed. The next scene is brutal assault by three teenagers who beat her and rape her anally. Thrown out of her apartment by her landlord, when she tries to track Ben down, she is also thrown out of the casino. As a result of this love, Sera is totally isolated and has lost even what she had before, both work and home, sinking to a new low in her life.

Nevertheless, in spite of this abnegation, she remains desperate to see him. In the next scene, as he lies close to death from his addiction, she goes to him and sits by his bed, a blond ministering angel:

SERA: Oh, Ben . . . you look so very sick . . . my love . . . you're so pale.
BEN: I wanted to see you . . . you're my angel.
SERA (VOICE-OVER): I think we realized that we didn't have long and accepted it. My charm, for him, was that I accepted him exactly as he was and didn't expect him to change. I think we both realized that about each other. Ben needed me and . . . I loved him.

She gets on top of him and they have sex in his final moments; it seems significant that she is in that position after she's been shown being anally raped. She has the power, at last, but at the cost of losing him for good.

Leaving Las Vegas is oddly ambiguous in its depiction of hopeless passion. For one thing, the soundtrack of classic, bluesy love songs such as "Come Rain or Come Shine" or "Angel Eyes" could either signal the romantic intensity of the character's emotions for each other or serve as ironic contrast to the degraded and neurotic relationship the lovers build, since on the surface this is far from a classic love story. Are we meant to take at face value Sera's view that this episode of unconditional love has opened the door for her to change in the future to an awakened and healthier self? Or is the film a dissection of self-deception? These questions depend on how much credence we give to Sera's claim that she and Ben loved each other unconditionally.

Critics have reacted with differing interpretations. The feminist critic bell hooks, for example, sees Sera as "letting go" into the vulnerability of love, which for hooks is the key to the empowerment of women. In hooks's view, "[Sera's] overactive sexuality serves to mask her desire to be loved. It is in the act of loving that Sera risks vulnerability, not in being sexual with men. In sex she can be indifferent—in control. To love she must let go. It is this letting go that makes it possible for her to be redeemed."[7] It's true that Sera seems to be at the forefront of the movie, the heroine who wants (both in the sense of desire and lack) and who must change because of what she wants, whereas the character of Ben is essentially static. But is *Leaving Las Vegas* really about the woman, or is it once again about the man's fantasy of the woman? She is constituted by desire for him ("He for God, she for God in him," said Milton), whereas he desires alcohol and death. So though Sera lives past her beloved's demise, his actions have driven the plot, while Sera mostly reacts to his decisions: What will he do next? Will he love her back or not? The end of their romance is in his hands—he controls the narrative as well as the woman's desire, which is to say her fate.

This is because what Sera wants is to be his "angel," which means to give him what he needs. The mythos of romantic love is that lovers mutually devote themselves to and sacrifice for each other, so the relationship of romance is equal and protected from abuse. But in accepting Sera as all-giving mother, Ben is in the position of the child who will be adored even if he is selfish. In the end, their relations weirdly resemble nothing so much as those of the Tree and the Boy in Shel Silverstein's oddly compelling children's classic *The Giving Tree*. Sera's love is "unconditional," as long as Ben is there to be loved, but Ben's is not: if she asks him to stop drinking, he will leave. Of course, one recognizes that he *can't* change for her because he is an addict, and her failure to recognize this—it's clear that she keeps hoping, "unconditional" love or not—pathologizes her.

What makes this story both interesting and also problematic is that the familiar scenario of codependence and recovery sets up the problem as one of individual psychodynamics and buries the role of the social system in which women are still valued through relations with males. This constitutes what has been called the " 'self as project' so characteristic of postfeminism."[8] And the movie seems to present that ideal as romanticism for women.

In the end we are left with some hope for Sera's nonneurotic future through the transformative experience of romantic love. But her desperate need to be loved underneath her "sexual liberation" can also imply that women still care most about love, unlike men, and will be rewarded for giving more than their share to men for love. How very Victorian.

Breaking the Waves (1996): The View from the Belfry

Breaking the Waves, an award-winning film by the famous Danish director Lars von Trier, opens with the pretty, naive, and childlike heroine, Bess, living in coastal Scotland. She shortly marries Jan, a hearty worker on the North Sea oil rigs.

Von Trier organizes the film with titles of "chapters," which helps frame the story as a kind of fable, though with realistic detail. Early on, the theme of ideal, selfless giving that defines Bess's commitment to religion is also emphasized by a speech at the wedding. Bess, says her friend Dodo, is generous and full of love: "You can get her to do anything."[9]

But Bess is not just the ordinary good-hearted heroine. She not only speaks aloud to God but startlingly, also answers herself in God's voice, as his ventriloquist. We are encouraged to see her as simple, in the sense of unaffected and unspoiled but also possibly "simple" mentally, or perhaps emotionally deformed, inadequate to coping with life. After her wedding, for example, she privately thanks God in church for the "greatest gift of all," her love, and answers in God's voice, a more severe version of her own, telling her to remember to be a good girl or he "could take it away" (37). She promises to be good, as would a child in the presence of a punitive grown-up. It is a scene that is deliberately, many assume, disturbing in its reminder of power and abjection as a part of the religious view.

Bess is a complicated character throughout the film because, as with Sera in *Leaving Las Vegas*, we don't quite know how to take her. Are we most meant to pity her limitations as victim or admire her stubborn heroic strengths? On the one hand, her overwhelming craving for her husband and inability to bear his absence when he returns to work on the rig seem extreme. Her sister-in-law, who is her only friend, warns Jan that Bess is very susceptible and he can get her to do anything he wants. She's not strong, says the sister-in-law, she's not right in the head, but Jan replies that "she's stronger than you or me" (42).

Bess doesn't seem strong, quite the opposite. Like an abandoned child, she can hardly bear for him to be gone: she screams and runs to the helicopter when he returns to work, banging on the door and clinging to him. Her sense of loss and fear is moving but also excessive. This is a woman—again—whose neediness reaches pathological levels.

In the next "chapter" of the film Bess is speaking with closed eyes in God's voice again: she knows she has been selfish. This positions us to defend Bess. She is already "good," and she is too hard on herself. On the other hand, Bess also has the strengths of a child: she sees what others don't because she is an angel and loves without holding back.

And if Bess is childlike and pure, she is also highly sexual. We see her (simple) pleasure in sex, which is an extension of her love for Jan; when they talk on the phone from a booth in the countryside, for example, they have phone sex: "You're so huge," she obligingly says, with her sweet, shy giggle (53). She even smiles with pleasure when she listens to him snore after their wedding night, so enchanted is she with his mere physical presence. Though in harmony with the modern idea that women may assert sexual desire as well as men, this seems not so much a hunger for pleasure as an expression of her purest truth: his literal existence makes hers worthwhile. As God must be near childlike Bess at all times so she is never alone, Jan must be, too.

Many folk tales turn on the hero or heroine getting what he or she asks for and finding it all wrong. At this point there is a terrible accident in which Jan suffers severe brain injury during an oil explosion. He will live, but doctors say he may be completely paralyzed and never walk again. Bess feels she caused this: when she converses with God, he tells her (with dark and cruel irony, it must be said) that he gave her what she wanted, to have Jan home.

Jan wants to "set her free," but Bess's sister-in-law reminds him that "she'd do anything for you, to see a smile on your face. She doesn't care about herself." She also tells Bess that it's all on her now: "You can give him the will to live." Jan comes up with a plan: she should have sex with others, which he calls "making love": "Love is a mighty power. I want you to find a man to make love to and come back here and tell me about it," he commands Bess. "It will feel like you and me together, and that will keep me alive" (75).

This "lovemaking" turns into a ritualized suffering very quickly. Bess's impossible task is that she has to pretend to enjoy her humiliation. She makes a clumsy pass at the doctor, which is rejected; gives a hand job to a startled but willing older man on a bus, which causes her to throw up; and finally puts on borrowed street-walker's finery to solicit sex. After that she appears gruesomely as a false sexpot, the innocent dressed up on sexual display, something like Sera in *Leaving Las Vegas*.

Meanwhile, the fate of the husband seems more and more tied in some way to Bess's "sacrifice" of her own body. In a chapter headed "Bess' Sacrifice," Bess goes to a big boat, whose bell we hear offshore. One man watches while another brutally has sex with her. She cries and tries to leave but is cut and beaten. Later, a traumatized and bedraggled Bess experiences utter abjection: taunting children follow her and harass her, stoning her and pushing her off her bike, calling her a tart. This scene is strangely reminiscent of Sera's scene of rape and humiliation in *Leaving Las Vegas*, the sacrifice of the good woman who only wants to love.

Bess dies from her beating, yet this is not the conclusion of the film. At the legal inquest, Bess is depicted as an unstable person who gave way to a perverse sexuality, but the doctor who loved her insists that, instead of neurotic or psychotic, she was . . . just *good*. Cut to the husband, who (miraculously) is up and walking with crutches. So, you see, our Little Woman has saved him after all— Christlike with her simple but strong, pure, unwavering love, dare one say something like the devoted dog figure in so many movies from Lassie on (though more so in the TV series, as in the children's novel *Lassie Come Home*, the dog is an adventure hero more than a rescue figure). The film ends when Jan and his friends bury Bess's body at sea, and (another miracle) they hear church bells, though we and they can see nothing. The last scene is the wide view from the belfry, as the camera pans the countryside.

But what *is* the view from the belfry? Is it the religious perspective, the idea(1) of eternal harmony and justice (as Fyodor Dostoevsky put it in *The Brothers Karamazov*), where an abstraction of purely unselfish love, like that described in the famous passage from Corinthians (love is "not self-seeking," "always protects, always trusts, always hopes, always perseveres"), enables miracles?

From one perspective, Bess is not childish (the "stupid little girl" that Bess believes God thinks she is) but rather childlike in her purity of intention. And Bess is not merely passively good but also strong, the holy fool who accomplishes what she sets out to do with an iron and righteous will. That is, Bess represents a certain kind of pure-hearted ideal: we should all be childlike in this sense. But once again, it's the woman who must rise to this ideal through love. The heroine cast in that role is the nineteenth-century female angel; we are back to the idea of the pure-hearted woman with a native (and naive) capability for moral action of a very particular kind, actively choosing to be acted upon romantically and sexually with proper humiliation, submission, and no complaining, to whom self-denial is the clear and natural path to fulfillment. Like Sera from *Leaving Las Vegas*, this heroine is noble only in the cause of true love, and sexual in a context that threatens to destroy her.

The belfry tower, though, is far from the human action of the film, and another perspective entirely is the semicynical view, the zooming-out shot of the moviemaker fantasist who is teasing us with this idea rather than outright giving us what we want or think we need. After all, much of the movie has convinced us that the viewer is meant to be on the side of women who are silenced, who are repressed by intransigent religiosity. We are shown in the film that the sexuality of womanhood is harshly and rigidly condemned and controlled, and the rights of women are not represented in their communities or religion, which see them as lesser than men. Then, too, the perfect love that heals the husband comes at the cost of the woman who is the sacrificial lamb. In this view the pure and simple love of Dostoevskian primitive Christianity is the adoration of a self-deceiving simpleton, one who allows herself to be abused. It is on her body that the offering required by the harsh God-voice is performed. And that is so because her desire, though of supernatural strength, must be used for his good at the cost of her own. The crux seems to be how we evaluate and respond to Bess's character, marked simultaneously as either God's true lamb or emotionally disturbed.

Many praise von Trier for the ambiguity of his viewpoint, though ironic ambiguity can be difficult to distinguish from wavering ambivalence and downright confusion. Each interpretation rests on its own set of ironic reversals. There is Bess as angel: see? Love really is a miracle, and Bess is a Christ-figure of universal love, o ye of little faith. But then there is Bess as victim of repressive religious misogyny: look how Bess has sacrificed herself for romantic love when she could have had what she wanted in the first place if she'd only been smarter about it!

Something sneaky is going on in these two tragic movies, some weird intertwining of women's sexuality and self-sacrificing romantic love. It is most telling that neither heroine, in *Leaving Las Vegas* or *Breaking the Waves*, privileges her own sexual desire, as opposed to the well-being of her beloved. The mythos of romance is that true love (what the sociologist Anthony Giddens calls "pure love") is an equal, "democratic" exchange of desire.[10] Lovers may put the beloved first because both are doing this to the same degree; the need of each lover for the other cancels out the power that being desired confers upon the beloved. The intersection of gender values with this deeply embedded modern idea is that women who are in love may desire without fear of harm if the true love returns that romantic desire. But these films frame a "test" (as it's called in *Breaking the Waves*): if the male beloved would but can't love back in the same way (because of his "condition," here addiction or paralysis), what can the heroine do but step up and be the self-denying one who lives for the other? And then we weep over her, and feel better, though perhaps rather troubled by the scenes of exploitation, humiliation, and downright brutality that are necessary to enable her (angelic) love.

In the end, we still can't decide if the pursuit of that unreturned love by the heroine is the ideal of the heroic self-sacrificing woman who just can't love enough for our taste or the unhealthy neuroticism of the woman who loves too much. In any case, the view from the belfry is the view of "those angel eyes."

THE COMEDIES

Tragedies often center on irrational passion (an unfulfillable craving for, say, alcohol, or for a man who can't respond) of the kind that frustrates the hope for a socially approved relationship. Comedies, on the other hand, are more frequently about overcoming those (wrong) emotions in order to rationally enable right ones. Of course, as a genre, filmed romantic comedy was born in prewar Hollywood.[11] But the contemporary rom-com, as much as the Hollywood tragedy, is often a mostly conservative (in the literal sense of conserving the traditional) solution, masquerading as one that proposes something new.

Because romantic comedies contain rule books for success at their heart (how to make a bad situation or character into a good one), there is a natural affinity between popular advice tomes and the rom-com genre. Ellen Fein and Sherrie Schneider's phenomenally successful *The Rules* (1995) and *The Rules for Marriage* (2002), for example, gave conservative advice to women about what they must do to snag and then keep the man. This is called "being smart" and "taking care of yourself" (the latter includes wearing makeup and reading fashion magazines), but in reality, as the authors proclaim from the get-go, their secret is to regress to the Victorian era of female withholding and passivity as a means to marriage: "The purpose of The Rules," they say, "is to make Mr. Right obsessed with having you as his by making yourself seem unattainable." Notice the phrase "making yourself seem": this is only a simulation of Victorian femininity, since it's a quite deliberate and false passivity, not supposedly inherent female modesty and reserve (much less self-abnegation). The fear behind the formula is blatantly stated: "When you do The Rules," the authors continue, "you don't have to worry about being abandoned, neglected, or ignored!" Some of the Rules include not talking "so much," smiling, refraining from joking, and never calling men, since men are said to *innately* desire The Hunt, whereas, oddly enough, women have to *pretend* they are passive by nature . . . as they are hunting for men.[12]

The iconic TV series *Sex and the City* (1998–2004) seemed designed to test out the reactionary advice of *The Rules* in a hip, urban environment in which women's desires could be both flaunted and fondly laughed at, as we chuckle at the image of Carrie in her tutu in the lead-up to each episode. And as with any serial narrative, the drive toward a happy or unhappy resolution always seemed possible but was not required, allowing a degree of ambiguity about questions such as how much one should settle for a relationship with little passion, or whether female promiscuity always leads to the punishment of being alone. That is, until the series ended in 2004, with all the characters well coupled up at last. Many viewers were delighted that Carrie got her prince, while others were disappointed at the conventionality of pairing up all the single ladies, with its prefeminist implication that this was necessary to ensure their emotional safety and the lifestyle they deserved. Where to go from there?

When *Sex and the City*, the movie, came out in 2008, the burning question was Mr. Big's commitment; Carrie had coupled up with her One, Mr. Big, at last, but would Carrie and Mr. Big in fact get married?

Sex and the City (2008): Some Rules Are Best Left in the Closet

The film *Sex and the City* picks up where the romantic narrative usually ends: on the last episode of the TV series, Carrie was finally told "You're the One" by Mr.

Big, in—of course—Paris. For years the TV show avoided final resolutions of romantic plots in favor of forefronting the tensions and camaraderie of the four single women who were friends; the subtext was always that men come and go, but sisterhood remains the same and is worth fighting for. The movie form, by contrast, more conventionally adheres to the standard formula: the rising arc of romantic problems, followed by a resolution meant to stabilize romantic uncertainty.

The first scene, however, starts with finding "the perfect apartment in New York City." "Do you want to get married?" Mr. Big asks Carrie unromantically in a discussion of her legal rights to his new apartment.[13]

Uh-oh. We see the problem immediately, even if Carrie doesn't, because we're trained in the rhetoric of romance: nothing good can come of a proposal that too bluntly reveals the pragmatism of marriage. Justifying her acceptance, Carrie later tells her girlfriends about making the decision to get married based on "what makes sense" for the future. This is the kiss of death, of course, because it implies that both future husband and wife are engaging in rational planning inimical to romantic passion. Carrie calls this "two grown-ups making a decision about spending their lives together," not indulging in "romantic clichés." The audience is signaled that both Carrie and Big need to be educated in love because they're not romantic enough.

Cut to Miranda, whose work as a lawyer and ensuing exhaustion are interfering with her marriage. We see her criticizing her husband, Steve, and flatly asking him during sex to "get it over with, we have to get up in four and a half hours." Miranda is clearly not loving properly. And soon after, Miranda leaves Steve because he confesses that he has had sex with someone else. The reason given for his one act of infidelity is that he and Miranda "hadn't made love in a long time," clearly Miranda's fault.

At the climax of the movie, Big doesn't show up on time for his wedding to Carrie and tells her on the phone that he "can't do this." He soon says he only freaked out for a minute, but Carrie is humiliated and won't hear of it, just as Miranda cannot forgive Steve his passing transgression.

Of course, there is one character who famously represents the anti-marriage perspective: Samantha complains that marriage is putting the other before yourself, planning your life around the man, in effect losing the self. But this is never treated seriously as a point of view, because Sam is a broadly drawn comic character: she is "flaky" and extreme in her desire, unable even to keep to a commitment to the gorgeous younger man she lives with.

Punishments are now doled out: Miranda misses Steve and being married. She is lonely on New Year's Eve, and so is Carrie. We see Big eating alone, too, and Steve is sleeping with his son alone. Only the female friendship remains: Carrie joins lonely Miranda on New Year's, but it's clearly a stopgap solution, not the right one.

It's a new year, however, and a new V-Day is near: Carrie looks again at the *Vogue* article about her wedding and discovers she "didn't say 'we' once." "The whole wedding was *my* point of view," concedes Carrie: what looked like a man's betrayal in leaving her at the altar was actually caused by the woman herself, you see.

Since Carrie has admitted that it was really all her fault, resolution of the romantic tensions can't be far behind. Miranda and Steve's marriage counselor asks them to make a decision deadline about getting back together. Sure enough, now that Miranda, too, knows it was really all her fault, the outcome is inevitable: she and Steve meet, embrace and, of course, have passionate sex, which will presumably never degenerate into banality and boredom ever again, if Miranda does her homework (and that means *home work*, as opposed to the job that exhausted her).

Sam's resolution comes when she realizes she wants to have sex with a neighbor and so breaks up with Smith, her boyfriend. Carrie's voice-over tells us (with a snicker) that "some love stories are short." This is what happens when you're too free-spirited and don't want to be married: you end up with no emotional anchor, only empty sex.

Meanwhile, Carrie discovers just at the right time, now that she has owned up to her fault, that Big has been sending her numerous love letters by e-mail that she hadn't seen. Ah, the sure sign of romance: the wish that was true all along, o ye of little romantic faith! On the last day that she can change her mind about selling their fabulous penthouse, Carrie goes back and sees him there. After the requisite makeup sex, Carrie allows that the funny part is that "we were perfectly happy before we decided to live happily ever after." Big adds, "And the way we decided to get married was all business, no romance." So that was the only problem! He then proposes to her on one knee—mocking, but also enacting, the traditional way.

When all the friends celebrate, Carrie asks, "Why is it that we write our own vows, but not our own rules?" It's not clear, however, what rules Carrie is breaking in marrying Big, besides wearing a glamorous pantsuit instead of a glamorous gown. And the movie concludes with Carrie's voice-over as she makes a sly reference to her love of individualistic fashion: "Maybe some rules are best left in the closet. We label people bride, groom, husband, wife, and forget to look past the label to the person." Apparently if the modern girl breaks the Rules and doesn't try to get married, she will win the heart of the recalcitrant male and get the cookie that she first denied herself. The heroine just has to go about loving in the *right way*. Sure enough, at the end of the movie, when all the rest are happy and have their men, Samantha is left with her dog.

Sex and the City 2: Women Who Don't Love the Right Way (2010)

Where could the "girls" of *Sex and the City* go after all find true love, you might wonder (or at least the producers did)—a question particularly well suited as a text for a time when marriage rates are declining even in marriage-happy America.

The sequel to *Sex and the City* attempts to reflect reality in marriage and motherhood, such as the "dark" secret that achieving motherhood is not just the fulfillment of a dream but also the beginning of nagging problems. By illustrating the exact ways in which the passion that leads to marriage is undermined, perhaps fatally, by the routine monotony of domestic life and its slowly accumulating irritations, the movie purports to examine what a "new" marriage is; beyond having the wedding one wants (as in *Sex and the City 1*), can women hope to make up its rules for greater personal liberation? Or should we rest on the bedrock of traditional rules and commitments as a safety net?

"Keeping romance alive" is a topic that is frequently treated as a problem in magazines and most other pop media, as well as self-help books, talk shows, and so on. But *Sex and the City 2* shows the doldrums more than most, as Carrie laments the loss of what she terms "sparkle."[14] Just as in TV sitcoms, where the husband is frequently a dummy who buys his wife a vacuum cleaner for Valentine's Day, Carrie's husband, Mr. Big, sincerely thinks she likes watching TV with him. Carrie nags and her husband is turned off. We see the perennial difficulty of "accepting the other person as they are," which he brings up as a defense, understandably, since that is the common advice for the relationship phase. The fact that it doesn't work for Carrie exposes the problematics of this concept: how much does the unconditional acceptance that defines romantic love get priority over "standing up for yourself" or "getting what you need"? Hmm. Is the woman going to do more accepting than the man?

So the setup of *Sex and the City 2*'s narrative arc is honest in the midst of the most offensive dishonesty, an idealized view of the privileged New Yorker as the reality of married life. For example, the conflict between having a career and being a mother is presented as easily fixed: when Miranda, the high income-earner in the family, quits her job, there is no worry that she won't get another or might have a problem affording the loyal housekeeper/nanny who does everything for her.

But as usual, the romantic-marital tension is only there in order to be resolved in a satisfying, conflict-free way. Here the central problem is one reflected in many modern popular magazines and self-help books: how to keep passion centered on one person for life (Carrie kisses a former flame, out of frustration with her husband's distance). Big's proposed solution of staying alone for two days a week even though they're married is meant to illustrate the same danger his behavior represented in *Sex and the City 1*, his lack of "commitment." Now there are two problems: not enough sparkle and not enough commitment. But it turns out, you see, that the lack of sparkle is really a problem of commitment, not working on it, not compromising with what the other wants to do in order to *renew* the sparkle. In other words, Carrie has just not been working hard enough at it.

A telling detail is that while the husband's idea of spending two days a week in Carrie's old apartment is presented as a debilitating danger to their relationship, no one ever brings up the possibility that Carrie herself might have more private time in that same apartment without threat. Somehow the husband's "leaving" the marital space is the issue, rather than Carrie's ability to control her own time and space. Why? Because it symbolically represents the greatest peril of all, that a man can and might leave the marriage (and narrative) altogether, leaving the heroine with no romantic story. And women must respond to this ultimate threat in order to get the audience behind the final compromise and the heroine's rejection of a "liberated" relationship.

Because conflict and ambiguity can't be dwelt on too long in pop culture, the climax of the drama has to be a narrative point that can be read in only one way. Carrie's extramarital kiss is the turning point of the narrative because it represents a clear signal that she was wrong to let her marriage get all unsparkly. Then, too, immediately after Miranda quits the overly demanding and ambitious job that makes her miss her son's science fair, she is rewarded by managing to walk (job-free) into the boy's classroom at the exact moment when he is about to get the science fair award. Of course, a scene showing she was demeaned as a woman at work is meant to make this veiled criticism of women's ambition into a feminist statement.

Most of all, Carrie's guilt over the adulterous kiss conveniently coincides with her husband "realizing" (everyone in Hollywood is always having permanent, life-enhancing epiphanies) that the kiss was ultimately his fault: he hasn't treated her well (that lack of commitment). This leads to the supposed immediate full restoration of sexual passion and sparkle, of course, just as Miranda's epiphany about her defective love for her husband in *Sex and the City 1* led to the same staged scene of joyful marital reunion and the implication that it will never get boring again. And since Big and Carrie are now sparkling, they also compromise on the question of watching television together. This is usually the quick fix to the nagging problem of how passion can be maintained as one navigates the next stage of romance, or how compromise has its built-in limits as a mediator of power: the problem is just dropped for an easy solution so we can all go home, both metaphorically and also literally from the movie theater.

As for the movie's opening question about "new" marriage and the possibility of making it up for oneself, the stance here seems to be that some modification of old rules is acceptable, as when the movie defends women who don't want children (Carrie) or who do want sex without the sanction of a long-term relationship (the independent but tellingly nutty, inconsiderate, and thoughtless Samantha). But in the end the point is that if women try to modify the bedrock of marriage, they will not gain in personal control or liberation but instead will lose the intimacy and all-important security that traditional marriage offers, or at least promises if you can keep up the work.

The problem is poignant: you're screwed if you're single because you don't have what you're supposed to, but when you get it, you're screwed because you're married and the sparkle is dulled. It's the romance that's great, not the before or after. Women live for the climactic moment of coming together, but in reality it's over in a moment, like a hit of a longed-for drug whose euphoria wears off only too quickly and leaves the user hungry again. This is the dark shadow beneath the dream-life of romance that has to be obscured with manufactured sparkle.

It might be useful to look at the two *Sex and the City* movies as parts of an instruction manual focused on the wedding as climax of romance (1) and the reality of the marriage of the heroine (2), each corresponding to those perennial magazine topics, "how to get the man to commit to marriage" and "how to keep the marriage going." The heroine's status as an independent woman in the popular TV series provides the challenge: just how independent can a woman be without threatening the marriage? In both films, the characters are really all parts of a whole, the modern woman, who must:

a. be successful but not work too hard (as Miranda is wrong to do in 1)
b. get a guy to commit (Carrie in 1)
c. fend off the threat of her own restlessness and desire for independence (Carrie in 2)
d. fend off the threat of adultery if she is not constantly sexy and giving to her man (Miranda in 1)
e. not be *too* sexy or promiscuous, or she won't get that permanent relationship in the first place (Samantha in 1)
f. be maternal while remaining calm and cheerful no matter how emotionally and physically debilitating it may be (Charlotte in 2)

Talk about a tall order. It's no wonder women escape to the movies.

He's Just Not That Into You: Creepy-Needy Women (2009)

Oddly, though not by the rule book of American media, a line from a *Sex and the City* TV episode "inspired" (if that's the word) an advice book of the same name: *He's Just Not That Into You: The No-Excuses Truth to Understanding Guys*.[15] This is a slim volume that purports to help women understand the lame excuses men give them for not calling, in order to—once again—empower the women to be realistic about hetero relationships and stop "waiting around for some guy." Women will be armed and ready to decode the man's signs by getting the skinny straight from the horse's mouth, since one author is male. The female coauthor of the book puts it this feminist way for the female reader: "It's good for us all to remember that we don't need to scheme and plot, or beg anyone to ask us out. We're fantastic." As in so many other works in the genre of self-help for women, the real problem is women's low self-esteem, not the overhyped romance or the inequality of women's greater interest in it.

In the wonderfully fertile way of pop culture, the book *He's Just Not That Into You* then became a modestly successful romantic comedy tracing the lives of a number of women struggling with modern dilemmas of love, all delivered with the same postmodern ironic wink as the *Sex and the City* TV series and movie.

Ever since Mary Wollstonecraft and Simone de Beauvoir, women have been castigated as contributing to their own subjugation. This movie pretends to scold like those feminists while turning those feminist "rules" to have the exact opposite effect. It's another example of Hollywood wanting its feminist cake and demolishing it too. Or rather, baking the cake so it can be eaten for profit.

In *He's Just Not That Into You*, virtually all the female characters are depicted as desperate for romance, clingy-needy, yet completely unable to read men even while obsessively trying to. Being out of control (passion) is bad: love is harnessing attraction to compatibility so it will be made to endure. These women don't only love too much, they also love the *wrong way*.

If the female characters are intensely manipulative, pulling out all the tricks to "get" men and hook them, like the girls in modern magazines, all the males are dumb as well as narcissistic. As in so many other movies, men are emotional oafs, eternally unable to feel properly, until a good woman finally makes a life-changing speech or stages a scene that will convert them by making them realize (mass culture's favorite rhetorical move) that love (the relationship leading to permanent commitment) is the answer.

"You don't need men to validate you" was the message of the book, not exactly original but at least approached from a funny and somewhat different standpoint, one that is arguably feminist. Once the scriptwriters made it a story in rom-com land, the grounds were shifted, however: in the movie, the women are rewarded in the end for the very obsessiveness they are castigated for. It's as if extrapolating the jokey "rule" into the genre of love story drops the ball into the same old hole by some imperative of gender relations.

The movie, with postmodern self-referentiality, includes a call for women to reject the conventions of the love story itself: "Girls are taught a lot of stuff growing up," narrates the heroine, Gigi: "If a guy punches you he likes you. . . . Every movie we see, every story we're told implores us to wait for it, the third act twist, the unexpected declaration of love, the exception to the rule." The voice-over features the usual nod to feminism, echoing the book's validation of women being happy alone: "And maybe a happy ending doesn't include a guy, maybe . . . it's you, on your own, picking up the pieces and starting over."[16] Notice the hesitation after the second "maybe," implying that's not what the heroine *really* wants or believes in her heart. You just know there will be an exception to the rule about not seeing yourself as an exception.

As it turns out, while women's hope to be that exception is ridiculed throughout most of the movie, the book's dictum that male distance does mean lack of feeling is belied by the main lovers, Gigi and Alex. She "reads" him right after all, and he "doesn't realize" that she was right until she makes her big speech about his shallowness and flounces out. At that point taking the self-help advice to stop "waiting around" and manipulating men, at first held up as a sensible and supportive warning to creepy-needy women, is suddenly recast as "giving up hope" (as Gigi says):

GIGI: But sometimes we're so focused on finding our happy ending we don't learn how to read the signs. How to tell the ones who want us from the ones who don't, the ones who will stay and the ones who will leave. Or maybe the happy ending is this, knowing after all the unreturned phone calls, broken hearts, through the blunders and misread signals, through all the pain and embarrassment, you never gave up hope.

God forbid that anyone in an American movie should ever be less than optimistic!

The potential boyfriend giving the advice is now cast as coldly cynical, thus (almost) forfeiting his own "chance at love," which is about trying hard, working at it, not about passion.

GIGI: I would rather be like that, than be like you.
ALEX: Excuse me? What's that supposed to mean?
GIGI: Oh! You think you've won because women are expendable to you. You may not get hurt or make an ass of yourself that way but you don't fall in love that way either. You have not won. You're alone.

Alex, the male who "plays doctor" in the sense of diagnosing and fixing what is wrong with the love life of the heroine, Gigi, and telling her what she "should" do, in the end gets his comeuppance for having rules in the first place:

ALEX: You were right. I'd gotten so used to keeping myself at a safe distance from all these women and having the power that—that I didn't know what it felt like when I actually fell for one of them . . . I didn't know . . . You are *my* exception.

Hollywood adores comeuppance: in the very smart film comedy *Up in the Air*, the coolly distant hero who beds many women gets his comeuppance when he falls in love with a woman who beds him but doesn't want an enduring love affair, because, as it turns out, she is married and simply uses men for sex. This would seem to be a clever rewriting of the stereotypical script, except that it's the same old idea about gender, coupling, and commitment: the hero is punished for his initial refusal to commit to love by being alone and lonely (perhaps forever) at the end.

Meanwhile, in *He's Just Not That Into You*, Neil, the man who has been living with Beth but won't marry her, shapes up only when the woman throws a fit and declares that the man is too infantile to want a "mature" love, punishing him by walking out and leaving him (horrors) "alone." As for Beth, the female chump who finally wises up and leaves the man who won't marry her, she is rewarded with what she wants when she stops trying to *get him* to marry her. The good girl who stops asking finds that she happens to be loved in the right way after all. So Beth is another exception, and hoping against hope is encouraged between the lines once again.

All you have to be is a good woman to get the results, unless there is an affair, in which case all bets are off. Everyone is happily coupled up at the end except for the adulterous married man and his (of course) shallow mistress, who obviously don't deserve love anyway. The victimized wife gets a divorce, but being conveniently gorgeous and still young, she, and the movie, are cheerily optimistic that she too will get a good man after all. In other words, women are criticized for being obsessive about romance in a movie that is obsessed with getting all the (good) women the romantic love they desire. It just pays to "believe in love," as our heroine Gigi does—it especially pays at the box office.

The last irony of this movie is that while the advice to women to stop being manipulative is supposed to empower them by bringing them the dignity, emotional independence, and agency they lack, it's only when the woman behaves in a traditionally feminine way, caring more than men do, or holding out for marriage as though it's a business deal, that she is rewarded by the breakthrough moment of the man's realization of love. Where have we seen this scenario before? Isn't it just a repeat of the same old Victorian dictum of feminine passivity yet superiority in love?

(500) Days of Summer (2009): The Woman Who Just Needs the Right Man

Why did the tragic movies examined earlier in this chapter have male and female audiences while the contemporary comedies are "chick flick" rom-coms aimed at female audiences? Aren't there movies about men who love too much, who are too dedicated to or needy for love? Actually, there is one, voted their favorite by many of my students.

All the above films are about women in love and their transformation—though the women themselves are focused on their men, and the problem presented is whether the women will get what they want—namely, the men. In other words, we watch the women watching the men, and the movies' real subject is the female desire to be desired.[17] This is not to say, of course, that all modern Hollywood movies are like this. Take *(500) Days of Summer*, for example, the young, hip, sweetly ironic movie that proclaims itself as different: it's the hero who is romantic, while the heroine, the ravishing Summer (who comes and goes like the pleasures of that season), is forthright and firm in her wish not to have a boyfriend or emotional commitment, just a good time with whichever guy she's involved with at the time, for however long it lasts. A liberated heroine!

The film proclaims: "This is a story of boy meets girl, but you should know upfront, this is not a love story."[18] In still another moment of wry postmodern self-referentiality (see *He's Just Not Into You* above), a character notes that "movies are responsible" for lies about love. The tone of the narration is cool and self-mocking, while the hero himself is still sincere enough to be "the boy" in the "boy meets girl" story. "Tom Hansen, of Margate, New Jersey, grew up believing that he'd never be truly happy until the day he met his . . . *soul mate*," says the narrator right at the start, as the movie seems to make fun of his romanticism before we can. What is he, some kind of girl in drag?

The hero, not quite a nerd in the sense of a Judd Apatow film, but certainly not dashing or clearly desirable in the way of Mr. Big, is stuck in a dead-end job writing doggerel for a greeting card company. Much of the comedy comes from the way he assumes the "feminine" role of nagging his Summer about where their relationship is going and exactly how she feels about him.

SUMMER: We're just friends.
TOM: No! Don't pull that with me! Kissing in the copy room? Holding hands in Ikea? Shower sex? Come on! Friends my balls!

He wants more than she does, which sets the stage for a Beauty-and-the-Beast scenario, that he will win her over by sheer devotion and goodness. But she really does not return his feelings, and the relationship is over before the movie is. We're not sure why this is so, exactly, since he is adorable, and in fact the narrative and its preoccupation with the feelings and mind of the hero have set us up to hope for a traditional ending. So yes, this seems unconventional, a challenge to the usual desperate search on the woman's part for love, or the typically unearned claim that the lovers onscreen are perfectly right for each other and will love forever after. And how refreshing that for once, *he* is the romantic and *she* is the free spirit, not to be pinned down, a modern girl who does not need emotional attachment or romance to enjoy a sexual relationship with someone she likes.

TOM: Look, we don't have to put a label on it. That's fine. I get it. But, you know, I just . . . I need some consistency. . . . I need to know that you're not gonna wake up in the morning and feel differently.
SUMMER: And I can't give you that. Nobody can.

Summer's critique of romance is equated with bursting the balloon of mystical explanations for romantic love as fate rather than coincidence, a view repeated by the narrator near the film's conclusion:

NARRATOR: If Tom had learned anything . . . it was that you can't ascribe great cosmic significance to a simple earthly event. Coincidence, that's all anything ever is, nothing more than coincidence. . . . Tom had finally learned, there are no miracles. There's no such thing as fate, nothing is *meant to be*. He knew, he was sure of it now.

But not so fast. First, the idea has been introduced early on that Summer's reluctance to commit to a relationship comes from her experience with her parents' divorce—in other words, from a neurotic, not a principled, place, no matter what she says. The distancing voice of the narrator coolly relates the story in the third person:

NARRATOR: The girl, Summer Finn of Shinnecock, Michigan, did not share this belief. Since the disintegration of her parents' marriage she'd only loved two things. The first was her long dark hair. The second was how easily she could cut it off and not feel a thing.

Of course, "cutting it off and not feeling a thing" applies to more than just hair; it's a *metaphor*. You see, Summer has that affliction common to heroes of romance fiction: she doesn't know how to love because she doesn't let herself feel. Liberation apparently implies pathology, no matter that this is a clever, postmodern take on romance with reversed gender roles as compared to a more conventional rom-com like *He's Just Not That Into You*.

This prepares us for the surprise ending, in which a sad and chastened Tom, the hero, discovers that Summer, the independent spirit, has become engaged, ring and all. He is crushed, but she explains it clearly and simply when they later meet unexpectedly after her marriage: the difference, she says, is that she "just woke up one day, and I knew . . . *it was meant to be*" with her husband. In other words, Summer found (yes) the One. And because everyone must have the One, if Tom is "open" to it, he will meet *his* One, who is "meant to be" for him.

Sure enough, while waiting to interview for a job that is the "right" job for him (a much higher status job as an architect, because this is still another film about self-development), he encounters a woman who, we understand, will be better for him than Summer. She is called Autumn, with the movie's sweetly smart humor, because she is associated with a more mature view of love. Maturity is about finding the One with whom one can make it "work" through perfect mutuality, but somehow it's also the mystery of fate in attraction: "What," asks Summer about her first meeting with her future husband in a café, "if I'd gone to the movies instead?" And when it all works, one has arrived, having mounted Freud's twin peaks of happiness through possessing both love and job fulfillment (though Summer's life beyond the fact of her marriage is not addressed at all, and Tom doesn't bother to inquire.)

Summer was just not that into him, but the difficulty is not romance, much less romance and gender, after all. Tom's initial skepticism about soul mates is now discredited as a result of his maturity, unless you consider the meaning of "soul mate" to be "the one who works out"—which is exactly what the movie means us to understand.

AUTUMN: Yeah, yeah I think I've seen you there.
TOM: I haven't seen you?
AUTUMN: You must not have been looking.

The real problem all along (just as it was in *He's Just Not That Into You*), it seems, was not working hard enough at looking for the One that he is meant to meet anyway, if you can figure out the metaphysics of that logic.

Why, then, does *(500) Days of Summer* proclaim itself "Not a love story"? Is it because the hero longed for Summer but didn't end up with her? The romantic Tom declared that "you know it's love when you feel it," but apparently you don't really know it (or *really* feel it?) unless it's conveniently mutual. None of this makes any sense, no matter how much covered over by repeated winking to the audience. But in fact the conceptual confusion about romance in the rom-com genre reflects the ongoing strain in the modern problem of hetero relations.

The tragic heroines in this chapter love too much, but that's because they are angelic rescuers, not just human characters with intense desire for the men they need so desperately. The tragic heroines' love is a subset of the larger problem of women's desire, which must be sacrificed in some way, but romantic comedy has cute, ironic laughter that saves face in our own era of unresolved problems of love. The noble (if misguided) tragic passion of the wounded angel is transformed into the more pragmatic concerns of a cute, slim, pretty, lighthearted woman who can learn to love correctly so as to render a relationship viable, releasing tension in the (supposedly) healing laugh of recognition. In romantic comedies, the heroine learns (in a well-placed epiphany) what to do in time to be rewarded with ideal love, the One. This is the man she should be with, who combines intense sexual feeling with permanent companionship, the "one who stays," as Gigi put it. The tragic heroine, on the other hand, was lucky to get martyrdom, or (if she survives at all) a few memories and more self-esteem, but she's not going to get the guy.

Both *Leaving Las Vegas* and *Breaking the Waves* feature strong central female characters who are undervalued and mistreated, much as fairy-tale heroines have always been. Both movies have prizewinning performances. And both play with ambiguous viewpoints, so they can be "feminist" and exploitative/misogynist at the same time. It is a sign of our modern times that the tragedies of the woman hurt by love are undercut with ironies about the validity of the heroine's desire that you may take or leave, just as you please. The optional tears, smirk, or condescension that result are not as important as the evolution of that Victorian icon, the self-sacrificing woman in love, into its modern afterlife: the beautiful, hurt angel as the female unknowable, an ideal enigma, whether as Freud's psychic woman-as-dark-continent or the icon of the mystery at the heart of life itself.

And if the heroines of our nineties tragedies have problematic sexuality (both are humiliated and prostituted, purely devoted though they are), the heroines of romantic comedy in the early 2000s have problematic hearts that must be governed and educated in loving as a woman, though they are depicted as women supposedly free to behave like men. To be fair, it isn't easy to take a simple stance that is politically correct when it comes to women and romance in the movies: if a heroine is either lonely as a single woman or vigorously pursues romance, (we) feminists criticize that.[19] Ironically, the liberal argument for gay marriage and the equal value of gay love utilizes the exact other view, that love is an essential part of life, that no one should be single who doesn't want to be, and who wants to be?

This contradiction is as much a red herring as questions about the privileged status of victimhood or whether female characters who rescue men through love are feminist ideals because they are "strong." In the end there's no getting away from it: heroines who love men in the movies are bounced between the unpleasant choices of being angelic victims of desire (tragedy) or goody-two-shoes troubleshooters of relationships (romantic comedy). No matter if they love too much or too little, whether they are holy fools and angels who choose to sacrifice themselves for love or rational smarty-pants regulators who need to love more lest they be too cool for marriage, it's still all on them to make the damned thing work.

7

FEMINISM AND HARLEQUIN ROMANCE
The Problem of the Love Story

> He'd give her some romance that would knock her out of her glass
> slippers.
> —Nora Roberts, *Cordina's Crown Jewel*, 2002

What is the problem with romance? Is it even a problem, besides to those whose hearts get broken? Actually, yes.

Romantic fiction is irresistibly delicious to many women. And many academic feminists have not been happy about that, or at best have had a vexed and ambivalent view of the pleasure women have derived from this genre. There is a whole body of scholarship out there that analyzes the heterosexual narrative of romantic love as a popular form, and at least in the past, it was seldom admiring.[1] I've (modestly) contributed to it myself.

In fact, much to my surprise, I recently came across a couple of references to this modest contribution in Pamela Regis's defense of the genre, *A Natural History of the Romance Novel*.[2] Regis infers that my own view aligns me with other critics who are "against" romance, while she seems vehemently "for" it. Analyzing romance seems to encourage choosing up sides, rooting for your own team while booing the opposition. This chapter represents my own attempt to describe how a feminist like me, who enjoys romance low and high and every which way, thinks about the feminism-and-fictional-romance kerfuffle.

But, you might reasonably inquire, why are feminists reading these books in the first place, and why should they care that others do? In fact, feminist scholars not only care but are quite passionate about it all, pun intended. What makes this odd is that in their long tug-of-war with faithful readers who mostly *don't* appear to care if feminists approve of them or not, only one side has been holding the rope. I wonder how many buyers of romantic fiction have given a passing thought to the feminist scholarship written about it (and I don't mean the tiny percentage of romance readers who are scholars themselves).

After all, as the critic Wendy Langford has said, as a concept, love remains "ill-defined, assumed rather than explained, seeming to reflect rather than elucidate a lived experience of something mysterious and impenetrable."[3] The mystery of what love is serves as both part of its glamour and a rationalization for not analyzing it. Why do fans of the romance want to see or read this genre? Not to understand it but to maintain the mystification. Mystification apparently sells well: a billion-dollar-plus industry, romance fiction dominates the U.S. consumer book market and accounts for as much as half of all paperback book sales.[4] When an industry has been as successful as the romance-publishing business, the business of pleasure is to make us consume the spectacle of that pleasure, not ponder it.

It's perfectly understandable that many feminist critics in the past have been critical of mass-market romances. Feminist criticism both analyzes and advocates at the same time, after all, for a fairer world where women can live better lives. Romantic fiction comes in for scrutiny because, for all its exaggerations and idealizations, it both reflects women's lived choices and practices and possibly—though no one knows exactly how or to what extent—influences them as well. The very fact that it is a widespread pleasure, written almost entirely by and for women, and overwhelmingly focused on men as objects of desire (or on men focusing on women as objects of desire) brings the whole genre under suspicion.[5] What are its values, in the literal sense of what should be valued at the expense of other possibilities? It seems fair, important in fact, for feminists to ask what it is accomplishing for us, exactly.

But are feminism and romance inherently opposed? In a way, sorting out their supposedly dueling interests is like trying to do counseling with mismatched lovers. As is so often the case with quarreling couples, the conflicts and issues that emerge turn out not to be the ones they at first seemed to be arguing about. I would say there are mutual attractions as well as antagonisms arising from the feminist and romantic perspectives and agendas.

A TROUBLED ROMANCE

In order to uncover these buried issues, let's first take a quick potted and admittedly incomplete look at a few important points in what might be called the love-hate relation between feminist criticism and popular romance. The association of women with what the eminent Victorian novelist George Eliot called "silly" novels (as opposed to serious, morally and aesthetically) is an old one, not only predating mass-market romance but perhaps as old as the genre of the novel itself. Certainly there was a tradition of highly fanciful "amatory" adventures written by and for women from at least the eighteenth century in England,[6] and the association of this kind of reading with the supposed triviality, shallowness, narcissism, and general fluffiness of women's tastes in general has been a charge leveled from various quarters pretty regularly since that time. Ironically, the accusers have grouped in two camps with opposing agendas: on the one hand, those such as the great eighteenth-century feminist Mary Wollstonecraft, who believed women's habits reflected their ignorance and social training more than their inherent abilities and therefore favored more education for women, and on the other, those whose low opinion of women's nature led to clamping down on their access to dangerously frivolous materials.[7]

Like women's propensity for the pleasures of gossip, cosmetics, or shopping, their apparent taste for the low arts and for consumer culture was perhaps a source of embarrassment for Second Wave feminists in the late twentieth century, but it was also a focus for criticism and a change in consciousness. Feminist critics Ann Douglas and Ann Snitow, both writing in the seventies, labeled mass-market romance as "soft pornography for women," a kind of emotional rather than sexual obscenity.[8] They saw the workings of the heart as a coy substitute for the desires of the body, concluding that the formula romance promotes the gender and sexual ideologies that denigrate women and serve to keep them in their place, subordinate to men and to the marriage and family system. Snitow's influential analysis, written at a time when heroines of popular romances had to be virgins and pursued only conventional female helping roles, analyzed the way romance constructs opposing traits of the male and female "as if they were two species," educating women's desire so that difference and distance are themselves rendered titillating.

Other critics took on a typical formula: the male is aloof, cool, distant, or gruff to the point of rudeness, verbally aggressive, and sometimes physically and sexually aggressive as well, so male and female engage in a kind of contest to see if she will penetrate his armor emotionally before he penetrates her sexually. Needless to say, the woman always won—at least in the short run, that is, within the narrative space of the text. But, the feminist critics asked, who comes out on top, so to speak, in the longer view?

So far, so good. This critique fit well with those Second Wave feminist views that have become quite familiar and much more acceptable in the decades that followed: it's no longer shocking, in contemporary Western societies, to say that women need not marry or be mothers to be complete, or that women have the right to pursue their ambitions. As the writer Katha Pollitt pointed out, there were few voices in the 2008 American presidential election deploring Hillary Clinton's or Sarah Palin's run for office on the grounds that they were women and mothers.

But as the critic Rosalind Coward noted in 1985, in the same decades that the core ideas of Second Wave feminism were becoming absorbed into the larger cultural picture, there was also a huge growth in the sales of Harlequin Enterprises Ltd., the powerful company that publishes many lines of popular romance.[9] As Harlequin and other publishers of romance adapted to the times by incorporating some aspects of feminist values—much greater emphasis on women's sexual desire and much less on the requirement to be a virgin bride, more career women and greater independence for the romantic heroine, for example—a countertradition of feminist analysis emerged that pushed back against this initial strongly negative critical stance.

This new feminist approach objected to the Second Wave feminist depiction of women as denigrated both within the romantic text and in the act of reading of the text. These defenders of mass-market romance often claimed that the romance genre is subversive rather than oppressive, in that it celebrates female power and adventure, echoing an older view of romantic love itself as rebellious against social norms. Just as Anglo-American women's right to choose their spouses became a mark of new individualistic freedoms in the eighteenth century (as in Samuel Richardson's masterpiece, the novel *Clarissa*), the power of women's choice in love was seen as liberatory in the twentieth. Still another type of analysis objected to the feminist disparagement of female readers who chose to read these novels for pleasure; why not instead reach out to those women in the name of sisterhood?

The new trend toward a more kind and gentle feminist understanding of the ordinary female reader took a stronger turn in the 1992 collection of essays called *Dangerous Men and Adventurous Women*, edited by a working Harlequin author, Jayne Ann Krentz. Krentz and the other authors in this anthology praise women's "courage" through the generations in reading romance in the face of a disparagement and hostility that the more "masculine" genres of mystery, thrillers, sci-fi, or horror do not elicit. Critics treat presumably female romance readers as if they were "children" who don't know how to tell reality from fantasy, an observation that is, again, rarely made about horror or science fiction. This charge against the critique of romance as *itself* anti-feminist cleverly aligns Second Wave criticism of the genre with the patriarchal dismissal of "women's reading" in the eighteenth and nineteenth centuries, depicting critics like Ann Snitow as snooty, stuffy elitists who are alienated from (and in turn alienate) the very group they claim they want to defend.[10]

In her introduction, Krentz avoids directly leveling the serious charge against the offending feminists that nevertheless informs the work throughout: that they are out of touch with the nature of "real womanhood," on the one hand, and with real women, on the other. However, she does imply that feminist critics willfully misunderstand romance because they perceive the genre as not politically correct—whereas, she argues, in fact romance "celebrates female power": "With courage, intelligence, and gentleness she [the heroine of the romance] brings the most dangerous creature on earth, the human male, to his knees . . . [and] forces him to acknowledge her power *as a woman*" (my emphasis). The romance novel, she says, "inverts the power structure of a patriarchal society," a view that clearly echoes the new trend of "oppositional" criticism begun by previous scholars (5).

Yet paradoxically, by taking the argument in favor of romance to its most radical "feminist" endorsement, the authors in *Dangerous Men and Adventurous Women* arrived full circle at the Victorian view of women as having a unique "power" within the circle of love and family (the Victorians liked to reference the moral "influence" of women in their "separate sphere" of home), to which a wider arena of rights, entitlements, and abilities is mere wallpaper. In this view, women are presumed to have a special kind of authority that seems mystical and spiritual, or else "natural"—anything but social or historical, and certainly not economic, political, or legal. "The fantasies in books have nothing to do with woman's politics," claims Krentz, who defended virginity in romance heroines, mandatory at the time, as a feminist "metaphor" for "female power, honor, generosity and courage."[11] Love is, as usual, above it all.

EVOLUTION, IF NOT REVOLUTION

An area of great conflict in the history of feminist ideas has been the desire of some (both in scholarship and popular media) to perpetuate and exalt so-called natural womanhood, especially those putative universal traits associated with women such as nurturance and emotionality. To examine the project of validating previously ignored or devalued so-called womanly traits or "powers," we might take another look at *Dangerous Women*. After all, the glorification of "separate spheres," as this notion was called in Britain and America, was popular with some Victorian feminists who wished for more public reverence for the feminized private sphere as the most acceptable and therefore immediately effective way to redress the imbalance between men and women. You can see how this new nineteenth-century appeal for higher value on "feminine" traits, space, and "power" was both progressive compared to the denigration of women in ages before and yet, at the same time, severely limiting compared to our own contemporary (Western) view of unfettered freedom of opportunity. It's as if, for these Victorians, the limits on behavior and potential were the price that had to be rendered for women's social progress.

Now, Krentz concludes in her introduction that romance is *about* "female power, intuition, and a female worldview that affirms life and expresses hope for the future" (8). The concept of tender emotion and subjectivity as aspects of a specifically female realm of competence and responsibility is important here: in Harlequin novels, unlike, for example, in other popular genres such as thrillers, westerns, or mysteries, the action tends to be entirely woman-oriented, in that the "life" affirmed consists of appealing to the hero's psyche (and testosterone) so that the woman gets what she wants. Accordingly, because these romances sell all over the world, the attraction of romance (and therefore of "female power") is said to be universal. Of course, one might argue that the danger of this particular approach is precisely that whatever is given in them is automatically naturalized, appearing as obvious and natural. So they are said to "celebrate the power of love" (17), without ever questioning—or even permitting the reader to have the vocabulary to question—what that power specifically is, how much one can really do with it, and what price is paid for it. In other words, what is left out of the discussion is whether the female lover's supposed power over the beloved is worth having in the first place, never mind what she has to do to obtain and keep it.

The claim of romantic love's disinterestedness, of its being exempt from issues of hierarchy and inequality in class society, is suspect to many critics. The feminist critique of popular romance may here be joined to the feminist critique of the classic novel, as when the eminent critic Mary Poovey argued that in Jane Austen's fiction, the force of love seemingly resolves the contradictions of a capitalist society by presenting the "struggle of desire against social constraint" and idealizing the "power of principled feeling."[12] Similarly, Nancy Armstrong's critically acclaimed study *Desire and Domestic Fiction* asserts that the nineteenth-century novel deflected social radicalism by substituting plots about love and domesticity for political issues, thus making the consciousness of the modern bourgeois reader into that of a conventional woman.[13] These critics argue that romance, high or low, provided women with temporary imaginative consolations, tending to defuse criticism of those very institutions (political, like the struggle for the vote, or social, like the economic dependence of women on men in marriage) that make those consolations necessary. If anything, high culture comes out looking worse than popular literature, since the courtship plot replaces serious social criticism that might otherwise be the focus. In fact, Poovey calls Austen "irresponsible" in promulgating the belief in personal fulfillment outside "configurations of power."[14] Clearly there are serious disagreements here in defining what power is, who has it, and how we know that.

On the other hand, the Second Wave feminist critique of romance has had its own problems and contradictions, revolving as it has around the uncomfortable idea that women readers must be said to act against their own best interests, with continual false consciousness. This view, which is easily criticized as condescending, is also part of a much broader scholarly disagreement, this one about the role the consumer plays in determining the meanings of popular culture in general, not just the romantic genre. The running controversy has to do with whether ideology is automatically reproduced in an oppressive and self-perpetuating manner, or whether popular culture represents a subversive attack on the patriarchal order. Critics of the latter camp see within pop culture a kind of resistance or undermining of social codes, all the more effective for appearing to acquiesce to the dominant ideology. Here the reader as subject is the issue at hand: does the consumer of popular culture have the agency to create its meanings for herself, and therefore, by implication, the meaning of her own life? To say no seems derogatory to the masses the intellectual wishes to study (and subtly identify him or herself with), but to say yes seems to deny the oppressive power of ideology. Thus the thorny dilemma, and the reams of paper and ergs of brainpower expended. The fact is that neither of these positions seems ultimately satisfying.

In the meantime, as feminists (self-identified) of varied stripes were debating the ethics and value of romance as a woman's genre, the popular romance itself continued to evolve. In the 1980s, the former mandate that the Harlequin romance heroine be a virgin and the prohibition against premarital intimacy beyond kissing were gradually discarded, though not quite at the rate they were discarded in real life. More and more, Harlequins included the titillation of what was called "petting" in the fifties and sixties, after which the heroine began to fall into bed quite soon. In Harlequins of the last few decades, heroines have engaged in premarital sexual relations more often than not (one study says 74 percent do), whereas only about half are virgins when they meet the hero.[15]

On a different but related side of mass-market publishing, in the 1990s so-called chick lit had become a separate genre with its own rules, one of which violated the formula that had sold so well: this heroine was no longer innocent and earnest when she fell in love but was self-deprecating, ironic, and interested in career and shopping almost as much as in her love life.[16] At the same time, in the real world, cohabitation rose to unprecedented proportions among Western couples, age of first marriage was postponed, and divorce lost its traditional stigma and became common and even (dare we say) expected. Alongside these social and literary developments, Harlequin fictions changed some old habits.

One extremely successful aspect of Harlequin Ltd.'s business model was to cultivate niche genres and audiences. Under the Harlequin umbrella, there are now specifically teen romances, genre divisions along the lines of race and ethnicity, and just about any other variation on romance you could possibly think up, including (but definitely not limited to) historical, paranormal, series like Harlequin Blaze that advertise their eroticism openly, Christian romance with more conservative standards of sexual behavior than the early Harlequins, and a series called Harlequin Presents Expecting, all of whose heroines are pregnant by the hero in or before marriage.

Romance also entered with gusto into the Internet revolution, proliferating with e-books, dedicated websites like that of Romance Writers of America, numerous fan blogs and fan-authored sequels to and spin-offs of well-loved romance novels, reviews of romance fiction for readers and booksellers, and online destinations for educators who are teaching romance. Lesbian and gay romance, while still excluded from a separate imprint in Harlequin Ltd., flourishes in online and smaller publishing venues as well.[17] In a parallel to the pornography industry, nearly any fantasy that turns you on romantically can be had somewhere: this gives readers what fans of romance call empowering "choice."[18] Alongside all these, there has been another "romance revolution": a new contingent of scholars united in common cause with fans has grown, emphasizing the variety, particularity, and complexity of romance fictions.

These new developments in romance criticism are, without question, positive and helpful; after all, particularity, in the form of close reading, is the bread and butter of literary studies, as well as of media criticism and cultural studies. But I am skeptical of the claim that a critic shouldn't generalize about romance on the grounds that it has so much variety, as if this implies that general observations are necessarily wrong. Romantic love comes in many forms, but I would argue it is still both possible and useful to extract a common (if complex) ideology of love from the family resemblances among them, both in imaginative texts and also in the language of experience.

Sally Goade, editor of a recent collection of essays called *Empowerment versus Oppression: Twenty-first-Century Views of Popular Romance Novels* (2007), calls her book's title "the question that haunts each study of romance's relationship with its readers." She asks, "Are women readers (and writers) oppressed by their commitment to a narrative with an essentially patriarchal, heterosexual relationship at its center, or are they somehow empowered by their ability to create, escape to, and transform the romance narrative into a vehicle for re-imagining women's freedom within relationships?"[19]

Goade sees these choices as a "false dichotomy" in the end, however, because she believes the answer to both questions can be yes, with "women romance readers . . . simultaneously bound to a patriarchal system and emboldened by their own choice and creativity within that system."[20] It's perhaps telling that Goade, in her effort to be evenhanded in introducing this collection of essays, uses the word "emboldened" rather than the usual "empowered." (What exactly *is* "emboldened"?) One wonders why.

It is now common to note that old-school feminist criticisms of formula romance are outdated because mass-market romance itself has changed so much that former critiques must not be credited.[21] For example, the critic Mairead Owen argued in her 1997 study of romance reading that the resolution of the romance plot occurs with the hero's declaration of love, rather than with a formal marriage proposal, thereby undermining previous critics' focus on the marriage plot as paramount.[22] In 2009 media critics Jade McKay and Elizabeth Parsons documented some of these changes in a study of depictions of marriage in 150 romances published by Mills and Boon between 1984 and 2004. They conclude that "marriage . . . no longer consistently occurs as the novels' closure," as it may be placed at the beginning or during the narrative.[23]

Not only is the heroine now freer to be overt about her own sexual desires, but most heroines are college educated, have a career, and are more financially independent than ever before: McKay and Parsons say that 87 percent have their own income. Therefore, the authors conclude, it is simply no longer true that the point of romance is to "get a husband and his money," and these changes contradict earlier theories that the heroine seeks protection, connection, or even nurturance from a powerful male, as the famous critic Janice Radway and others claimed. McKay and Parsons characterize the relationship between the hero and heroine as "equal" in an impressive 82 percent of the texts surveyed.[24] This is progress any feminist should get behind, one would think.

In fact, McKay and Parsons go further; they claim that feminism as an ideology is overtly foregrounded in about 25 percent of the novels they examined, contrasted with only 4 percent of the novels from the 1980s. This "upward trajectory" leads to their conclusion that "the statistics thus indicate a promisingly feminist trend in romance, a genre long derided by feminist scholars for selling regressive stereotypes to women."[25]

The "upward trajectory" certainly is promising until one looks at the critics' stated criteria for counting "equality" in these fictional romances: their evidence for equality of power was "mutual love, mutual dependency, and no set roles for either . . . as dominant or dominated." But what defines who is "dominant or dominated"? To determine the balance of power, it turns out the authors posed questions such as "Does the hero appear to love the heroine equally as much as the heroine loves the hero?"[26] With such a question as the determinant of feminist ideology, it's a wonder they only came up with a mere 82 percent of the novels surveyed, because entirely mutual love has always and everywhere been the case in formula romances. In fact, it's the whole point of mass-market romance, is constitutive of the genre itself, and is the basis of exactly what Second Wave feminists objected to: the entire enterprise works on the idea that women can expect to have both pleasure *and* power from a love that is conveniently perfect in its mutuality, and don't have to worry about any other inequality as long as the emotions and dependency on each side of the fictional characters balance the other out. Since love is not defined as "real" unless it is a reciprocal dependency, all the heroine has to do to is find "true" love and those nagging questions of social power, authority, and value are automatically erased. There is something oddly circular about this logic.

In regard to those admirable transformations in the genre that now "challenge the traditional power relationships between men and women,"[27] there is no question that popular romance has diversified its target audiences and adapted to the new (Western) cultural codes; it's also no coincidence that romances became much more profitable when they abandoned virginity and embraced sexuality after the sexual revolution of the seventies.[28] In order to survive and flourish, romance publishers had to adopt (one might say "co-opt," in the sixties sense of the word) the most common rhetoric and representations of equality between men and women.[29] Other, more controversial feminist demands, such as the legalization of abortion, have been given a wide berth (the Expecting series of Harlequin romances, based on a heroine who is pregnant with the hero's child, celebrates her decision to have the baby against all odds; you may guess the ending). Given the widespread acceptance of certain versions of feminism in mainstream culture in the West, it's not very surprising that romances of recent decades have incorporated some of the less controversial ideas (or modified forms of the ideas) of the feminist revolution, though it should be said that not all these changes, such as the increased legitimacy of women working outside the home or cohabiting before marriage, are directly attributable to feminist thought alone, rather than to complex socioeconomic developments in post–World War II society. These developments in popular romances are optimistically interpreted by Goade and others as "the power of readers to help transform the genre from within."[30] One might just as well say they exemplify the profit motive and the commodification of romance.

After all, lip service to feminism has now become so prevalent a cliché in popular media that celebrities and public figures of all stripes, including very conservative, regularly declare themselves—if not feminist (there is still considerable hostility to the term)—at least *pro-woman*. Almost everyone is "for equality," but what that actually means is not always so clear.

What precisely does the modern "romance revolution" say about the relationship between popular romance and feminist values? These changes don't so much resolve the nagging question of the possible inherent antagonism of romance and feminism as beg the question. I am reminded of students who argue that the passive, near-silent, self-denying, obedient Fanny in Jane Austen's *Mansfield Park* is a feminist heroine because "she's just being herself, and isn't that what feminists want women to be?" Or take the new forms of outspokenness and independence in heroines, mentioned by everyone from Krentz to Regis to Goade. What could be more of a hallmark of feminist strength of character than openly expressing what you desire and doing what you want (the very opposite of Austen's Fanny)? So what if your one focus is love, and getting what you want boils down to the same old idea of finding the perfect man? By the time we define the feminist heroine as both the silent one and the outspoken one, the passive one and the assertive one, just about everything begins to look like modern feminism and qualify as feminist.

Here, for example, is one Amazon.com reader's comment on the publishing sensation *Fifty Shades of Grey*, an erotic romance in which the naive young heroine learns to love being whipped by a handsome billionaire who supposedly likes to dominate because of dark childhood trauma: "As far as the feminist outcry over this book . . . are you blind to the fact that Annastasia Steele is a very strong female character exploring her own sexuality and consents to everything that Mr. Grey wants to try. Her strength as a character changes Mr. Grey into something he never thought he would be or their relationship into something he has never had."

In reality, the "strong heroine" is not a new feminist phenomenon at all; there have been spunky (now often called "courageous") heroines in romance going all the way back to Samuel Richardson's *Pamela* and Fanny Burney's *Evelina* in the eighteenth century, young women who are "spirited" and speak their minds and get what they want (the guy they want, who enables all the rest) . . . by the machinations of plot. But yes, conventions have changed with the times: Burney's Evelina could not say "I love you" first, much less propose marriage. However, heroines still don't do either one that often in formula romances. And it's true that, unlike our modern liberated heroines, Jane Austen's Elizabeth Bennet did not have a career (duh) and so depended on her husband for her social and economic status—though McKay and Parsons admit in their 2009 survey that "many of the male heroes in contemporary romance are still rich," which they explain as "arguably necessary . . . to free the narrative and the lovers to concentrate on their attentions to each other rather than mundane issues."[31] Hmm: is this a persuasive explanation for what seems like more of the same old thing?

What, then, are we celebrating, exactly? We are down to what McKay and Parsons call the heroine's "sexual freedom."[32] And certainly, with the exception of the so-called sweet romance lines and specifically Christian ones, most romance heroines now go at it like rabbits at any opportunity and constantly think about their own sexual desire when not directly acting on it. On the other hand, it almost always turns out that all that much-expressed desire is aimed at the hero alone and, equally as important, predicated on the love he will eventually show her and her only.

Take, for example, the 2008 novel *Indulge Me*, by Isabel Sharpe, from Harlequin's avowedly super-sexy (but not pornographic!) Blaze/Forbidden Fantasies imprint. Darcy, the heroine, who has "spent her life as a good girl" (14), decides in the first chapter to seduce the gorgeous, hunky house painter (he's actually a college professor, needless to say) who is working outside her window. To that end, she strips in front of that window as an invitation, then waits for him naked on the bed. Bold! Forbidden! Blazing! When she tells him she lured him in because she "wants to come," he responds with equal lust, and a long, detailed description of their romp follows. But even before he has boiling hot, electric sex with her, we get his point of view, and what do we learn? He feels "emotions, swirling within him—desire, and something softer, like tenderness, which he didn't understand" (23). We know how to interpret the code when he has "a sense that he knew her even having just met her" (21). That is, the heroine is permitted her bit of limited sexual license only because it's not really just sex for the hero from the first minute. Apparently the erotic can't have value for its own sake, even at the start.

Though Darcy reveals that she is not only not a virgin but even had sex with a stranger before (only once in college, when she was drunk), a confession that certainly would not have appeared in the Harlequins of yesteryear, she quickly adds that she's "never taken the initiative like this with someone I didn't know" (26–27). In other words, the daring, adventurous, "liberated" sex that makes this novel a "feminist" enterprise depends wholly on the authorization of the same old paradigm. Although this imprint is at the most erotic end of Harlequin's spectrum of choices in category, the heroine's limitations on her sexual behavior seem requisite to her "goodness." These boundaries, along with her ability to evoke the safety of the hero's deep emotional response in the most unlikely circumstances, make her appropriate as a heroine whose reward will be love. And by the end of this bold and courageous adventure, the heroine is engaged to marry the fabulously muscled hero, whose "heart swelled with so much love he could barely take in what was happening." They will "spend the rest of their lives having sex all over the city" (212), in a state of unflagging sexual arousal so sweetly contained in legitimated form that even the Victorians might approve.

As with all the other "transformations" in the genre of formula romance, whatever is currently acceptable in women's social relations is simply integrated into the old romantic paradigm: the heroine is beautiful but not egoistic, stubborn but willing to bend for the right man, highly responsive sexually but a one-man woman, who loves a hero who is powerful and untamed but uniquely susceptible to the heroine, whose unjustified specialness he values as no one else has or can, enabling her to obtain a permanent emotional and sexual commitment, implying marriage (or a committed, marriagelike relationship), without really trying. Underlying the overt changes—the heroine, already not a virgin, has premarital sex with the hero and is free to choose education and career or domesticity—the essential romantic ideology remains. The outside of the box may have more color and variety, but the gift within is the same, thanks to its enormous power to please . . . and sell.

Nicole Kennedy, Romance Writers of America's public relations manager, defined romance by two basic elements in 2005: "There has to be one man and one woman and, no matter the ensuing complications, an emotionally satisfying and optimistic ending," that is, one in which "they either get married or are going in that direction."[33] Regis and others insist that whether or not there is a marriage at the end of a romance, it's the process of overcoming barriers to love that defines the genre.[34] But at least in Harlequin romance, the process works because of the security the reader feels in the formula ending of enduring monogamy, just as the heroine Darcy's willingness to "indulge" her erotic desire was permissible only because we knew in advance that she would invoke transcendent love in his lustful masculine heart and wind up as his adored wife.

I would speculate that the reader's attraction to Darcy's "free" sexual choice of a stranger and its happy consequence in *Indulge Me* emerges from anxiety surrounding the still-fraught value of women's sexuality, more confusing than ever now that it is seemingly so open yet also held ever more cheaply in public displays and private expectations. Because the end is foretold—we know the hero loved her from the beginning and is therefore in her power—it appears as a "solution" to these problems. The structure itself is designed to provide surety, not to complicate, examine, or challenge; that's the payoff of pleasurable fantasy, and it's what distinguishes pop formula from the great classic romance novels, such as *Wuthering Heights*, that do raise disturbingly complex questions. This easy out—a kind of get-out-of-jail-free card—allows a contemporary romance to begin by looking radical while framed within a conservative agenda. For me this does not square well with romance as the "vehicle for re-imagining women's freedom within relationships," in Sally Goade's formulation.[35] At best, such a view seems partially true and partially not, depending on how you spin it or what you leave out of it.

Looking at the fraught history of the feminist response to romance fiction, one almost gets the impression that both former attacks on and the recent defense of the genre may have little to do with the complex value of the texts at all; rather, the nature of the critique sometimes seems to turn on whether or not the critic enjoys popular romance. The Second Wave feminists came down hard on formula romance because its preoccupation with fulfillment through heterosexual love clashed with new values of autonomy in women's professional and private lives; more recent critics have struggled to establish romance as a genre with literary credibility (if not street cred) and readers who must be taken seriously. Oddly, both have seen themselves as protecting the interests of "ordinary women," meaning the readers of romance.

Can popular romances ever be compatible with feminism? Perhaps the answer is not a matter of finding the one right and proper place on the continuum of criticism that wants either to castigate or justify the romance genre, nor positing an essential nature of romance itself that is universally or timelessly expressed, as both vehement critics and defenders have done.

Feminist discussions of mass-market romance often relate in interesting ways to the extraordinarily vexed topic of female desire and pleasure.[36] Arguments about the nature and value of woman's self-defined desire and pleasure in romance can be compared to the equally entangled feminist arguments about pornography, especially about the depiction of female sexual pleasure with a dominating man who is fulfilling the woman's masochistic wishes. Anti-porn feminists have argued that the legitimating of this desire entails the endorsement of an illegitimate supremacy over women. As in the related case of pornography, feminist insistence on a woman's right to pleasure in romance is often presumed to be oppositional to the feminist imperative to understand and change the social and political economy of power that shapes what pleasures are available, and even shapes desire itself.

What about the contention that there is a liberating aspect of romance in female readers *choosing* a fantasy for themselves? This idea rests on the point that the woman is in control and orchestrates the fantasy herself. The counterargument here is that as long as some variant of emotional domination is being eroticized, the danger of reading romances is the reader's enacting some version of this dependency and subordination in real life without the consciousness that she is doing so.[37] The presence of power in the fantasy makes all the difference: do most readers of Harlequins live out their lives conscious of power in their romantic relations or not? I tend to suspect not (students very rarely address the issue of power in romantic love, in my experience). It's not just choosing a satisfying text or selecting among a menu of fantasies that imparts the sense of agency that women might experience in reading formula romance, but the specific shape that power takes: supposedly malleable and educable on the part of the male, who is transformed by the emotional allure of the female. Emotions are the prize, and what is erotic is the *apparent* lack of mutuality that the heroine must overcome, transforming her from the one-down position to the one-up.

After all, the risks of bad love affairs are unpleasantly real: emotional relations are particularly serious for women's lives because the stakes are still higher for them than for men. If women care more about love and marriage than men do, and invest more emotion, time, and energy, cling harder and stay longer, they will also get hurt more and more often, sometimes even physically. The love and marriage market is still the major context for the social and material realities of women's lives, the currency by which their value is judged.

FEMINISM, CYNICISM, AND PLEASURE

When the critic bell hooks undertook to analyze the problems real-life women face in love, she noted that when women meet men, they first typically try to decide if the man is a threat.[38] This is exactly what romance addresses: the double-edged sword that women who desire men are often uncertain who the man is and what he thinks, even when in a relationship with him. It's hard to see how pop romance, which offers an irresistible heroine and a fake glimpse into the (adoring) male mind in a "scenario of extreme heterosexism," to use Alison Light's phrase, can do much more than temporarily render these problems invisible.[39]

The contexts for the fictional representation of successful love, however that is defined in the past or present, are real social conditions and readers' personal experience framed within those conditions. I do not think it is necessarily condescending for feminists to point that out or to be interested in investigating the connection. Romance is a problem because love can be politically problematic, not just because women's creativity is denigrated or because emotions are narrowly associated with femininity, though these are also true.

Neither anti-romantic academic feminist theory, the dark cynicism of contemporary serious literature, nor the crassness of sexual representations in commercial media allows the ordinary reader to find her own experience of romantic feelings reproduced and interpreted in a way that leads to pleasure, while giving her a sense of mastery over her own sexual and emotional desires. But does this necessarily mean that mass-market romance serves feminist interests? What interests me most is not an up-or-down jury decision on whether pop romance is good or bad, or even good or bad for women, so much as why there is an enormous gap left in the interstices between feminist theory, modern literature, and the actual lives of women.

I would speculate this is because feminist thought hasn't yet really found a way for a woman to love a man romantically in a historically and socially one-down situation. This is understandable, just as we lack a clear path to giving and receiving sexual pleasure in the context of female sexuality as public spectacle and product. But in trying to erase romance, feminists sometimes have erased needs that many certainly feel. To tell masses of women they should not like or want romance, or would be better alone rather than in a less than perfectly politically correct situation, is like telling a child living in poverty that she should not want the toys she sees at Walmart because this is a consumer society with false values. You can't blame anyone for answering, "Oh, shut up. Easy for you to say."

"You *should not want*" is not a fair or effective message in parenting, on the analyst's couch, in romantic relationships, or in feminist theory. I don't believe our deepest desires, either existing or those created at some buried level, conveniently go away with even the most advanced intellectual consciousness. How often, for example, can women have free access to sexual pleasure or emotional involvement with men—or women—without running into opposition from other women who are disapproving, or from men who are sexually conservative in using the double standard? It seems to me that our sexual system is still a mess, a better but perhaps more confusing mess than in the Victorian era, with arguably more subtle permutations and more bright-sounding rhetoric about the choices available, but no less a mess for all that.

My own position comes from my belief that it is necessary to be both sympathetic to and politically conscious about the double bind of modern women. Why must these be inimical? We need to point to the ways in which women do and do not benefit from the couple system, instead of just trying to make women feel good *within* the system, as those who exalt women's "talent" for love do. Worst is not questioning it at all. But there also ought to be a role for intensity and passion in our lives, as there already is for domesticity and stability, and most importantly, *they should be liberated from having to be necessarily yoked together.*

I would therefore like to question the oppositions that are drawn in feminist critical agendas between the pathetically passive consumer of mass-market romance and the smart, subversive reader who carries her agency around like the briefcase she takes to her office; between the female right to pleasure and the feminist necessity to analyze and critique (and yes, mock) the sources of that pleasure, including romantic fiction; and between literature as a medium that uncritically transmits ideology and literature as a medium to resist or change it. Our social and personal worlds are too complex to admit simple oppositions like this, and the problem of romance has too many implications for women in the real world to be solved by recourse to either simple denigration or easy enthusiasm.

If in fact popular romances "celebrate life," as Jayne Ann Krentz claims, I am all for that (who wouldn't be?), but I would want to know first what in the world that means: what *is* life, anyway, for women, in and out of romance? Though Pamela Regis may be right when she asserts that the romance novel "is about women's freedom," I need to understand just what the heroine is supposedly "free" from, or for, exactly.[40] Personally, I enjoy the warm comforts of *not thinking* as I watch the heroine meet her perfect match, but then I also want to grasp how the world works, since I have to live in it. Here is an example of what the sociologist Shere Hite called an "unequal emotional contract" between men and women:[41] polls tell us that American men believe in love at first sight somewhat more than women do, yet it's women who are overwhelmingly the audience for romantic fiction and other forms of popular romance. What does the inequality of male and female interest in romantic representations say about how heterosexual romance in real life will be conducted?

As a (self-declared) feminist, then, my position is that I am neither in favor of nor against romance, popular or otherwise, any more than I am for or against fantasies in general. Pro-romance critics resent the charge that romantic fiction is merely a silly fantasy. I agree that popular romance has been treated badly relative to other genres because it is identified as "feminine," but I think this critique goes only so far. More importantly, fantasies are not necessarily silly so much as they are simplistic in that they negate contradictions. Simple pleasures are more straightforwardly satisfying—and I am not against simple pleasures, silly or otherwise. For this reason I believe that the polarization between "regressive" and "progressive" that has marked the criticism of romance is something of a red herring, for the reader of romances and for feminism itself.

In the modern world, hetero women have every reason to fear giving up the privileges of traditional romantic love, when they still struggle, perhaps more than ever, to live up to impossible standards of desirability. Until we have solutions to these problems, a certain kind of utopian fantasy about the equality of the genders in love is our fallback. We can't remake society overnight; on the other hand, ignoring the connection of social issues to a certain kind of fantasy seems unhelpful.

I have suggested that much of the conflict about the political meanings of romance has to do with our ambivalence toward female pleasure. And indeed, romance itself remains a murky area in feminism because it encapsulates such larger issues that remain tangled and unresolved within feminist theory. Sometimes pleasure has to be enjoyed for its own sake, whether it's neurotic or rational, silly or serious. We like to think we have control over the irrational even while we pretend to extol its "magical" qualities. For all the rhetoric, it seems the only passion we really revere in our culture is one that will get you something, such as a passion for fitness or success. Efficiency, hard work, and speed are all American virtues that legitimate intense feeling. Speaking for myself, I want pleasure, *and* I want to understand pleasure, not necessarily at the same time (maybe *preferably* not at the same time), just as I can think critically about a movie after enjoying it. Don't tell me to eat my peas when I want a sweet, and don't tell me my Mars Bar is dinner.

What, then, do we do about a problem like popular romance fiction? As the psychologist Jerome Bruner has said, "Narrative solves no problems. It simply locates them in such a way as to make them comprehensible."[42] My own answer is this: let's cede to popular romance fiction the pleasures it brings and try to make the problems of gender relations comprehensible, so we can do something about them.

8

A GENRE OF ONE'S OWN

African American Romance Imprints and the "Universality" of Love

They [Negroes] are more ardent after their female [than whites]; but love seems with them to be more an eager desire than a tender delicate mixture of sentiment and sensation.
—Thomas Jefferson, *Notes on the State of Virginia*, 1788

When Harlequin Enterprises, the hugely successful company specializing in formula romance, began publishing the Kimani line of black romance novels in 2006, its general manager, Linda Gill, announced: "While the current tastes for African American fiction includes quite a bit of street lit, we've heard from black women they want to see more sexy and sophisticated love stories that reflect their lives," adding, "These captivating novels will provide all readers of romance with wonderfully passionate romances!"[1]

I can't help wondering about the self-contradiction in these statements. After all, the first implies that black women are a special audience with distinct sorts of lives and therefore a need for a genre of their own; the second seems to assume that "all readers of romance" are in matters of the heart really sisters under the skin, merged into oneness by the universal desire for the same type of "passionate" story.

From a marketing point of view, one can easily see the agenda: target a neglected niche audience while advertising that the product will also appeal to the widest possible audience, nothing less than "all" readers. But therein lies the rub: while many consumers of specialized categories of romance (historical, erotic, paranormal, cowboy, medical, Christian, and so on) may enjoy multiple genres and form crossover markets, African American and "white" (which is to say, majority) romances primarily cross over in one direction only.

There is unquestionably a world of profitability in mass-market romance publications (well over a billion dollars in worldwide sales), and some sources estimate that from 10 to 30 percent of all readers are black.[2] But there is a troubling disparity between readers and writers: though black women seem to have always formed a sizable part of the devoted readership for the overwhelming majority of Harlequins featuring white lovers—and the industry claims that African American readers make up the fastest-growing segment of the romance-reading community—only a small percentage of the many authors in the majority of Harlequin imprints are African American.[3] Some black authors have complained that publishers treat them differently, failing to promote their books and selling them in special sections of books for African Americans segregated from mainstream romances.[4]

The publisher's idea that black women want their own imprint of romance novels seems linked to the assumption that white women would not buy mainstream books featuring heroines of color. But why should this be so? If a white American woman can identify with a heroine living in England during the Regency era, why can't she identify with a contemporary black American heroine? The fact is that Kimani's "passion-filled pages" (as one article on Kimani Press puts it) do not attract anything close to a similar proportion of white readers, in spite of Gill's hopeful prediction that "all readers of romance" will be captivated by these stories.[5] Apparently "reflections" of African American lives do not trigger the romantic fantasies of a broader swath of mass-market readers.

What exactly does it mean to say that a particular *brand* of love story will mirror the actual lives of African American women, the history of whose intimate relations is as complex as that of American race relations?[6] Whether or not romance is a universal, the social context of a segregated genre of pop romance is the way in which long-term relations between men and women skew differently by race. If one goes by statistics, the conventional formulas of mass-produced romance are problematic when mapped onto the lived experience of many black American women, even more than for women in general. While the core principle of traditional category romance is the formation of an enduring romantic couple, implying a happy and secure future in marriage,[7] in American society, according to the latest census figures, the rate of marriage among the black population is close to half that of whites and Asians, and the rate of divorce among African Americans who do marry is higher.[8]

Sociologists report that relationships between African American men and women changed dramatically within a few decades.[9] In 1950, one scholar shows, approximately two-thirds of all African Americans were married and living with their spouses, declining to 32.5 percent in 2003; less than 25 percent of African Americans had never married in 1950, rising by 2003 to 43.4 percent.[10] (It's important to note that there is a class correlation to this decline: In 1960, 83 percent of those of *all* races in the working class were married. Now only 48 percent are.)[11] This precipitous decrease in marriage rates among African Americans in the second half of the twentieth century had a significant negative impact on income of households,[12] as a widely quoted study by the Pew Research Center reported in 2010. Then, too, data from the National Survey of Black Americans show that compared to whites, black women marry men who are significantly older and were more often previously married,[13] while after divorce, black women remarry at a lower rate (32 percent after five years of divorce) than either white women (58 percent) or Hispanic women (44 percent). These are all astonishing disparities.

Yet in one study, conducted in 2006, more than half of black men surveyed said they place a high value on marriage—compared with 39 percent of black women—though 6 in 10 of the same men said that black men in general disrespect black women (that would be *other* men).[14] It's no wonder that the sociologist Anthony King could remark, "Younger African American males and females are engaged in a low-level gender war, sparked by the declining fortunes of African American males and the tremendous social, economic, and political gains African American women have enjoyed over the past three decades."[15]

It's often noted that educated black women, who increasingly outnumber their educated black male peers, have been hit particularly hard in the marriage market. Most people marry mates with similar backgrounds and education, but there are far more college-educated black women than men; females comprise a towering 71 percent of black graduate students, for example, and 70 percent of professional black women are unmarried.[16] Statistics show that "marriage chances for highly educated black women have declined over time relative to white women."[17] In addition, as black men become more educated, they are more likely to marry those in other races: More than 1 in 5 black men who married in 2008 wed a nonblack woman, a huge increase from 7.9 percent in 1980.[18] "There's a pool of middle-class women who don't have educationally comparable men to choose from," according to sociologist Lynda Dickson, "so they are essentially having to marry down."[19] The fact that black women disproportionally marry lower wage earners may be related to their high divorce rate. Of the well-educated black women in one study, only 45 percent believed their black dates were trustworthy, 50 percent said that black men were not committed to relationships, and 59 percent said men of other racial groups were more committed.[20]

On the other hand, one might question, as does the commentator Melissa Harris-Perry, why marriage must be the necessary outcome of romance, either in fiction or real life. Responding to a story on ABC News' *Nightline* entitled "Why Can't a Successful Black Woman Find a Man?" in 2010, Harris-Perry resists the "Disney-inspired assumption that marriage is an appropriate and universal goal for women," or that being single must be seen as somehow "pathological."[21] After all, both cohabitation and serial coupling have been mainstream in Western society for decades now, and the super-glued bond between romance and marriage has begun to loosen in popular romances, too. When the sociologist Belinda Tucker asked black men and women about their romantic lives, she found, not surprisingly, that "the decline of marriage has not signaled a decline in romantic involvement," though the terms of romance may have changed.[22] Most African Americans still enter into some kind of long-term committed relationship as do the majority of all Americans, but for many, marriage, sexuality, and parenthood have become separate experiences that are not necessarily joined.[23]

However one interprets these statistics, these are facts of modern African American life that provide a very different context for the desires, hopes, and expectations of romance readers. By contrast, the publisher's unspoken assumption of the universality of love is one that comes easily in Western society. "Modern Romance explores emotional themes that are universal," say the Guidelines for Writing at Harlequin.com. The idea that "love" is "the same everywhere," no matter who you are or where you are, has been so normalized that it is seldom questioned in mainstream media. I would suggest that the presumed sameness of all romance exists in a paradoxical tension with the particularities of social conditions for African American women, troubling simple celebrations or condemnations of a separate genre of popular romance aimed at a black audience.[24]

BELIEVING IN LOVE

As we have seen, feminists have long debated whether romance is a genre that is progressive for women, with some defending it as no less valuable for its "feminine" narrative pleasures than other popular "masculine" genres such as science fiction or thrillers, and others deriding it as "dope for dupes," essentially a tool of patriarchy. The film scholar Norma Manatu relates that when she was lecturing on the absence of black women as romantic figures onscreen, an audience member asked, "Why would black women want to go back into the patriarchal ideology of the feminine when women were working so hard to escape it?" The question vexed Manatu because she believes the questioner's generalized term "women" erased racial as well as class distinctions and therefore ignores discrimination.[25] Fair enough; feminist battles in the seventies showed us that the identification of "women" cannot be used unproblematically.

Nevertheless, this is a question I'd like to take seriously: Why *would* black women be drawn to a genre that has (as romance lovers often complain) a low status in society? If many African American women are, as one sociologist put it, "happily living busy lifestyles as a single person,"[26] why buy a book (many, many of them) that narrows the definition of happiness to romantic love? If romance disempowers black women by elevating the importance of men in their lives, perhaps they should not rejoice at having their "own line" of books. On the other hand, it seems reasonable to argue that because romance is a great pleasure for millions of women, African American women ought to be able to participate in any way they like in this general (if not universal) pleasure.

For most of America's history, neither black men nor black women were allowed admittance to the category of the "romantic" in dominant white society. Romance was the realm of the delicate Victorian ideal heroine, which is to say, fair-skinned and middle- to upper class, based on highly orthodox racial, gender, and class-based notions of masculinity and femininity. Historically, love in nineteenth-century white culture was not only a supposed *sign* of superior sensibility, but its just *reward* as well. Women of color were shut out from mainstream published stories of love in Anglo societies as a direct result of the fixed presumption that they were unworthy of being adored.

This history of black women's exclusion from mainstream romance was inevitably tied to their sexual position in slave societies. When Thomas Jefferson confidently asserted in the epigraph to this chapter that the entire "race" was not capable of the tender sentiment of love, he expressed an ingrained belief that barely needed articulation: black men and women were fit only for a bestial and emotionless lust. All too frequently, African American women were subject to horrific assumptions of degraded sensuality, stereotypical beliefs of their hyper-sexuality that served as ideological scaffolding for the racist practice of sexual exploitation of female slaves. The widespread notion of the erotic "nature" of dark-skinned peoples that we see in Jefferson's comments made the so-called tender passion an excluded term for nonwhites.

Not only were black women seen as oversexed, viewed as so-called unbridled sexual animals throughout American history, but they were also frequently caricatured as excessive in their attempted dominance over their men. Large, strong, aggressive black girlfriends and wives have appeared and still appear in mainstream popular culture as occasions of comedy and contempt in equal measure.[27] Their strength as well as their sexuality were coded as unfeminine and unladylike, and therefore unromantic. In Manatu's view, African American females, treated as "masculine women whose central interest lies in raw, impersonal sex," tend to react with ambivalence: they "hardly know whether they want to stay on the 'feminine' pedestal or if they wish to get off." Until they are allowed to participate in the category of the "feminine," she says, they "can hardly join in a fight to escape that to which they have not been privy." Romance, Manatu argues, is "rarely, if ever, treated as a natural outgrowth of their male-female relationships."[28]

In addition to the trials of sexual exploitation and negative stereotype, African American women have always borne the enormous burden of the diminishment of black women's beauty in our society. As one sociologist has put it, though black women have sometimes been reported to have a better body self-image than white women, "Black women are also clearly (and increasingly) affected by hegemonic depictions of feminine beauty." Both black men and women internalize toxic massmedia images, both of themselves and of an idealized femininity.[29] How could romance not be affected by what has been called "finding love under the specter of the Lily Complex"?[30] Romance for men and women of color could hardly avoid being politicized, and these conditions were problematic for the depiction of love in litera-ture from the beginning of African American women's writing.[31] The critic Lisa Guer-rero has a good point: "[White] chicks are looking for love because, as white women, they have been taught to believe in their preciousness and the fact that they should be loved, even worshipped," while black women must begin with the opposite domi-nant social assumption, that they have been disqualified for love.[32]

Yet though the best-selling imprints of black popular romance series were created near the end of the twentieth century, there already existed a long history of fiction and blues music by African Americans that centered on love stories, as several well-known scholars have illuminated.[33] In spite of their exclusion from the mainstream idea of romantic love as a union between bourgeois, delicate fair women and suc-cessful, high-status Anglo men, African American women had long constructed their own subversive history of love stories, including historical romances.[34] Then in the 1970s, some rising stars of late twentieth-century black American literature such as Alice Walker, Toni Morrison, Gayl Jones, Ntozake Shange, and Gloria Naylor began to publish fiction, poetry, and drama about love and sexuality from a woman's point of view, to great acclaim and some critical controversy. The scholar Ann duCille and other influential critics lauded the way modern black women writers began at last "making ourselves the subjects of our own stories, our own lives."[35]

The impulse of these new chroniclers of black love relationships was to draw attention to the abuse that African American women have suffered at the hands of men, both white and black. This sparked a so-called gender war that was the sub-ject of public discussions and, in one or two famous cases, the object of black male resentment.[36] Ironically, the charge of these male critics was that while these female novelists were resisting pernicious traditional images of black women by celebrat-ing them as sympathetic heroines, *both* white dominant ideology and best-selling black women's writing were stereotyping the ghetto culture of the macho male.

This development in American literary history may have influenced race-oriented category romance fiction: if a reader of any race bought a book by a well-known black female author published at this time, she would be likely to en-counter heroines represented as sexually exploited, held back, or abused by love for men who were unworthy of them, a trend the scholar and filmmaker Carmen Coustaut calls "a perpetual stance of victimization."[37] As one romance author put it, "If novels gave us black women who were about something, they still gave us jerks for mates."[38] This popular and respected literature offered women high-quality imaginative art with pointed social criticism but did not fill the still-wide gap, the lack of "real" romance with happy outcomes, by and about men and women of color for the general public. Why, one might wonder, should the black female audience be deprived of love stories with "emotionally satisfying end-ings"?[39] Where were romances of the sort that is the backbone of the great novel tradition of the nineteenth century, or the popular entertainment of the twenti-eth? Where could African American women find a modern black Jane Austen?

For over forty years, women of color had been reading mass-market category romances while they were shut out of the categories. Amusingly and poignantly, the romance novelist Evelyn Palfrey writes about her youthful reading of romances snuck from under her mother's bed: "There was a time when I had to pretend that the heroine had short, nappy hair like mine, instead of long, flowing and blond tresses. A time when I had to pretend that the tall, dark and handsome hero really was dark."[40]

Into this opening sprang two forms of popular love stories aimed at black women, beginning in the early 1990s: a variation of "chick lit" for African American women sometimes called "sistah lit," and the adoption of black imprints by the hugely profitable formula romance industry. While both these genres are largely written by black women for a black female audience and center on romantic plots, "sistah lit" and formula romance are quite different in their approach.[41]

You might think that sistah lit is closer to the chick lit genre than to Harlequin romance. White chick lit, starting with Helen Fielding's wildly popular best seller *Bridget Jones's Diary* in 1998, was itself a revision of traditional popular romance. In Lisa Guerrero's sharp analysis, romance in white hetero chick lit tends to be treated as "an ironic fantasy, at once coveted and mocked."[42] Nevertheless, the ideal of monogamous coupling was left intact in the chick lit genre, and the problem the narrative must solve is the difficulty of finding the proper man while achieving a certain chic lifestyle.

Sistah lit, so-called, has had a somewhat different approach, as much linked to the love-and-trouble tradition of black women's love stories as it is to its mainstream cousin chick lit. It was defined early by the huge crossover publishing success of Terry McMillan's *Waiting to Exhale* (1992), which shows African American women as part of a female community. The difference between the British *Bridget Jones* and *Waiting to Exhale*, Guerrero says, is between the white romantic fantasy that "chicks" are allowed to believe in (as well as mock) and "the real-life experience that sistahs are forced to live in."[43] These developments in mass publishing filled an opportunity left wide open by the twentieth-century critique of love, adopted by serious writers of all races, including the Harlem Renaissance author Zora Neale Hurston. Not long after *Waiting to Exhale*, Kensington Publishing became the first major publisher to create an imprint of African American romances in 1994, called Arabesque.

Arabesque was so successful that it was bought in 1998 by Black Entertainment Television (BET), which has turned many Arabesque novels into made-for-TV movies (Harlequin Ltd. subsequently bought the BET imprints in 2005).[44] As the black readership for romantic fiction grew, so did romantic comedy featuring black characters in films and television, magazine articles (like "*Ebony* Celebrates Black Love: 10 Hottest Couples" or *Essence*'s "Is It a Fling or the Real Thing?"), and self-help books such as Jeffrey Gardere's 2003 *Love Prescription: Ending the War between Black Men & Women* (he recommends devoting more time to foreplay). One interesting study compared ads in four magazines, including *Ebony* and *Life,* and discovered there was a "disproportionate selling of sex-romance to Blacks and a subtle overuse of affluent images for whites."[45] It's no wonder, then, that one psychologist claims, "For a long time we have lived with the idea of the strong black woman, who by implication can do without a romantic relationship if she must, but the truth is that she would rather not." Best-selling Arabesque author Donna Hill concurs: "Black women still believe in love," she says.[46]

Terry McMillan, author of *Waiting to Exhale* and *How Stella Got Her Groove Back,* herself volunteered in an interview that no one should feel embarrassed about wanting love: "The Eighties said that we [women] should feel okay by ourselves, but after a while it gets lonely."[47] In the sense that publishers began providing African American women with a slice of the pie that had been out of reach in the bakery window, these new romantic imprints seem an unequivocal sign of progress. And in fact publishers in the 1990s jumped on the profitable enterprise with a message of social redemption: "Now," they seemed to be saying to black women, "You can have *your own romance!*" as if it were equivalent to founding black colleges. But why offer "your own" rather than simply publish authors of varied backgrounds and colors within the same imprints, featuring stories about lovers of similarly varied backgrounds and colors (or genders, for that matter)?

After all, the great general success of *The Color Purple* or *Waiting to Exhale* belies the usual answer, that white audiences overwhelmingly do not read (or publishers presume they will not buy) stories about black love. But could it be that there was a huge mixed-race following for these novels *because* relations with males are troubled in them, and the white audience does not want to read about black women who get the romance they *want*?

Of course, labeling a line of romance as African American is not likely to increase white readership of that imprint, since it could signal to the reader that the genre is separate and exclusive to one audience. The experience of difference is foregrounded from the moment one views both the Anglo and African American romance novels, most often distinguished by the skin color of the impossibly gorgeous man and woman on the cover. One blogger offered this solution: "What would happen [if there were] no distinction made on the spines of books, what if generic covers were given to all romances?"[48]

In addition, it seems significant that women of color—or men of color—are rarely featured as important characters in mainstream "white" romances, in any role at all.[49] The implication is that while romance is widely held to be "universal," it isn't also ever simply human, but more often colored either black *or* white.

Or perhaps the reason for this ghettoization of romance by race lies in the desires of African American women themselves; that is, many black readers enjoy *their own* romances because they do want them to be distinct from the mainstream form of the genre. Osborne quotes romance readers she interviewed who "chafe at the mere suggestion of removing Black characters from the covers . . . 'women who look like me.' "[50]

If African American women have a "double consciousness," to make use of W.E.B. Du Bois's famous term, as to how they are seen as well as how they identify themselves, the opportunity to shape a new tradition should be uniquely empowering. Romances by, about and for a black female audience, in which the women themselves control how the terms are defined, could be an entry into the prince's castle, where both the prince himself and the castle that is the scene of the story are subversive versions of a privileged pleasure.

But is this what these fictions do? It is one thing to theorize in the abstract about a genre, but whether black formula romances are essentially different from the "white" Harlequins is (perhaps literally) another story. Do the general rules for white romance apply, and if not, how do they specifically differ? If the features of romance do turn out to be the same in both mainstream and black romance, this might confirm the shared essential nature of "romantic love" in ways that bring the neglected black female audience into the fold at last. In that case, could it be that popular romances expressly aimed at and about black women are somehow actually better for them (in the sense of more progressive) than they are for women in general?

READING EACH OTHER

Black category romance may sell because it defines and shapes "the romantic" as antithetical to the specific real-life conditions of African American women, not because it mirrors them. The guaranteed "happily ever after" ending might have a special meaning for African American women for this reason.

Traditionally, the (hetero) romance story turns on male recognition of the heroine's special value, an affirmation of self-worth that lies down in the same bed with the fear of sexual exploitation, abandonment, and emotional suffering. All romance may be said to contain these fantasized elements of desire and apprehension in precarious balance with one another, but this intensified doubleness of "pleasure and danger" (to paraphrase the title of a well-known collection of essays on women's sexuality) is inflected in African American women's history in a way that is more socially or politically fraught than for privileged white American women. To put it another way, popular black romantic fiction is the rosy representation of exactly the same impulse that drew hard-hitting twentieth-century black female novelists to the subject of love and trouble. You might call it "love and trouble . . . and then more love *without* trouble."

The critic Ann duCille asks, "As black men and women, our racial alterity makes us perpetually other, perpetually beheld. But what happens when blacks read each other?"[51] What difference does it make to the genre of popular romance when the genre is written by and for black women? One way to find out is to look closely at what actually happens in formula black romances.

While a great deal has been written both in mass-media and scholarly circles about the prizewinning fiction by black women in American literature, relatively little attention has been paid to black formula romance, and even less to the re-lationship between Anglo and specifically black-targeted formula romances, ex-cept by readers themselves.[52] For this reason, I decided to take an unusual ap-proach and directly compare category romance novels written by and for African American women with category romances overwhelmingly written by and for white women, with a focus on their distinct details. How is race represented as a frame of reference in black romance imprints, and how does the conscious-ness of an overwhelmingly black audience shape the stories and the way they are told?

I am aware of the irony in questioning the separation of black romance im-prints in a chapter that is itself separate from a more general study of popular romance. But as a political statement, this can cut two ways: one might empha-size the separation of the imprints as exclusion (equal but still separate), or one might see it as disrespectful to fold black romance into a general study, as though it were merely a footnote to the real thing. This ambiguity perfectly mirrors the problems of gender and race in these novels, and makes the examination of dif-ference all the more significant.

To begin my investigation, I read and made note of recurring language, im-agery, motifs, and plot structures in ten African American romances and ten Anglo Harlequin romances, all randomly selected from contemporary diverse imprints. I was especially curious to see how closely the black imprints followed the dominant white romance formula.

I concluded that black genre romance is very much like Harlequin's main-stream romance in many ways, but with some striking differences. One ironic similarity is that the segregation of the white romances, confined to one class, race, and sexuality, is mirrored in a parallel segregation of race, class, and sexual-ity in African American romance. Just as there are almost no women of color—or *people* of color—in white mainstream romances, in any role at all, there are also almost no Caucasians in the African American romances I sampled.

As a reference point for comparison, there was an amusing gay best friend in two of the ten black romances I examined and in one of the ten Anglo romances, a fairly high proportion. Yet there were no black characters (or characters of color in general) in the Anglo romances at all, while two black novels had white characters in very minor roles as bitchy or trashy women to contrast with the heroine's superior nature.

This isn't a matter of separate but equal genres, since we know that black women constitute a disproportionate percentage of all romance read-ers, whereas African American imprints are a small percentage of romances published. The exclusion of white characters perhaps reflects the wish of the princess, having achieved access to her fantasized castle, to draw up the bridge behind her and seal it against rivals and enemies. In any case, race in both worlds—that of African American imprints and Anglo imprints—is not associated with difference or variety but naturalized as the condition of that particular genre.[53]

Black romance is very much like its white Harlequin sister in its basic gestures, driven so much by its genre that it barely seems to resemble its African American sister, prizewinning literary feminist black fiction, at all. For example, African American romance imprints, like all formula romance, have a set of core plots and standardized vocabulary.

Similarities

Both male and female characters are stunningly beautiful, and their body parts defy gravity.

> *White imprints:* "When he moved it was like watching a wild stallion in its prime." (*Bound by Marriage*)

> "His chest—God, it was perfect." (*Feels like Home*)

> *Black imprints:* "Being extremely beautiful only made her reputation worse." (*A Merry Little Christmas*)

> "He wasn't sure what he was expecting, but it wasn't this vision." (*Chances Are*)

The heroine is usually accomplished but often feels inexplicably empty and restless.

> *White imprint:* "She paced the floor of her sumptuous suite. . . . 'I have no direction, no skills. . . . Where's my passion?' " (*Cordina's Crown Jewel*)

> *Black imprints:* "I just feel empty, and I don't know why." (*A Merry Little Christmas*)

> "*Then why do you feel so empty?*" (*All for Love,* original emphasis)

The pivot of both black and white category romance is a super-masculine, powerful man—"very alpha," as the Harlequin guidelines describe him for the aspiring author.

> *White imprints:* "Without looking, she was aware of his strength, the broad expanse of his shoulders." (*As Big as Texas*)

> "A man who knew what he wanted and exactly how he wanted it. . . . The faded burn scars . . . contributed to the overwhelming sense of masculinity that surrounded him." (*Bound by Marriage*)

Black imprint: "Lord, he was so much man, power, self-confidence, he exuded it. . . . He had an elegance, an air of authority that commanded respect and compliance." (*Learning to Love*)

He has trouble with emotional commitment, possibly because he was hurt by a woman in the past, and has to "learn to love."

White imprints: "He'd decided long ago that love would play no part in any marriage of his." (*Bound by Marriage*)

"Ethan had sworn off marriage, given up any hope of having children." (*As Big as Texas*)

Black imprints: "After finally giving someone his heart and getting burned, Khamil had vowed to never let a woman hurt him again." (*Flirting with Danger*)

"Since his breakup with [his childhood sweetheart], he'd been emotionally dead inside . . . afraid of losing himself in total commitment." (*Distant Lover*)

Men can be threatening or dominating, not least around sexual contact.

White imprints: "Her cheeks burned with humiliation—not just because of the paper tissue way he clearly treated women . . . but because of the very fact she wasn't walking away. " (*Expecting His Love-Child*)

"Deliberately he raked his gaze over her, an insulting pass down her body and back up again. . . . She'd never been treated so rudely, so carelessly in her life. It was beyond her comprehension why she enjoyed it." (*Cordina's Crown Jewel*)

Black imprint: "Vincent made Nina think of a predatory jaguar ready to pounce on its prey." (*Distant Lover*)

Fortunately, it turns out they are sensitive and tamable in the end:

White imprint: "His face was all harsh, masculine lines when he glanced at her, but she thought she heard a buried thread of unexpected gentleness." (*Bound by Marriage*)

Black imprint: "Thanks, but I'm not drinking coffee right now. Angel [the heroine] can't have it, so I drink herbal tea with her. I was just about to put the kettle on." (*A Merry Little Christmas*)

There is something special about the heroine that makes her different from the rest; love is being mysteriously drawn to that particular woman.

White imprint: "Disquiet moved through his marrow at how this woman moved him so." (*Expecting His Love-Child*)

Black imprints: "He couldn't explain it. He barely knew her. Yet he couldn't get her off his mind for more than a minute." (*Distant Lover*)

"There was something different about her that piqued his interest." (*Flirting with Danger*)

She gets "under his skin," code for emotional investment.

White imprint: "Because he'd tripped over his own unspoken rule and fallen flat on his face in love with her." (*Cordina's Crown Jewel*)

Black imprints: "That little woman had gotten under his skin from the first moment they met." (*A Merry Little Christmas*)

"But as a quick as a pop of your fingers to the beat, Dione had gotten under his skin." (*Chances Are*)

"What was it about this Nina . . . that had slipped beneath his skin?" (*Distant Lover*)

Possibly because of her adorable stubbornness and/or toughness . . .

White imprint: "Wasn't she aware that her frosty attitude was challenging, and that a man with success exuding from every pore of his being found the idea of such a challenge irresistible?" (*Accidentally Pregnant, Conveniently Wed*)

Black imprint: "He'd known she was trouble the moment he'd laid eyes on her." (*Southern Comfort*)

. . . which cause her to lift her chin quite a bit:

White imprint: "He stared at her for a moment, taking in her lush mouth and the angle of her stubborn chin." (*Off Limits*)

Black imprints: "He looked at her fists on her hipbones and the upward defiant tilt of her chin, and nearly doubled up in joyous laughter." (*Learning to Love*)

"She angled her chin in a challenge." (*Chances Are*)

Much is made of an adoring male gaze, during which the hero contemplates the heroine's charms. More and more in contemporary romance, the heroine is occasionally seen through the eyes of the male, as we overhear the hero thinking about her through the third person indirect style. (As such, it operates something like the joke that goes, "But enough about me, let's talk about what you think of me.") This switch in point of view expresses the tension hetero women feel about the power men have over women's all-important love lives. The reader, but not the heroine, gets to understand how men (supposedly) think by observing the thoughts of the hero. As his mysterious attraction to the heroine grows, he registers the consuming intensity of his desire for her, and he muses about the future he would like to have with her . . . long before he proposes and often while a misunderstanding exists between them so she doubts his good intentions. The following are typical of the hero's thoughts:

> *White imprint*: "Damn, he loved Kara Brand, and he probably had for a while now. He'd been so busy telling himself he didn't—couldn't—that he hadn't noticed that he did." (*Feels like Home*)

> *Black imprint*: "He loved everything about Katherine—her face, her body, and the ecstasy she was able to arouse in him just by sharing the same space. She was perfect—in and out of bed." (*Stand-in Bride*)

This device is especially popular for making mild fun of or explaining the hero's chauvinism or misogyny.

> *White imprint*: "He wouldn't have some woman cluttering up his space. Cluttering up his mind." (*Cordina's Crown Jewel*)

> *Black imprints*: "Women . . . He knew it would be hard working with a group of females who epitomized everything he despised." (*Chances Are*, original emphasis)

> "American men must have a hard time with their women." (*Learning to Love*)

The hero and heroine have nothing but incredible, fetishized kisses . . .

> *White imprints*: "But this time, the kiss didn't end in a hard flash. It was an inferno." (*Bound by Marriage*)

> "His tongue savored while his will plummeted." (*As Big as Texas*)

> *Black imprints*: "She parted her lips for his foraging tongue . . . she pulled his tongue deeper, feasting on it as if she were starved." (*Learning to Love*)

> "Her tongue danced with Khamil's in a desperate song of passion." (*Flirting with Danger*)

. . . followed by world-rocking sex every time, including multiple orgasms for the heroine, and occasionally oral sex for the woman but rarely for the man.

White imprints: "Never in all her years of dating, had she reached release this often or quickly, and they hadn't even had intercourse yet." (*Off Limits*)

"As Lavender spilled his full cup, taking her to the brink of insanity, she knew this was once in a lifetime." (*Expecting His Love-Child*)

Black imprints: "His seeking mouth finally found what it yearned for, the most feminine, intimate part of her that yielded up its sweet nectar as he pleasured her beyond imagination." (*A Merry Little Christmas*)

"And just when she thought she would die of ecstasy, Khamil . . . began daintily caressing her most private part." (*Flirting with Danger*)

However, it's made clear that the heroine (unlike the hero or the heroine's bitchy rival) enjoys sex only in the context of (eventual) enduring emotional commitment. The woman is "empowered" by her sexual hold over the man, which is always accompanied by his profound and enduring emotional investment and never wanes through the course of the narrative.

White imprint: "She'd never experienced this kind of tenderness, the sensation of being adored." (*As Big as Texas*)

Black imprints: "He'd thought time and her absence would ease Sharon out of his system, but it hadn't. His desire for her had become a driving need, a hunger that he didn't even consider assuaging with another woman." (*Learning to Love*)

"When her cry of fulfillment came, he was there with her, holding her as he always would." (*Southern Comfort*)

And, of course, there is what the online romance-reading world calls the HEA (the "happily ever after" ending):

White imprint: " 'I'll spend the rest of my life trying to be worthy of you,' he vowed." (*As Big as Texas*)

Black imprints: "It probably would become the most talked-about wedding of the season . . . because of the woman who'd managed to land one of Savannah's most eligible African American bachelors." (*Stand-in Bride*)

"I want you all to know that I'm a very, very fortunate man. I have the privilege of being married to the most incredible woman in the world." (*A Merry Little Christmas*)

Are there strong similarities in the black and white imprints because of the universal nature of love or because of the rigidities of the formula that constitutes the readers' understanding of what "love" is? The answer is not so easy: for one thing, these structural similarities are shadowed by *differences* between mainstream and black imprints, some of which seem more progressive than others.

Differences

For example, four of the ten black romances I looked at made a self-conscious effort to be "Afro-centric," referencing and celebrating African or African American communal values and traditions, thus countering black invisibility in mainstream novels.

> "Her grandfather had petitioned the state for a charter to establish a bank for the city's African American population." (*Stand-in Bride*)

> "If she was going to get his help setting up her project in Nigeria, she'd have to hold her tongue." (*Learning to Love*)

> "The African American museum is talking to me about having an exhibition." (*A Merry Little Christmas*)

> "She sat in her small but neat afro-centric office." (*Chances Are*)

On the other hand, there are also ambiguities about black identity in these same novels. In *Learning to Love*, for example, where the heroine is American and the hero is an African prince, the heroine expresses a distinct preference for her American identity.

> "He was a Prince, and she knew she'd never settle in Yorubaland. Being a foreigner wasn't fun, especially in an African country where she wasn't considered black." (*Learning to Love*)

Several heroines of African American romances identified with the South or the tradition of the southern lady, while ignoring the irony, to say the least, of the legacy of slavery or racism this identification might entail.

> "She swallowed again, thought what a proper Southern lady should do when faced with temptation. . . . Then Vincent closed his hot mouth over her nipple and she was lost." (*Southern Comfort*)

Rochelle Alers's *Stand-in Bride* gestures toward the pre–Civil War southern plantation, with one scene mirroring the famous moment when Rhett carries Scarlett up the stairs in *Gone with the Wind*: "Gerald swung Catherine up in his arms and headed for the staircase." Whether you see these as politically forward, possibly ironic, co-optation of the plantation setting by the descendants of the slaves or as a mind-boggling erasure of history depends on your point of view.

Though race was treated ambiguously in the black imprints, sometimes fore-fronted and more often invisible, I saw more nods to feminism in which love breaks down chauvinism if it is present in the hero in the black imprints than in the Anglo imprints.

> "Most of the men she met . . . thought she was too outspoken and aggres-sive. They wanted a woman who stayed in the background, who was non-threatening and demure. She'd never be that." (*Southern Comfort*)

> "He [former husband] wanted a stay-at-home wife. Out of his circle of friends, I was the only wife who worked outside the home." (*Campaign for Love*)

Heroines are achieving women, educated, professional, and intelligent, per-haps more often than in Anglo romances.

> "She earned a solid six-figure income plus commission as the Senior Vice President of Development for the Burns Corporation." (*Distant Lover*)

> *Hero*: "She's beautiful, she's brilliant and talented and she's funny, com-passionate and kind. She is the most fascinating woman I've ever known and she can do anything." (*A Merry Little Christmas*)

> "Charlotte Duvall, political fundraiser extraordinaire, longtime friend of the bride, meet Vincent Maxwell, financial wizard, Vice President of Fi-nance for Oratech Petroleum Company." (*Southern Comfort*)

The standard formula of mass-market romantic fiction, in which the emotion-ally distant, difficult, and noncommittal hero is converted by love for the special heroine into perfect husband material, has a distinct meaning in the context of the black romance. When the heroine expresses (unfounded) fear that the hero will be a "player," she is speaking, overtly or not, to a common stereotype of black men. There are many successful and stable African American males and authors and readers who have specified their desire to write or read romances that "honor black men" by showing them in a relationship defined by respect and commitment. Palfrey, like many other black romance writers, speaks about her intention to honor "good" black men, as opposed to mainstream media de-pictions: "Our good men get their glory in our romance novels."[54] This makes for an odd counterpoint to the so-called bashed black men in black feminist fiction, an exaggerated positive response to the same negative perceptions of black men as lovers and husbands:

"He placed her on her bed as if she were a piece of fragile crystal." (*Stand-in Bride*)

"In her opinion, her employer ([the hero] was the total package: wealthy, attractive, smart, attractive, charismatic, and attractive." (*Unforgettable*)

On the other hand, the high level of professional achievement in hero and heroine seems to go hand in hand with the mandate to position the story among a class of elites, where wealth seems natural and universal, and poverty is either completely ignored or, less often, relegated to a "hardworking past." One type of story suggested for Harlequin's Kimani authors that doesn't appear in the guidelines for other imprints is "über-wealthy romances." I saw a great deal of explicit description of upper-class housing, material possessions, and clothing.

"He shrugged. 'It's late, and with seventeen bedrooms, there's plenty of space.'" (*Unforgettable*)

"Nina settled back against the butter-soft leather of the limousine." (*Distant Lover*)

"She wore a full-length cream-colored cashmere coat." (*Chances Are*) (This is worn by the "Director of a non-profit for unwed mothers" who is struggling to keep her agency afloat.)

Similarly, there is ambiguity in the description of the black heroine's typically high-level beauty. On the one hand, black imprints contain an unusual and refreshing recognition of other kinds of beauty than that found in most Anglo romances.

"Next year I'll be forty. I'll never see a size ten again—a twelve on a bad day." (*Distant Lover*)

"Men like to have something to hold onto. My brothers all say that nothing wants a bone but a dog." (*A Merry Little Christmas*)

On the other hand, there is also a definite emphasis on the texture of hair and color of skin not found in white romances.

"golden streaks in her light-brown, chemically relaxed, shoulder-length hair" (*Stand-in Bride*)

"I ran my hand over my hair . . . now it reached to my shoulder blades, turning just under. It looked like black satin." (*All for Love*)

"thick, shiny black hair" (*A Merry Little Christmas*)

"warm deep sienna skin" (*All for Love*)

"flawless, sable-brown skin" (*Stand-in Bride*)

"His skin was the color of the darkest polished mahogany." (*Distant Lover*)

"They both had café au lait complexions." (*A Merry Little Christmas*)

"a smooth, toffee-toned body . . . toasted brown skin" (*Southern Comfort*)

In one passage, the hero's skin is said to be "a touch darker than Jefferson's, *but* his face was lean and chiseled in masculine grooves" (*For All We Know*). In other words, the author implies that the hero's "darker skin" is less attractive, "*but*" that is outweighed by the attractive grooves of his "masculine" face, lest the skin tone tarnish the hero's desirability.

In order to appreciate the uniqueness of this emphasis on skin color in the black imprints, compare typical descriptions of the hero and heroine in white romances, which emphasize their beauty but only rarely mention the color of their skin.

"The Audrey Hepburn cheekbones, the delicate jaw and perfect nose, the wide set of her eyes, thick lashes, so much natural beauty." (*Feels like Home*)

"Light brown hair and chocolate colored eyes dominated her girl-next-door features." (*Off Limits*)

When the heroine's skin was mentioned in the following novels from white imprints, it was the "clear" texture of the skin rather than its tone that was described.

"Her eyes were more gold than brown, and seemed impossibly rich against the cool, clear skin." (*Cordina's Crown Jewel*)

"her nearly flawless skin, with its dusting of freckles across the nose" (*Dear Maggie*)

In some romance novels, children appear as minor characters. In the romances I examined, white children's skin color is similarly absent from the description, while the black children's skin tone was always included.

White child's appearance: "Hair too thick and a little too long, a mixture of honey and amber, eyes usually sparkling with mischief and intelligence." (*Feels like Home*)

Black child's appearance: "She was a mirror image of her mother, with velvety chocolate skin and big golden eyes." (*A Merry Little Christmas*)

Most striking of all, however, I observed more sexual conservatism and focus on marriage, including in some cases virginity before marriage, in the African American than in the Anglo imprints. This is significant, given that the rigid requirements for both have been declining in mainstream Harlequin imprints for decades. It was true for nearly every black romance I sampled.

"She'd permitted him to kiss her, but whenever he'd made an attempt to caress her body, she'd pushed him away." (*Stand-in Bride*)

"She thought she was in love and she'd given away the one thing she could never regain: her virginity." (*Chances Are*)

"The more Khamil thought about it, the more he realized that it was the women who were the boldest who turned him off the most." (*Flirting with Danger*)

Some of this conservatism is no doubt produced by the Harlequin writing requirements for black imprints, which resemble those for the explicitly Christian imprint, Love Inspired. The mandated formula is detailed and specific: "In Arabesque, the story line should be well developed and reflect the ups and downs of relationships, but without the kinds of issues that would diminish the qualities and appeal of the main characters." Now, what kinds of issues that diminish the characters could they mean?

Helpfully, Kimani Arabesque provides guidelines a writer should "adhere" to: no profanity, drug use, or alcohol abuse, and minimal violence. As for sex, the couple should be single, must use condoms, and "not be sexually or emotionally involved with anyone else." In general, "the hero and heroine should exhibit good character and not be dishonest, unethical or otherwise morally corrupt." Oddly, and tellingly, none of the many other Harlequin imprints (except for the specifically Christian Love Inspired line) has any such restrictions—not even Harlequin Teen, which you'd think might be interested in curbing inappropriate depictions of sexual behavior, violence, or drug use.

ROMANCE IN BLACK OR WHITE

Does a line of romance devoted singularly to African American authors and characters (and most probably readers) represent a long-overdue entrance into a world of human pleasure previously denied? And if so, is it therefore a mark of progressive equality, or is this publishing phenomenon a representation of white privilege in blackface, a false promise of happiness that masks and distorts the problems that surround race relations?

Your answer derives from both your estimate of romance in general and how "authentic" you think the representation of black women's identity is in any given literary form. From one critical perspective, we might say the similarities-but-differences between the Anglo and African American imprints fit well with the black tradition of appropriation outlined by the scholar Henry Louis Gates.[55] According to this interpretation, romance writers are enacting Ann duCille's praise of modern black women writers in general, who "pay less attention to male gratification and more to our own" and find "subversive ways" to use the traditional marriage plot to their own purposes.[56] On the other hand, in African American imprints, the powerful conventions of genre romance intersect with the publishers' mandate to make the characters and scene "authentically black," whatever that has come to mean to different audiences, often in ways that coexist in tension. It should be expected, then, that self-contradictions will emerge.

For example, Gwynne Forster, a beloved black romance author, has been quoted as claiming that black romances "represent us as we are."[57] But such a statement imagines that there is a homogeneous "we" that is a racial category. How *do* these formula black romances represent race? Most often by a set of features and contexts (skin, hair, community, traditions such as food or church) entirely outside of the white world. As we have seen, neither Anglo romances nor black romances represent the tremendous variety of ethnicities, classes, religions, and race mixtures in American society. For the most part, they simply avoid the complexities of any use of "us" by ghettoization into black *or* white.

However, from another point of view, since African American characters are not usually part of the landscape of mainstream romances, it seems understandable that the world of the African American romance is entirely black. If you're not welcome in white neighborhoods, for example, why is it wrong to head to an area populated by "your own kind"? Yet the doubling of segregation hardly seems to push the issue of racial alienation to a better place. For example, without a representation of the white world, no critique of race or racism in America seems possible.

Also, the fantasy of wealth and success found in much dominant white romance is especially poignant when mirrored in black romance, where the social situation of many black women's lives and the crisis-level correlation of African American unemployment, housing, education, and male incarceration are simply excluded from its imagined world. "Us" becomes an elite class with a privileged lifestyle. Kimani's website characterizes its novels as "*Aspirational* love stories that feature appealing characters who have made it and yet are still seeking love," with the explanation that these will be "role models" for readers. Yet the series guidelines of Anglo imprints, such as those of Harlequin American Romance or Harlequin Presents, apparently don't feel the need to specify class and riches, much less "über-wealthy romances" specified for Kimani. Most white heroes and heroines are middle-class or upper-class (if not actual royalty) anyway, without the reminder or task of heavy-handed "modeling."

Now, whether or not the genuine motive is role modeling, you may say it's a positive development that, as the Harlequin Kimani website specifies, "the hero and heroine should be . . . upwardly mobile and educated individuals that our readers can admire." But interestingly, there is also a relatively new series, a division of Kimani aimed at black teenagers called Kimani TRU, whose guidelines instruct: "The main characters should both be young adults . . . and should represent a broad spectrum of incomes (poor, working class, middle class, and wealthy)." This is apparently tied to the wider range of plots and themes in the Kimani TRU line, namely, "relationships: those with peers, family members, love interests, and with other adults that influence the characters' lives." It says a great deal about both romance and Harlequin's view of its African American audience that when these novels center exclusively on romance—but especially *black* romance—only one fantasy of class supremacy is permissible. Other types of stories can engage with "a broad spectrum of incomes," as the Kimani TRU guidelines advise, but *only* the love story is rigidly tied to wealth. The princesslike image of the desirable young white woman who is at the top of the hierarchy in wealth, beauty, and desirability is ubiquitous in contemporary media and growing more so, but it's the Glass Slipper princess of romance in particular who becomes a queen of society by being recognized as special and chosen by a man. Apparently this is the only model—or modeling—encouraged by the mass-market black romance.

Above all, depictions of sex and marriage in the black formula romances seem to bear the weight of responding to stereotype. Take, for instance, the fraught issue of women's sexuality. Just as romantic ideology in modern magazines is still steeped in Victorian values, with threads of twentieth-century feminism somehow twisted in as the gloss on its commercialism, romance fiction has run on a parallel track in our own age, post–women's movement and post–sexual revolution. Harlequin, for example, has several series that emphasize sexuality, such as Harlequin Desire or Harlequin Blaze: "The Blaze line of red-hot reads is changing the face of Harlequin and creating a continual buzz with readers. The series features sensuous, highly romantic, innovative stories that are sexy in premise and execution. . . . Writers can push the boundaries in terms of characterization, plot, and explicitness," explains the Harlequin website.

The rise of black formula romance in the 1990s coincided with this new "feminist," sexy form of genre romance itself and of its more mainstream sister, chick lit. As we have seen, modern scholars of romance often present the expansion of sexual behavior in romance novels as evidence of their implicit feminism.[58] Sex is now the primary power a woman has in most formula romance, and female sexual irresistibility is a way of gaining male attention and exerting control in hetero relations. Almost all modern romance (except explicitly Christian romance) stresses sexual attraction, combined with commitment. But both female sexuality and the institution of marriage have been problematic in black experience and are therefore problematized in black literature.

Modern women of all colors struggle with their conflicting roles as creatures who must be both sexy (but not skanky) and nurturing (as mother and wife), but this conflict is especially fraught for black women, who carry the historical double load of a hyper-eroticized but supposedly unlovable/unbeautiful sexuality along with their *other* stereotype as hyper-nurturing mammy. The deep contradiction, for all women but especially for black women, is that when women's subjective pleasure is emphasized, it can be read as a positive feminist assertion, but when representations of female sexuality seem to affirm the stereotype of promiscuity, the subject herself loses.[59] Romance, through its preoccupation with both female pleasure and emotional power leading to the hero's lifelong adoration and respect, seems to solve that particular double bind.

The historian Nancy Cott is famous for her theory that nineteenth-century "passionlessness" was a survival strategy that allowed white middle-class women to control their own bodies at an uncertain time of social change;[60] it might not be far off to hypothesize that romances are a way for Kimani's black readers to imagine having control of men's emotions in a social context that is in some ways parallel to the situation of white women in the Victorian era: transitioning to a time of new liberties, yet still limited and oppressed.

But men won't be controlled if they are not listening, and we know there are not many male readers of formula romances. Surely there is a far greater male audience for conservative voices like Tyler Perry, who says in *Don't Make a Black Woman Take Off Her Earrings* (2006), that "having sex will get you dinner and a movie. That's all you're going to get out of it. But holding out will get you diamonds and furs and Cadillacs and marriage proposals."[61]

In the 1970s, when black feminists spoke out loudly to voice resistance to men who abused them, the writer Gail Stokes cried, "Here we are, you and me, loving each other in our blackness . . . but then my arms grow weary as I work harder straining myself in order to build you up."[62] Category romance writers and readers don't want to strain themselves, and black romance writers may not wish to encourage further diminishment of black men, and so practice a super-benign response to the so-called war between black men and women.

The signature move of hetero romance is that it embraces gender conflict as a flirtatious, erotic tension that is legitimated by the certainty of emotional commitment and permanent devotion. Invariably whatever goes wrong is a prelude to emotional utopia once the misunderstanding is cleared up or (male) conversion to marriage takes place. The eminent critic Patricia Hill Collins says that men need to choose to love black women, and black women must demand that their black male sex partners respect them for "who they are."[63] Does the idealization of the hero in romance help women "choose" better partners in a climate of privation? Some might say yes, and Harlequin would agree. Collins herself concludes that black women must be educated about social issues instead of "searching for the elusive good 'catch' in a sea of Black men as an endangered species," which only generates intense competition among females and an attempt to be more desirable by submitting to traditional gender expectations.[64]

It is questionable how the audience is affected by this tension between the presumed universal entitlement to love and what the psychologist Renée Redd called African American women's "resign[ation] to never really being able to find a fulfilling love in their actual lives."[65] Perhaps all this analysis and history is too much fuss? Says Jeanette Cogdell, editor of the popular website *Romance in Color*: "When reality gets to be a bit too overwhelming for you, romance novels offer an escape to a world you may never live in."[66] Is romance reading merely an innocent "escape" to counteract what she calls "stress"?

One scholar, Patricia Dixon, argues that African American women may be unrealistic in terms of what they look for in mates: her work shows that female black college students expect to marry a man of superior economic, educational, professional, and income status, even while two-thirds of college degrees earned by African Americans are earned by women. Research has also shown that, although African Americans believe in egalitarian ideas in general, they still "subscribe to neo-patriarchal gender roles, especially the expectation of provider husbands and nurturing wives."[67]

As to having "a genre of their own," black romance author Monica Harris has protested: "How many white writers think about being white as they write their novels? . . . Both black and white writers write about and for human beings."[68] In the end the separation of race in romance genres might serve the master of corporate profit more than it serves the audience of any race.

Because the core narrative structure is the same for both black and white formula romances while the conditions of the gender struggle are different, black formula romance fiction is a kind of racial as well as emotional idyll that pretends to operate outside the "real lives" of women. But real life intrudes, wanted or not: where features of hair or skin color are strongly marked only in the black romance, where views of women's sexuality or the imperative to marry are more conservative than in other imprints, it's not because the fictional world is *outside* social conditions, but because its roots are still caught in the swamp of historical and present injustices.

In the end the "universal" is not love so much as the desire to make a story out of the materials of conflict in our culture. What the reader of black romances wants is no doubt what all romance readers want: to solve a set of irresolvable conflicts as if they were pieces of a puzzle whose finished picture is provided on the box. It comes down to this: romance is the attempt to mold the political and social forces that drive and limit our intimate lives into the shape of a wish come true. But if this wish is the same for "all women," the boundaries they imagine they have escaped are certainly not. Entangled in an invisible web of history and strained social values, popular black romance is both part of the solution and part of the problem.

ROMANCE NOVELS CITED

Harlequin Ltd.

Bowers, Celya. *Campaign for Love.* 2004
Byrd, Adrianne. *Unforgettable.* 2004
Casper, K. N. *As Big as Texas.* 2005
Hill, Donna. *Chances Are.* 2008
Kendrick, Sharon. *Accidentally Pregnant, Conveniently Wed.* 2008
Kitt, Sandra. *For All We Know.* 2008
Marinelli, Carol. *Expecting His Love-Child.* 2008
Novak, Brenda. *Dear Maggie.* 2001
Perrin, Kayla. *Flirting with Danger.* 2001
Roberts, Nora. *Cordina's Crown Jewel.* 2002
Schuster, Melanie. *A Merry Little Christmas.* 2004
Shayne, Maggie. *Feels like Home.* 2005
Singh, Nalini. *Bound by Marriage.* 2007
Summers, Jordan. *Off Limits.* 2000

Kensington Publishing

Manees, Raynetta. *All for Love.* 1996

St. Martin's Paperbacks

Alers, Rochelle. *Stand-in Bride.* 2001
Forster, Gwynne. *Learning to Love.* 2001
Hill, Donna. *Distant Lover.* 2001
Ray, Francis. *Southern Comfort.* 2001

9

IS FEMALE TO ROMANCE
AS MALE IS TO PORN?

> We (romance writers) think of pornography as something exploit-
> ative and dehumanizing. . . . That isn't what turns women on. . . .
> Women are turned on by . . . romance.
> —Candice Proctor, "The Romance Genre Blues or Why We Don't
> Get No Respect," 2007

The pairing up of women with romance and men with pornography has a comfortably familiar ring in our society. And yet, as the anthropologist Sherry B. Ortner wrote asked about the close association of women with nature in a famous
article from which I take this chapter's title, "What is our evidence that this is a
universal fact?"[1]

Actually, there's something odd about the formulation in my title that
doesn't exactly hold up when closely examined in our society. It's common
knowledge that far more women buy romance novels and watch romance
movies than men do, and that more men than women are fond of hard-core
porn. Yet we also know that men do fall in love regularly, with profound consequences for their lives, and still marry for love, so they say, in shockingly high
numbers (though even Americans marry more infrequently than formerly).
Moreover, women have become the fastest-growing audience for pornography.[2] So it does seem that men have emotions and women just may be interested in sex, after all.

All this tells us that pleasure, whether "romantic" or sexual, has a complex relation to genre as an expression of imagination. Just to confuse the picture even more,
the defining gestures of desire in the stylized genres of romance and pornography,
like the actual social enactment of both sex and romantic love in people's personal

lives, are steeped in the dye of gender, as feminism has made us aware. It's impossible to talk about these categories without also talking the talk of gender.

But again, the connection between gender and genre isn't as simple as it appears in heterosexual romantic and sexual stories. For example, a fascinating aspect of romance and porn *as representations* is that both frequently play with the reversal of gender expectations: romance by depicting the emotional power women have over men, and porn by representing the assertiveness of women's desire. In romance the man is often reduced to jelly in the hands of the woman he adores, while in pornography the fantasy woman who actively invites or demands sex is arguably as popular as the one who has to be seduced or forced.[3] And surely the way these switches play with clichés about emotionally aloof men and sexually virtuous women enhances the pleasure of these genres. By the time you consider both traditions and the enjoyable reversals of traditions, those die-hard stereotypes of gender, sex, and love start breaking down in ways that yield no easy answers to the question in my title.

One way to explain these nuances in the genres is to see that they are as much about power as pleasure. If romance is the dream language of the dominated, porn is that of the dominator wishing for the slave to be happy, or at least on call. We might say romance explains brutality in men—"If you can't lick 'em, you might as well love them"—whereas porn says, "If you can't love them, you might as well lick them." Each contains wishes for power through personal manipulation, and each also may contain its own contradiction, wanting to be ravished and swept away.

But power and pleasure are never simple concepts, and the power *of* pleasure, or pleasure *in* power, even less so. Texts designated as pornographic and romantic have been called liberating or oppressive at different times and places, and either might be elevated as high culture (as when sexual representations have been part of ancient religious ritual, or romance demonstrates noble, chivalrous traits) or denigrated as harmful or silly. My point is that they are not natural categories or natural opposites, as they are often assumed to be. It might be more useful to see them as parallel investments of meaning, permitting us to experience a need whose possibility of existence may not be fully recognized in social relations, reified in the body of the desired.

THE INTERDEPENDENCE OF PORN AND ROMANCE

They do share complementary traits. Porn appears to divide the world into good and bad in order to enjoy the bad, as if it can only be enjoyed if it *is* bad; romance similarly divides the world, as if it can be enjoyed only if one is good, or at least good enough to get the guy. Their acts and objects of desire seemingly break from the constraint of all "shoulds." Desire isn't a "should" but rather appears as an "is." Since the narrative world is experienced as of one's own making, the result of both genres is an inflation of the self: the fictional world comes to look like you as you really are inside. To put it another way, both porn and romance are hyperbolic, utopian fictions of hope, imagining a universe moving in harmony with one's innermost wishes.[4]

What hopes and wishes, though? Pornography is notoriously hard to define (the Supreme Court has never come up with a very clear definition), but so is the genre of romance. It seems both narrow and crude to reduce them to their focus on sexual coupling and emotional bonding, respectively. Moreover, attempts to justify their presumed nature by finding their origins too often resemble "just-so" stories, in which the characteristics we have come to expect as modern Westerners are universalized when looking backward. Modern definitions of romance and pornography often seem subject to that well-known bedevilment, finding what you're looking for . . . because you're looking for it. As scholars have shown, there is no historical basis for assuming that explicit sexually stimulating materials have always been "bad," or that the essence of romance is passionate emotion pointed toward domestic bliss.[5] And there certainly is no historical basis for assuming that love has always been the particular domain of femininity, or concupiscence necessarily seen as exclusive to men.

Nevertheless, porn and romance in recent cultural history seem to depend on each other, in much the same way that an old married couple who have hated each other for decades organize their existence around that hatred and would be lost if they did not have one another to define themselves against. While both kinds of texts construct a fictional world in which absolutely everything appears to either help or hinder the rise and fulfillment of desire, it used to be that the distinction between them turned on what *kind* of desire. This boiled down to the concept of sexual virtue: romance is self-consciously good (noble, in the strong version), porn is self-consciously bad (or at least naughty, in the mild version). Women as objects of *romantic* desire are sexually virtuous, women as "mere" objects of *lustful* desire are sexually denigrated. "She is sacred to me," says the hero of *The Sorrows of Young Werther* (1774), Johann Wolfgang von Goethe's extraordinary account of suicide by romantic love. "All lust is stilled in her presence." Before the so-called sexual revolution of the 1970s, such a distinction was generally comfortable and easily made: there was wife material and then there were those other women.

The nineteenth century saw the rise of literacy and technologies of mass culture, leading to more romance in both esteemed novels and popular reading, alongside a whole new world of seemingly invisible prurience. Each world rigorously eschewed recognition of the other as natural and inevitable descriptions of desire, with the organizing principle of the "tender passion" (as the Victorians used to say) versus raw sex to differentiate their orbits. In the Victorian view, the two categories of pornography and romance grounded their self-definition on each other in a way that presupposes opposite terms (the body and the "heart"), and so could never be the same—though, as Steven Marcus showed in his groundbreaking *The Other Victorians*, they shared a historically specific ideology of sex and gender.

With the twentieth century came a radical revaluation of sexuality, as part of the modern "revaluation of all values," leading to famous court battles over the social value of sexual language and representations and legal definitions of obscenity and hard-core porn.[6] Equally hard-fought was the later conflict in the women's movement between anti-porn feminists who believed that pornography victimizes women and sex-positive feminists who were anti the anti-porn group.[7]

For our purposes, it is striking that some feminist critics of pornography tended to focus on its presentation of desire in terms of "use-value for others" as its distinction from romance.[8] Gloria Steinem, for example, made much of the difference between erotica (good) and pornography (bad), resting on the male *using* the female for his own pleasure ("Erotica and Pornography: A Clear and Present Difference"). This distinction echoed the celebrated diarist Anaïs Nin's argument that women are attracted to erotica rather than pornography, which she equated with "the animal" in her essay "Eroticism in Women." In other words, women should be allowed to have sexual desire and the freedom to pursue it, but this has to be good sex rather than bad. "Good" sex incorporated the warm and tender elements of romance, the affections rather than the low, dirty sensations. It seemed the heart was not so much a part of the body in romance as the body was part of "the heart."

The problem with this neat differentiation is that we have to buy the idea that romance is *not* about someone else's value based on her ability to give us pleasure, or that the emotional pleasure we receive from love is superior to and therefore ennobles sexual pleasure. But it isn't obvious that this is so unless we already believe it, or clear why that should be. The idea that women intrinsically like (or at least *should* like) only "good" sex hovers close to the Victorian idea that they are kinder and purer by nature than men.

Similarly, the still-popular view that romantic love is entirely unselfish, about caring and *caritas* for the individual, is that becomes more dubious the more you look at it. For one thing, if hetero pornographic stories make women into cartoon figures, in hetero romance fiction men are likewise cookie-cutter shapes of instant arousal and perfect buffing. No hero in a Harlequin novel is ever bald and overweight, has chronic potency problems, or is emotionally distant after his declaration of love (as opposed to before, when he is often an iceberg there for the melting). Are fictions of romance any less vehicles of "objectification" because men's "feelings" are depicted, even though these "feelings" are fictional representations tailor-made to female fantasies?

Why, then, don't men complain of being "love objects," as women do of being sex objects? Try to imagine it: "I'm nothing but a love object to you!" The absurdity of this idea comes from the historical Western tradition, based on the Christian ethos that the spirit is higher than the flesh, that "real" love of any kind is measured by the degree of concern for the other, not intensity of passion. Love is pictured as the protector and guarantor against sexual "use" (a term that is used synonymously in this context to "abuse"), as if emotionality or even emotional commitment provides a kind of insurance policy against what we don't like. But does it?

What, I would like to ask, is so noble about emotional commitment, anyway? One can be committed to an unequal or manipulative relationship, after all. My guess is that many batterers would say they love their wives or girlfriends and never want to leave them. Certainly a "committed relationship" feels better to a great number of people in some ways (though it can be uncomfortable in others), but there are many reasons why people might like to be in one besides selfless devotion: to name a few, the social status of being in a couple; a sense of claim and control over another; the relief of insecurities, including fear of change or loneliness; and motives of vanity, material betterment, social mobility, or escape from an unwanted prior situation. These niceties seldom appear as agendas in the representations we call romance.

The romantic lover is usually presented as hooked by some mysterious essence of the heroine, not by the advantages of being in a relationship, so romance seems to be defined by committed emotion, while pornography is about selfish power. But if we accept that porn demeans women by depicting them as permanently sexually aroused, as some critics have charged, we must also admit that romance often depicts women as permanently *emotionally* aroused. In romance, just as the home is supposed to be a pressure valve regulating the tensions and contradictions of a stressed and competitive society, so the committed relationship is always pictured as the safe space instead of the producer of tension. A hero's sexual desire is a sign of sanctified love in hetero romance, as it is not always in real life, where desire can be irritating, threatening, or even dangerous to women. Conversely, in porn a woman's pleasant behavior is always a sure sign of sexual availability; she's never just being nice because she's a friendly person. Part of the pleasure in consuming these texts is the magic trick of erasing the other side of the story.

BEYOND PORN AND ROMANCE?

In our own time, when both romance and pornography have proliferated, thanks to ever-growing mass media and the post-Freudian value placed on intense feelings in general, one would think the two genres would be more similar to each other than not. As we know, romance in all media, including formula romance, has become ever more sexually explicit in its depictions, warmly (if you will forgive the pun) embracing female sexual desire and sexual fulfillment in general—at least between the monogamous hero and heroine in the context of long-term emotional commitment, as, for example, in the publishing phenomenon *Fifty Shades of Grey*. And not coincidentally, while pop romance got ever hotter after the sixties, the idea of a new kind of pornography, one that did not objectify or demean women, also gained some traction. These developments were the result of a double-barreled shot heard round the world: the success of the almost-simultaneous sexual and feminist revolutions.

It was exciting to think of the blurring of long-held boundaries as modern society left behind traditional views of sex and gender. How might it affect the genres when a romance is written by a modern male, for example, or when porn is produced by and for women? Would the whole sex-gender system collapse, be revolutionized, permit a new way of looking at the world?

It's interesting to look at two texts that broke traditional bounds within the genres themselves, namely, the popular *Herotica* series (1988–2003), erotica written by and for women from a feminist, multicultural, and mixed hetero-and-gay viewpoint, and a novel (later a movie) by an extraordinarily successful male writer of romance fiction, Nicholas Sparks. Compare, for example, this description of lovemaking (one dares not call it sex) from Sparks's highly romantic *The Notebook* (1996) . . .

They lay back, close to the fire, and the heat made the air seem thick. Her back was slightly arched as he rolled atop her in one fluid motion. He was on all fours above her, his knees astride her hips. . . . She buried her face in his neck and felt him deep inside her, felt his strength and gentleness, felt his muscle and his soul. She moved rhythmically against him, allowing him to take her wherever he wanted, *to the place she was meant to be* [my emphasis].[9]

. . . to the following excerpt from *Herotica*'s "women's porn":

Amara spread her legs, dug her ass deeper into the yielding sand and moaned, waiting for the next ephemeral kiss of the salty ocean. . . . Her anus was like a tiny whirlpool on a heaving ocean, the deep brown ridges twirling inward, daring Yasmin to come closer, closer still, to spin ever down and into *a place without time,* to *the place before the beginning.* . . . She moaned, catching the tiniest trickle from Amara's anus before it dropped, blessed, onto her clit [my emphasis].[10]

Is the "place she was meant to be" the same location as "the place before the beginning"? I'm afraid so, even though we get more explicit body parts and fluids in the "porn" and a bit more earnest grandeur in the "romance." In the male-authored romance, the noble alliance of "muscle and soul" substitute for the tiny whirlpool of Anara's anus in the heaving ocean of the female-authored porn, but it seems to me window dressing. Rather than finding "the place without time," these popular examples of men's romance and women's porn appear to meet in some limp and soggy patch of inflated prose that only renders each less capable of doing its job.

Sadly, I would suggest that the crossover liberates neither male romance nor female porn. The authors themselves no doubt see their work as transgressive and empowering—sexual scenes embedded in exalted romantic emotion from a male hero's point of view, and women controlling their own sexual representations. Instead, the erotic romance and the woman-pleasing erotica, both about sex in a loving, mutual, committed relationship, seem to founder on their mutual driving need to be everything to everyone.

You may have noticed that in spite of the presence in these texts of formerly unmentionable body parts, both the sexy romance and the romantic porn have the same sincere, elevated tone that distinguishes them from what is called hard-core porn; this is connected to the odd fact that both were aimed at a female audience. I say "odd" because you might think, after all this boundary-breaking between sex and romance, that men, too, would want to read these works, or for that matter head in droves to the soft-focus date movies made from Sparks's novels. But though it has been claimed that the male audience for romance texts has grown, perhaps even doubled, this is actually a tiny increase, nowhere near the rise in texts that depict women's sexuality; in that way it's similar to the increase in the number of men who want to tend house and raise children, which has not exactly been a major surge. This is another way of asking a question not posed often enough, in my opinion: why does romance appeal much more to one gender rather than the other in our own liberated era?

Perhaps the science of sex studies can help us out here, since female sexuality compared to male has been a hot topic (again, it is difficult to avoid such puns when writing on a subject like this one) in psychology for decades. Given that women have been allowed their own sexual desires and granted sexual freedom as never before for nearly half a century now, do they still *feel* differently than men in some essential way that gives sex and romance a distinct meaning for each? Surely *female is to romance as male is to porn* as a paradigm has been tested in the numerous studies of males and females responding to pornography.

It has. Yet much social science research on the subject of romance and pornography has turned on the same conventional distinction: the acceptance of the mutual antagonism of "lust" and "love," or, as it has often been phrased, sex and emotion, as if these were transcendentally discrete categories. The science journalist Daniel Goleman summed it up in the *New York Times* by grandly concluding, "The differences between sexual fantasies of men and women seem to run deep in the workings of the male and female minds." He was referring to an oft-quoted study of men's and women's sexual fantasies by Donald Symons and Bruce Ellis (1990) that endorsed, as so many have since then, the idea that female sex fantasies are "more likely to emphasize themes of tenderness and emotionality" and contain only implicit rather than explicit sexual content. Therefore, the authors assert, women are more likely to be emotionally rather than physically aroused by their sexual fantasies. The problem with this, however, is that it begs the question of what a sex fantasy *is*.[11]

This study, which may stand in for the many before and after that reach the same conclusion, would seem to answer the question in my title with irrefutable empirical evidence, but some further probing in the archives of social science turns up complexities in the picture. For one thing, though Alfred Kinsey's original study appeared to demonstrate that females require greater expression of emotional commitment to maximize arousal, women in the decades following the rapid decline of rigid gender restrictions on expressing sexuality were increasingly likely to engage in and enjoy casual sex. Similarly, following confident claims all the way from the Victorians to some contemporary evolutionary psychologists that women are *naturally* the monogamous sex,[12] rates of female adultery leaped to unprecedented heights practically overnight following the sexual revolution and the invention of reliable birth control methods in the seventies. Did half the women's brains suddenly turn male? This is enough to make one scratch one's head about what runs deep in the so-called innate workings of the male and female minds.

Moreover, in one study from about the same time, *both* males and females rated high romantic porn as more arousing than low romantic porn.[13] What to make of all these contradictions? When the researcher Ellen Laan asked whether women were more aroused by woman-made films in which females initiate sex and that are softer in ambience, the answer was yes and no—women reported liking them more and feeling more aroused, but their genital arousal, measured by vaginal probe, was equal to men's.[14] An interesting difference was that for women, the man-made films aroused more shame and guilt. And how did Dr. Lonnie Barbach, popular self-help author and therapist, explain why women say they are aroused by romantic sex when physiological tests show increased vaginal moisture and blood flow after viewing the same stuff men are aroused by? "For women there is a predisposition to . . . become turned on [by] romance," she tells us. "This wouldn't necessarily be measured by genital arousal."[15] I ask again, what, then, does "turned on" actually *mean*? Are we twisting the meanings of key terms so the results come out to confirm what we already think we know?

The recent work of sex researchers Meredith Chivers and Amanda Timmers confirms that "women are capable of greater sexual responsiveness than previously thought and can experience genital response in the absence of a subjective experience of sexual arousal" but also finds that one of the fantasies that most arouse women is sex with strangers. While "women might be expected to report greater arousal to cues of relationship commitment," there was no real difference in women's sexual responses to narratives of casual one-off hookups versus long-term relationships.[16] You might think this would settle it.

Nevertheless, in the media we still hear all the time that women *naturally* prefer tender erotic stories rather than unromantic sexual representations. Is there something about women's brains that draws them to the story form, and is that part connected to the clitoris? Evolutionary psychologists and the pop science writers who love them think so: there is "a profound difference in the brain software of men and women" in the area of sexual desire, conclude Sai Gaddam and Ogi Ogas in the commercially published *A Billion Wicked Thoughts: What the World's Largest Experiment Reveals about Human Desire* (2011). They offer the usual reason: "Unconscious software has evolved to protect women over hundreds of thousands of years [because] sex with the wrong guy could lead to many unpleasant outcomes," specifically "single motherhood."[17] Well, yes, it could, though given the unprecedented rate of nonmarital births in countries where women have the *most* choice in their private lives, you'd expect all that evolved software to work better. But wouldn't the obvious burden of maternity (not to mention the danger of sexual assault and rape) for women mean we *don't* need evolution to explain women's greater caution about actual sex, as opposed to fantasy sex? Until we have a way of separating out neurology from social context, it seems unreasonable to say for sure whether there is a *naturally* hard-wired "profound difference" in male and female responses to porn and romance.[18]

Moreover, that is only one side of the equation: women's response to porn has been studied a great deal more than men's gender-specific response to romantic media, perhaps because women have become more publicly sexualized than men have been converted to romance. I would suggest that this disparity has less to do with inherited gray matter than with the difference in the relation of the romantic fantasy to the social and economic realities of men's and women's lives. That is, the ever-growing importance of romance in mass media expresses the historical and material conditions of "love" for modern women, which have raised newer forms of angst, uncertainty, and, underneath, a hidden cynicism.

Part of this disturbance comes from our contemporary culture's ambivalence about the sexuality of women: where does a woman's value and power lie, in being a hot sexual object or in her emotional nurturance of hetero men? "True love" in the Victorian age was viewed as a protection against the dangers of lust, but modern romantic love is *supposed to* include sexual passion (while reframing its meaning), so it can be confusing. In fact, one might say romance has become the fault line for women in defining the difference between being "used" for mere lust and being respected, even revered, in romance (as if a sexually desirable woman cannot be respected without being loved). The story of a love affair redefines sexuality as something personal that women can understand and control, rendering its social context invisible or irrelevant. For this reason, many women deeply want to see romance as a script for their *total* lives, hoping for the mate who through choosing you merges strong emotion, sexuality, partnering, and childrearing, forms of experience not necessarily fused in the past.

I have said that modern cultural developments have blurred the line between romance and pornography, but not necessarily in ways that would bring happy mist to a Second Wave feminist's eyes. Contemporary Western depictions of female sexuality as a stripper/hooker display have recently further clouded the picture considerably. The writer Ariel Levy made an important point about the gender asymmetry of modern hyper-sexualization: "Proving that you are hot, worthy of lust, and—necessarily–that you seek to provoke lust is still exclusively women's work."[19] I would suggest a new genre entirely has sprouted up in mass media, combining the idealization attributed to romance with the dirty and forbidden attractions of porn: call it the rom-porn of class vulgarity, in which the audience mock-celebrates tastelessness in the working class (drunkenness, peeing in public, and fighting on *Jersey Shore*), or the trashy glamour of the newly wealthy class (*The Real Housewives* franchise and its ilk).

The imagery of the latter is everywhere now, featuring women who sell "looks" and "style" (they "go for it," they "own the look," they "label out") as romantic objects of envy to each other even more than as objects of desire to men, competing for the prize by displaying decorated and augmented bodies or real estate. Though this seems not to be about either sex or romance in actuality, enlarged breasts notwithstanding, it has helped define the terms of both for many women. How confounding this must be to twelve-year-old girls who dress like glammed-out Real Housewives to go to a dance: are they displaying their "sexy" makeup and clothes for the twelve-year-old boys they hope to date or for an invisible audience that will evaluate them as women are judged on TV and in music videos?

Adding to the confusion is that the mandate to be a sexy bitch for desirability, power, and success as a celebrity is still at odds with being a sweet romantic object of emotional desire. It's telling that the figure of the bitch as a villain in formula romance is alive and well in Harlequin novels as a character who suggests to the reader that being sexy without goodness should not and will not bring love.[20] Take K. N. Casper's *As Big as Texas* (2005), in which a cold and manipulative bitch-rival wears "tight jeans and a T-shirt that clung provocatively to her full, round breasts and showed the outline of her nipples."[21] The heroine herself may also wear tight jeans and of course has wonderfully shaped breasts, too, but would never allow a glimpse of nipples, it goes without saying.

It seems to me that contemporary women are caught in a difficult bind. Feminism worked hard (in tandem with the sexual revolution) to demand women's right to own their desire and act on it freely, along with control over reproductive rights. But pop media further the traditional double standard in a new way, as on *Jersey Shore*, *The Bachelor*, or the *Real Housewives* franchise, where women constantly criticize other women for their looks (however much they all look and dress alike) or categorize each other as "sluts" and "skanks." Meanwhile, conservatives hardened their attack when they brought women's sexuality into play in the 2012 elections. Romance represents an easy path out of that bind because it still often appears to turn on the idea that any romantic image or story is *not* porn, embodying the wish that the story itself protects and insures against sexual exploitation of another.

What, then, can we conclude about that old formula that *female is to romance as male is to porn?* First, as we have seen, it is not really all that old and certainly not universal, even if it has stuck around long enough to feel traditional. And now? The terms have shifted: while sexual desire is supposedly for both sexes, and romantic love encompasses hot sex, oddly, interest in romance as a genre is still mostly confined to females. Because of this imbalance, only women must hope to be both as dynamically sexy as a sizzling figure out of porn and sweetly cuddly at the same time. It seems unnecessarily exhausting for women to have to be good-yet-hot while men need only be hot-to-trot—except in stories of romance for women, where men melt like cream puffs before the emotional and sexual power of the heroine, and neither sex would ever dream of checking out pornography on their computers.

10

MODERN ROMANCE

Two Versions of Love in Reality/"Reality"

> Mass culture is a machine for showing desire: here is what must inter-
> est you, it says.
> —Roland Barthes, *A Lover's Discourse: Fragments*, 1978

Victorian magazines often featured manufactured anecdotes and stories that
were presented (if only with tongue in cheek) as true. Our modern culture, in
ironic reversal, presents filmed stories of actual people in a simulacrum of reality.
Similarly, the relatively recent explosion in memoir presents its own challenge to
the idea of truth: "my" truth is real enough if it's a good story. I hope to show that
romance, too—fictional or not—is a *version* of reality, and for lovers, or just lovers of love stories, it becomes a fictional but necessary truth.

There has been much scholarly commentary on the relationship of these multiple realities to lived experience, blurring the line of the true and untrue in all
sorts of bewildering postmodern ways.[1] But, you might object, the dividing line
itself, however queasily wavering, is still there; even a postmodernist uses an umbrella when it rains. Romance in texts and in life, after all, seems pretty clearly ap-
ples and oranges: romance fiction is deliberately removed from actual life, often
labeled mere entertainment or "escape," whereas when a living woman appears
on a sort-of-unscripted TV show or writes about herself on an Internet dating
site, it's presumably real (or at least real to her). Even where romance specifically stands for another world, the world of wondrous fables or (in the modern
American sense) fabulousness, that unreality is still one of our realities.

Given all this, it seems futile to ask what love is in the real world; a better
question might be, How do we understand "real" romance—one that is lived
out in actual time, by oneself or others? I would argue that there is no getting

away from story entirely when it comes to romance. Traditional narratives are threaded into our experience; fictions become real to us as we try to live with and through them, while "reality" becomes fictionalized. Just as our culture's fictions are often the undercurrent of our reality, so we view those fictions through the lens of our experiences and the choices they present.

In this chapter we will look at two versions of "real" love: a dating reality show and women's Internet dating profiles. These romantic forms, while obviously diverse, stand as connected examples that defy the widely understood sense of the "real" in romance, the notion of what "real" love is. They also rebuke the idea of the "self" as a unitary form. The patterns of our love stories are organized according to the demands of representing the multiple, often contradictory possible selves that we fear, or seek, or imagine. As a multifaceted and ambiguous idea, love is peculiarly suited to this kind of representation, a fluid mold into which to pour the fluctuations and layers of selfhood. This may in fact be so whether the stories are "true" (narratives of lived experience) or named as fiction.

The visions of romance in the two genres of reality TV and the explosively popular phenomenon of Internet dating reproduce forms and scripts we recognize in our lives, while providing us with a "meaning," a way of understanding our feelings and relations that appears natural and universal. In both these genres, one finds people becoming characters, or using characters based on actual identities. Professional and nonprofessional become one, the body gives way to the avatar, and we invest these others with our dreams, if not laugh at foolishness, following Friedrich Nietzsche's dictum that we discover both "the hero and the fool" in our art. Now, Nietzsche might not have recognized either reality TV or Internet dating profiles as art, you will point out, but my view is that they are, in fact, as carefully constructed as any artistic form.

REALITY/"REALITY" TV

It's not difficult to see why reality TV has had such unprecedented appeal to the public; for one, it has the same appeal as gossip, and really, how can anyone be above good gossip? You have to have the imagination of a termite not to enjoy the capricious (and naughty) ways people behave when it appears that others are not looking. Of course, they do know we are looking, which makes it even more delicious that they can't seem to help making utter fools of themselves or don't seem to know how transparent their self-serving behaviors are. But is this really so different from social life in "reality"? In reality TV, people pretend the cameras are not there and we're not watching, whereas in real life, we often behave as though the cameras are there and we are the center of attention.

The oft-repeated objection that what is presented on so-called reality shows isn't really "reality" seems to me absurd, the sort of stupid thing smart people are wont to say; *nothing* on TV is "real" by definition, any more than a filmed documentary is a straightforward picture of life, or a politician's replies in an interview are spontaneous. For that matter, when we non-TV folks are in any social setting, we act in constrained and self-conscious ways. What could be more scripted than the first conversation between two actual people who meet in a bar, or on a blind date? "What do you like to do?" "Where are you from?" "Do you enjoy your work?" Linguists will tell you that there are always unspoken rules attached to situations in which we regularly encounter other people, as when we take part in a classroom discussion or pretend we're having a great time at a party. I perform, you perform, reality show participants perform: we all put on a show, whether in competition for prizes monetary or social or romantic. In other words, though reality TV is artificial, social life is, too, fascinatingly so. There's a reality show always going on, whether for the camera, other eyes, or one's own eyes in the mirror or memoir. It's turtles all the way down.

The Bachelor: He's Just Not That Into You . . . or You, or You

As Mr. Rogers used to say, we are *all special* . . . aren't we?

This very American ethos accords beautifully with the modern democratized idea of romantic love. We are more and more encouraged to have confidence that being chosen by the Right One (the One, in its short form) is like becoming a superstar, at least to one's beloved, and to family and friends on the day of the wedding itself; as one scholar put it, being in love means Starring in One's Own Movie.[2] Similarly, and not coincidentally, "hope" and "belief" that what *should* happen *will* happen are foundational blocks in the discourse of the modern Western version of religion. Destiny, magic ("magical nights"), fantasy, and fairy tales are the lingua franca of *The Bachelor* franchise, all associated with the folk religion of romance: "My fairy tale is *supposed to be here*. It was my destiny. I believe I will have a man to love me and take care of me," exclaimed one contestant. In other words, the romantic expectation of being elite (though still average) and special, if only to the One, is assumed to be a universal entitlement. As a female contestant put it, "I believe there's one person for each person; you have to find the right person." In other words, build that castle and the prince will come.

Because *The Bachelor* as a spectacle reproduces our anxieties and hopes about romance in concentrated form, like a little petri dish of desire deliberately cultivated to grow into a familiar story, the show can tell us a lot about the way we see the interactions between gender and romantic love now. For example, if the new form of success is celebrity at any cost, romantic love is simply the new face of celebrity. In fact, on *The Bachelor*, some are scorned for "not being here for the right reasons," that is, they seek media exposure rather than pure feeling and relationship in front of a massive public audience. Bachelor Prince Lorenzo of 2006 dismissed "bachelorette" Lisa because he thought she "is there just to be on a TV show"—as though the spectacle is irrelevant and must be ignored, even while *he* is speaking into the camera.

A common thread in televised contests is that we, the audience, both pity and enjoy the humiliation of the losers, but in *The Bachelor* the loss (or rather, punishment for not winning) is in the coin of emotion rather than money or fame. If multiple people are not "heartbroken" (a word repeated endlessly) in *The Bachelor*, its job is not done. Yet at times, the genre of romantic reality TV more closely resembles home decorating shows, in which the choice of luxury items provides the excitement, than it does last-one-standing competitions for "survival" on an island or talent contests like *American Idol* or *Top Chef*. The desirable girls paraded before the Bachelor are the equivalent of the marble bathroom.

What We Want, and How We Want It

The largest audience for *The Bachelor* is almost certainly women interested in the drama of what succeeds on the marriage market, or at least those who wish to measure their own value against those well-groomed visions of loveliness in gaudy clothes who stand in for the rest of us.[3] The Bachelor's job is to distinguish and shuffle out various good-looking women, gaining the young woman of most value (though the rhetoric is "the One who is right for him") and rewarding her with true love. Many nineteenth-century novels, if it comes to that, are also about knowing how to discern and catch the One, and that story, isolated from a greater social context, ritualized, and greatly sped up, is replicated here.

The fuel for *The Bachelor* is nostalgia for *courtship*, the wooing of a young woman by a man for the purpose of marriage, as opposed to modern *dating*, which has taken on so many varied forms—one being hookups, casual or temporary connections based on sexual attraction—that the distinction is understandably confusing in our contemporary world. We all know that the highly ritualized, controlled, and strictly chaperoned world of courtship, as it appears in nineteenth-century novels, was based on deeply held notions of strictly gendered roles, especially the woman's passivity and the man's active pursuit of her hand in the unquestioned ideal of marriage. Signposts were clear: pursuing a woman without marriage in mind indicated a "dishonorable" purpose, and while a woman (if she was lucky) might have more than one suitor, encouraging more than one was a sign of bad character.[4]

The ethos of dating, on the other hand, begun in the 1920s, and tied to consumer options such as the newly available automobile, was completely different: unmoored from the strict control of parental supervision, couples could get to know each other in a casual way while having fun, especially fun that involved spending money.[5] In the later twentieth century it was often presumed that both young men and women were "playing the field," including increasing degrees of sexual play, until their emotions for one person grew strong and mutual enough for a monogamous relationship whose right end was a wedding. *The Bachelor* wants to combine the lighthearted, casual "fun" of modern multiple dating (with its forced laughter, silliness, sexual flirtation, and desperate small talk) with the narrative through-line of Victorian courtship, implying serious, sanctified emotion, sentimental drama (always including "heartbreak"), and high purpose: love that will last forever, or at least till the new season begins.

The very language of the show reflects this ambiguity toward the turn romance has taken in contemporary society: the man is the "bachelor," which as we all know is a far more esteemed condition than the "spinster," or even the *Cosmo* girl, who is single and looking for fun and love, not necessarily in that order. A single young woman, always an object of desire, may now express her own sexual desire, thanks to the feminist and sexual revolutions, but we are still missing a single word for an unmarried woman that is not fraught with uncomfortable meaning. So what to call the women who become enamored of the bachelor? Cutely, they are "bachelorettes," a title that has the invented sound of an all-girls singing group from the fifties.

Surely this small gesture marks the show's effort to modernize its attitude toward women, which explains why the female contestants are not called by the sexist epithet for grown women, "girls." Yet the host and the Bachelor himself always refer to the women as "ladies," to signify that they are not just a bunch of women but have a kind of nineteenth-century dignity to their status (actual and typical line from the show: "I'm going to take these ladies down Sunset Strip"). On the other hand, when there are multiple men, as on *The Bachelorette*, the contestants are frequently called "dudes," implying a casual, rough-hewn masculinity in contrast to the formality of "the ladies." So while the femininity of the female contestants invokes Austenish old-fashioned nostalgic upper-class chivalry, masculinity is defined as the more modern charm of eternal raw, boyish wildness.

For centuries, courtship was arranged by parents or at least conducted under the watch of those who monitored the social and financial worth of each suitor. *The Bachelor* succeeds because it replicates the uncertainties of actual dating, where women themselves must "catch" desirable men's attention and hold them fast by achieving the men's emotional investment. The conclusion of each show, when roses are given out to those who are passed on to the next week's installment, pits the women against each other in the twitchy atmosphere of increasing scarcity, something like romantic musical chairs.[6]

But it's not just the fun of picking a winner that is the appeal for the audience. We judge what should be expected in the winner by the valued Bachelors' reactions. What they like teaches us not only about gender but also how to be loved; we need to know what and who is valuable in a world of dating that has become uncertain because the old rules have melted away. The woman who is going to be chosen is inevitably young, beautiful, bubbly, sweet, and "fun," which is to say charming in a feminine way. "Smart" is always thrown in for good measure (with no evidence at all) in a gesture toward feminism. However, the "nutty" contestants are just as important in that they crucially define the outer limits of what is deemed appropriate in getting the man, such as the exact line that separates when assertive attention-getting is cute and when it is shameful and embarrassing "stalking."

It's important that on the show the women must be sexy but use just the right *amount* of sex and the right *kind:* cleavage (but never nudity), flirting, giggling, and hot-tub bikini-showing are all emphasized. Kissing, an allowable form of romantic sexuality, is so fetishized that the camera lingers for endless minutes on mouths that are meeting and working (usually without tongue, as the Bachelorette Jillian admitted in an interview with Anderson Cooper, famously causing him to gag) and the juicy sounds of lips smacking together are much amplified for our envy and delight. This extreme heightening of the kiss replicates what has long been a fictional device in Harlequin romances. Bachelors and Bachelorettes kiss in helicopters, on bungee jumps and beaches, with sunsets in the background; they go at it in hot tubs, on picnics, and underwater. Both emotions and sex are then carefully calibrated, ranked, and judged as to what is permissible and what is low status, differentiated by gender: "too aggressive" or "drama queen" moves for women, and for men, being "too reserved" and "not opening up" (defined as not "sharing hopes and dreams").

You would think that for the female audience, identifying with the women who are in the humiliating position of competing with each other for the only prize in sight would be stressful and unpleasantly angst-producing. But in fact the show works by invoking that anxiety, as in any story with a happy ending, and then encouraging the female viewer to identify with the one who overcomes, who masters the master. The feminist critique of the Cinderella story, or for that matter a Jane Austen novel, is that women are passively dependent on being chosen by a man. For fans of a formulaic and ritualistic show like *The Bachelor*, if you know the happy ending in advance, you don't need to experience the weaknesses of that position. Or rather, its abjection is ritually expunged from the story when the not-chosen are "eliminated." One woman, in theory the most deserving one/One, will triumph, and if she doesn't, we get to vent our wrath at the ingrate Bachelor who *won't fall in love.* This reminds me of a student who angrily objected to my reading list of fictions about love, many with unhappy endings: "I'm tired of reading about love that doesn't work," she wrote. "Real love isn't like that."

Victorian Values and Modern Women

The era that is evoked by the performance of the show (as opposed to its rhetoric) is the nineteenth century and its traditional gender divisions. Though some of the women on shows like *The Bachelor* are labeled "independent" in character (like Harlequin heroines) and nearly all have jobs of their own, however vague ("consultant"), the structure and values of the show are steeped in Victorian ideas. This is not often directly expressed, though one contestant on season 9 actually said, "I believe I will have a man to love me and take care of me." Victorian ideology is more often apparent in the categories of women: for example,

good-hearted and modest (femininine), or calculating and aggressive (unfeminine). There is frequently a virgin who plans to delay sex until marriage, a slutty
oversexed one, a drunken loud one, and a bitchy one, all roles that the audience
knows how to read. Both the virgin and the slut are titillatingly abnormal compared to the rest, and the show works the pleasure of this marginality.

Often there is a contrast between the woman who "throws herself" at the
Bachelor sexually and emotionally, violating the Victorian definition of the lady
as modest, passive, restrained, and restraining (too modern), versus the woman
who risks being seen as cold and withholding of sex and emotion by modern
standards (too traditional). Both of these are risky positions. No wonder it's difficult to "win," especially for those "ladies" vying for the Bachelor, whose show-
arranged matches have been uniformly unsuccessful compared to one or two of
their female (Bachelorette) counterparts.

The pleasure of watching *The Bachelor* is not unlike the reason many women
love to read female authors of the nineteenth century, or buy self-help books on
love: learning how to discern hierarchies of value, follow rules of behavior, parse
out popular ideas about men and women. You may have noticed that the fun of
it—sorting out the worthy from the unworthy, understanding the enigmatic intentions of others (what psychologists call the theory of mind)—is reminiscent
of the pleasures of reading Jane Austen. How do you get that man, what do you
do? *This* is how you succeed. And just as the Austen heroine marries only for love
but somehow manages to love and be loved by the man who has a comfortable
income or better, *The Bachelor* fuses "finding" the Right One with a picture of a
lifestyle that is as close to the American Dream as the viewer imagines. The problem then takes the storied form: how do you make your way into the symbolic
luxury of the "Fantasy Suite" and all the wealth and the lifestyle it represents?
You may say that wealth and luxury are metaphors for the value of love, or you
may say it's the other way around.

It's a zero-sum game, and emotions are said to be the stakes. But what emotions, exactly? The show often tells us defensively that "these emotions are *very
real*," inadvertently underlining the slippery definition of what romantic emotions are and how they originate. My own view is that the much ridiculed "unreality" of "reality" dating shows reflects real dilemmas in women's lives in general,
not just in dating: the trade-offs and risks of gendered behavior. If too modern,
women will miss out on being adored and forfeit the privilege of male protection; if too traditional, they will miss out on the privileges of hard-won freedom.
Rhetorically appealing to the "modern" independent, strong, and spirited working woman, while playing out the opposing mode of traditional gender roles,
shows like *The Bachelor* soothe and resolve women's doubts and unease by seeming to take the risks, and therefore the sting, out of both.

For example, *The Bachelor* season 10 (2007) featured Andy, a "naval officer"
who was all floppy sincerity. A doctor and an athlete, he was said to be "every

girl's dream." As usual, when the girls marched in, they were filmed from the shoes up—the classic pumps getting out of the car—as they were told they had to make the Bachelor remember them in the "race for Andy's heart." Again, Andy's rejects were often floozies or too pushy. For example, Stephanie was a called a "hussy"—so labeled because she asked Andy to go look at the pier with her. Another contestant remarked that "everyone hates Stephanie" (as if it were high school). In a no doubt deliberate contrast, Alexis was a virgin at age twenty-six who was home-schooled and had "conservative values." One girl observed jealously that Alexis "has an advantage because she's a virgin—what guy wouldn't like that?" Well, did he? Apparently not all that much, but it's informative she'd still think so in an age when virginity at marriage is no longer the norm.

At a postshow reunion of "the ladies," the women called each other "whore" and "slutty," with the outrageous one, Erica, saying that one of her fellow contestants was "like a prostitute." (Of course, that's the function of the outspoken one.) Since sexual contact, if not full sexual relations, is implied by the nights the Bachelor and his three finalists share alone and unfilmed in the Fantasy Suite, you would not guess that sexuality would be treated with such Victorian judgmentality. And of course this is where modern social beliefs shape the judgments: the implication is that monogamous sex accompanied by "feeling" is *the* mark of difference between the good and bad, real and fake women.

Love as Mystery, Love as Shopping

I have argued that our conflicting definitions of romantic love as both irrational, spontaneous passion and enduring pragmatic "relationship" are usually resolved by the theory of stages, in which passion morphs, with due attention and hard work, into "mature" attachment. But *The Bachelor* skips the development of intimacy as it evolves into an attachment, one that is equivalent (as Jillian kept saying) to having a "best friend for life" who is also a passionate and monogamous sexual partner and committed, devoted co-parent.

As in my students' belief system, *The Bachelor* has it both ways: a great emphasis is placed on "chemistry" and an innate attraction to the contestants who survive the competitive winnowing-down (what Judith Halberstam has cleverly called Darwinian "survival of the cutest");[7] this is termed "making a connection," both using and teaching the audience the signs (however faint and unreliable) of future potential for intimacy. On the other hand, the show's structure is all about consumer selection; in effect, the Bachelor is shopping, that is, looking over, sampling, and testing out the wares on offer for his future gene pool. American audiences are entirely comfortable with this familiar scenario, since the world of advertising has inured us to the supposedly necessary delights of lifestyle choices in taste and opportunities. (Shall we go to Aspen or cruise in the Bahamas? Shall we select the Audi or the Toyota? What's the better buy as opposed to what will code us as upwardly mobile?) The relationship between taste, choice, and shopping for superior goods or a good bargain in romance (someone who "likes you for yourself" and is family oriented, for example) is something we all know but don't like to talk about, lest we appear . . . "insincere."

The Bachelor's choice of one woman over another is supposedly based on an indisputable emotional logic: who would make the best wife according to what the Bachelor is "looking for." Yet when Jason of season 13 (2009) shortly changed his mind after choosing Melissa—because he hadn't known her well enough and had true "chemistry" with Molly, the runner-up that season—it was treated by the other "ladies" in the reunion show as a kind of sadism on his part. Unsurprisingly, Jason's reversal was given a lot of play in the media, both TV and Internet; we loved to hate him because he "broke up with her on TV." This though we are expected to relish the sight of heartbroken runners-up weeping in the limo on their way out of town as well as the schadenfreude of seeing Melissa humiliated by her rejection—*also* on TV. Suddenly the theory of chemistry, connection, and the mystery of passion, celebrated for bravely breaking social rules, was less important than the violation of the expected trajectory of the story itself. Perhaps what caused all the audience outrage online was that Jason's story exposed the carefully guarded fault line between the rationalization of love and the irrationality of "chemistry."

And do the "ladies" on the show actually fall in love? They certainly tear up (and not infrequently sob uncontrollably, allowing their makeup to run most unattractively) when the "hopes and dreams" attached to this person fall through, and claim to be joyously happy when they have "won." Yet the losers are seldom still heartbroken when the reunion special comes around a few months later, and the "success" rate of the relationships formed to date is, as everyone knows, dismal. Cynics usually remark on this as a comment on the "fakeness" of the emotions themselves, as compared to love in real life; I would suggest rather that it throws into question what people actually do feel when they believe they are "in love," and how the context for what we are *supposed* to be feeling shapes what we experience. Maybe "fake" and "real" love are just as indistinguishable in actual life, our own reality show.

Is *The Bachelorette* a Feminist Version of *The Bachelor*?

Not surprisingly, *The Bachelor* has been an obvious target for feminist media critics, who all note the absurdity and regressive nature of the marriage plot, as women perform their most alluring version of femininity for the pleasure of the Bachelor.[8] Katherine Frank, for example, compares it to the Miss America contest.[9] Since the Bachelor has all the choice and the women appear single-minded, if not hysterical, in their pursuit of him, the metaphor most often invoked is the harem (as in Frank's "Primetime Harem Fantasies"), in which one powerful male controls the sexual fate of multiple women, apparently getting much in the way of his own pleasure while dominating them with the power of his high status. The

spectacle is too reminiscent of the way women in the past were forced to depend on men for their future not to leave a sour taste in the mouth. In addition, the show has never featured a black or Latina Bachelorette, or a contestant of color who makes it past an early round. Among twenty-five women, no one is ever less than perfect-bodied, young, glammed up, and high-heeled, which defines "hot."

Perhaps out of sensitivity to that critique, or else elated at finding a new twist to a show that threatened to repeat itself tiresomely, the producers began to vary the formula with an occasional Bachelorette at its center in 2003. The first Bachelorette was Trista, who had been one of the last two standing in the first season. Since Trista's choice resulted in the only actual marriage with the winner (as of this writing), a great deal of talk followed about women's superior ability to choose wisely. Still, it would seem that putting the woman in the power position of chooser does appear to silence the "harem" objection. One can imagine the producers and executives congratulating themselves as they flipped the show's coin over from shaggy heads to well-shaped tails, from the sexual objectification of the harem to the subjectivity of the princess who has the power to decide her own romantic fate ("deciding one's fate" being something of an oxymoron).

In practice, what happens when the Bachelor is a Bachelorette is much more interesting than a mere reversal of gendered power positions. That is, the show itself simply takes a different but similarly regressive tack. The story of the women who must fight (in a modest and ladylike, "feminine" way) for the desirable man of high status to get him to marry one of them is switched back like a train on a track to the even older story of the chivalrous knight who competes and battles for the lady he adores, a narrative similarly appealing for its traditional gender values. Not coincidentally, the Victorians loved all things medieval, too.

The Bachelor may be like a Miss America beauty pageant, but The Bachelorette is tailored for women's fantasies of being the lone center of male attention and devotion, a narcissistic wonderland in which single men (thirty of them, in Jillian's incarnation) pronounce you "smokin' hot!" (yet wholesome) multiple times. Men say things like "Because she's here, it's the best place I've ever been." In other words, they act the way men are "supposed" to act when they worship a woman. But while the regressive appeal of the The Bachelorette is the woman as object of adoration, she is put on a peculiarly modern pedestal, that of transitory reality celebrity.

Presumably the women in the audience identify not only with the Bachelorette's beauty and the compliments she gets but with the control she has over the men. If the dream moment of The Bachelor is the Glass Slipper proposal of a prince by which the "ordinary" woman becomes a princess, the vision at the heart of The Bachelorette is to be the queen who is idolized no matter what she does, just by virtue of existing. The fantasy is that the Bachelorette's superior nature induces men to perform for her as she orders them around, just as Queen Guinevere's great knight Lancelot is rendered helpless by love even as he protects her with his superlative

strength, courage, and skill. In *The Bachelor,* the chosen one is a "good catch" for marriage—his success or wealth (upper middle class to upper class) and status are emphasized, whereas in *The Bachelorette,* the woman at the center has power over the men for the traditional reasons, her beauty and entertainment value.

So, is *The Bachelorette* a feminist version of *The Bachelor*? The answer cannot be simple.[10] Look at the way contemporary versions of feminism and conservative values intertwine in a revealing scene from Jillian's turn as the Bachelorette. In the postshow dissection of who lost out and why, David, a verbally aggressive competitor, learned that Jillian was put off by a compliment he'd given her: he'd said he "liked her ass." David, flabbergasted that she was not excited by this praise, turned to the mostly female audience and asked indignantly, "Wouldn't you like *your* ass to be complimented?" "NO!" the women yelled, supporting Jillian's and the host's contention that praising a sexualized body part on a woman, even one you "care for," was not "respectful."

It's interesting to unwind the dense social meanings of David's puzzlement. The first thread that informs this discussion is the support for important change in sexual mores by Second Wave feminism in the seventies, with its plea for equalizing women's freedom in sex. This history is what allows women to dress and speak in a way that expresses (even flaunts) their sexuality in Western societies, but it comes with mixed messages that are arguably both progressive and regressive for women.[11] If we compare *The Bachelor* and *The Bachelorette* as to allowable sexual behavior, we can see the clear consequences of both the women's movement and the sexual revolution in the way the Bachelorettes loudly voice their own sexual attraction to the men, but the comparison is ambiguous. When the host offers the last couples standing the opportunity to spend the night alone together in the Fantasy Suite, some female contestants turn it down, but a man rarely does. Jillian, for example, refused the sleepover with a contestant named Kiptyn because she "needs to know first that I'm the one he wants to spend the rest of his life with, that he can't live without," that is, "what direction we're going in." He solemnly claimed he "respected that." The men apparently don't have that "need." Is this progress for women or not?

The second thread is that women uniting and *demanding* that an exploitative and out-of-bounds male cease a kind of verbal sexual harassment, as the female audience seemed to do when outraged about David's "compliment" on that reunion show, is also the product of feminism, and is the progressive source of the camaraderie expressed in the audience for Jillian's rejection of David's behavior. What is not discussed, however, is the third aspect of this: the idea of "respecting" the woman through adherence to strict sexual codes is a derivative of the Victorian idea of "the lady" whose gentility and femininity imply her need for protection from the sexually improper world of men who desire her.

What an episode like this does is to emphasize the feel-good aspect of both the Bachelorette's strength and freedom as a modern woman *and* her privileged

status as a beautiful woman, while maintaining the traditional rules that many modern women rely on to keep their romantic value in an increasingly ambiguous and bewildering world of sexuality, love, and marriage. This is not just having your cake and eating it too, but stirring up oil and water and hoping they'll mix.

But isn't this how many women think of romance in "real life" as well? *The Bachelor* and *Bachelorette* simply do what all pop culture does: they first raise and then soothe unwanted discordances in our beliefs, which titillate but also disturb. We crave the authenticity of extraordinary phenomena, but we also want the familiar artifice of narrative, a shaping and selection that allows us to process "meaning" in a simplified way as "message"—for example, that we are lucky or unlucky, that what happens is meant to be or isn't, that we do or don't deserve our romantic fates.

Next time someone derides *The Bachelor* as pure escapism, think of it this way: nothing reveals our values like a good reality show. When you have immersed yourself in a program like *The Bachelor* or *The Bachelorette,* you have not escaped at all; rather, you have learned to experience the multiple and contradictory longings and obfuscations that impel us to trap ourselves in the past. As the slogan of the Disney show *Cinderella on Ice* goes, "Believing is just the beginning"; it's for the student of culture to figure out what you are taught to believe when you enter the magical world of popular romance. Though few have found true love on the show, the most wonderful thing about romance on reality TV is that no one can ever actually lose at love—because the contestants' "real" lover is not another person (nor an actor impersonating another person) but the audience itself. Happy ending or not, "success" is beside the point, as long as someone is watching.

THE ANTI-ROMANCE OF INTERNET DATING

"How an Advertisement Got a Wife," a tongue-in-cheek fictional account of a young man of twenty-six who seeks a wife through a personal ad in a newspaper, appeared in 1859 in *Once a Week,* a well-known British magazine. The story begins with the narrator sitting by his fireside and sighing—he is lonely, and his loneliness makes him ready for love. But "how was the matter to be accomplished?"

The writer's situation might appear quite familiar to modern readers, accustomed as we are to "the personals" or "dating online." Like many modern subscribers to Internet dating websites, the narrator has been too busy, distracted, or shy to put in what we might call face-time: "I had been too much occupied, too idle, or too indolent to devote the time or make the effort to 'form an attachment.' It was through no disinclination or difficulty to be pleased . . . but I was too bashful to adopt the initiative." With charming (and almost postmodern) irony, the writer mocks himself: "Most men at my age would already have adjusted their inclination to some object; so that having made up their mind and counted the cost, little more would have remained to be done than to decide upon the day . . . this however was not the case with me."

What a strangely unromantic way to describe romance, the modern reader might observe: "adjust inclination to some object" or "make the effort to 'form an attachment'!" It's as if falling in love were conceived as a deliberate act of the will, a kind of ritualized manipulation of one's own emotions for pragmatic purposes. Isn't this the very antithesis of the spontaneity and unfettered feeling that is the essence of romantic love?

Why is the writer bashful? "This weakness came from . . . a want of acquaintance with female society, which want arose from another cause in my case—namely, too close an application to business." Now surely the modern reader can relate to this "cause" of difficulty in finding dates; many in our own corporate society work long hours and have little leisure to pursue the social networks in person that might lead to romantic relationships.

In any case, our hero places the following ad in a newspaper: "WANTED A WIFE—None but principals need apply. The advertiser does not require cash, but only a companion. . . . As men go, he believes he has a moderate share of temper, and want of time is his only reason for having recourse to the newspapers. He has enough means for himself and a second party, and is willing to treat at once."

This fictional ad is probably a parody of what must have been a commonplace in Victorian newspaper conventions. Our writer's brief self-description—what will evolve in the next century and a half into an electronic "profile"—tells readers he has a reasonably good temper and is only posting an ad because of "want of time," that is, not because he has been rejected elsewhere and is desperate. Note that other than the putative responder's sincerity, *nothing at all* about the woman he seeks is designated. The important point here is not so much the character of the individuals as the conditions of the arrangement itself. This is not what one critic has called "the great supermarket of desire" found on the Internet.[12]

When our hero publishes his ad, he receives a response from a lady who proposes an interview "in a neighboring city." On the coach ride there he makes the acquaintance of a gentleman who invites him to tea with his wife and five daughters, all of whom, the father jokes, "are spinsters, young ladies whom an undiscriminating world seems disposed to leave upon my hands." At tea, the family does not inquire about his married state, "for where there were five young unmated daughters, the question might seem invidious," but he volunteers that he is a bachelor. At once his suspicions are aroused when this information elicits a "glance of arch intelligence from one [sister] to the other." That very evening the young lady confesses "that she and her sisters had conspired to bring me up to G____ on a fools errand, never meaning, of course, to keep the engagement. 'Then,' said I, 'since you designed to take me in, you must consent to make me happy!' "

"Make me happy" was a common euphemism for accepting a proposal, as anyone who has read Victorian novels knows. The story then concludes in the fictional present with the narrator's young daughter asking, "And what did she say, papa?" "Why, you little goose," he replies, "she promised to be your mamma, and she has kept her word." The practical joke played by a young woman led to a happy marriage, while the woman's intentions were pure, which is to say, she wasn't actually planning to snag the man at all.

Is this a romantic story? Apparently the Victorian audience thought so. Though it gently satirizes the growing trend in advertising for mates, the article ends with the typical Victorian sentimentalism of the future perspective from which marital "happiness" is recollected. This plot is something like that of a popular television sitcom, *How I Met Your Mother.*

But there is something extremely peculiar about the absence of elements we like to think are intrinsic to a romantic story: the decision that it's time to marry preceding the choice of partner, the swiftness of the decision to marry in two days with no development of intimacy, and, most startling, an entire absence of emotion. Even for standards of fiction in the nineteenth century, this picture of "love" is not all that far from the hilarious proposals of Mr. Collins in Austen's *Pride and Prejudice* or of Mr. Elton in Austen's *Emma*, where speech is laced with practical considerations dressed in flowery rhetoric and stylized gestures rather than driven by feeling or even personal connection. This story may have made sense as sentimental humor, a form of romantic comedy, to the Victorian audience, but it is strangely, even disturbingly, incoherent to us as a love story.

Yet online dating as a contemporary social practice follows much the same logic, however many quintessentially modern strands of "romance" are now twisted in. In fact the ethos of work in personal ads, and more broadly in self-help discourse, fits very well with the Victorian hero scolding those who are "too much occupied, too idle, or too indolent to devote the time or make the effort to 'form an attachment,'" as he says. Relationships we now call "romantic" are often said to require initiative and concentrated effort to begin as well as endure—in other words, *work*, whether the labor involves the seemingly passive effort to "be open" to romance or the arduous industry of self-promotion.[13]

Judging the Book by Its Cover: The Profile

Personal ads are not as old as the so-called earliest profession, but the business of publicizing oneself in print in order to find a spouse has been traced back to at least the mid-eighteenth century.[14] By the nineteenth century there were British magazines dedicated specifically to the search for marriage partners, such as the *Matrimonial Journal*. And in the present time "the personals" are doing very well indeed, as they evolve along with the media that contain them, from the spread of advertising columns in newspapers and magazines in the nineteenth century to the advent of the present-day online dating site. As a business model, dating websites have posted record subscriptions and profits even in a major recession. An oft-quoted study showed that "1 out of every 5 singles in the United States have dated someone they met online." As they have grown, these enterprises have become more "successful" at forming relationships, and as they become more successful, they have become ever more ubiquitous.[15]

In the typical format, the customer writes a personal "profile," which you would think would be a site for freedom of expression in a virtual paradise of creative individualism. Given that there are few limits on the length or content of these, it might be expected that these would be romantic, exciting, imaginative life stories, designed to distinguish the writer from the herd of would-be daters and lure in desired lovers through the writer's unique style or by the power of a good narrative. After all, the literary genre of romance started as a story, an adventure narrative (the very term "romance" is related to the French word for "novel," *roman*).

But in fact, "romance" is no longer a story on most online dating sites, but rather a compilation of traits summarizing "who I am," side by side with a shopping list of "what I want you to be like." Like many others, the largest online dating company, Match.com, *discourages* narrative by emphasizing the "right" way to profile. On its website it provides successful examples in which both the profiler's identity and the potential date/mate's identity are reduced, for practical purposes, to a few hundred efficient words of genotype, situation, and personality attributes. "Start by telling us a little about yourself and who you're looking for," purrs the Match.com website. "We'll use the information to help you find a great match and to help the right people find you. So go ahead, put yourself out there and get the attention you deserve!"

The idea here is that one can best find love by "matching" traits: "Looking for someone who loves sushi, the Mets, or runs marathons? We [Match.com] provide a variety of powerful search tools to help you find people based on their interests, background, age, location, and more." The rigid structure of each subscriber's two consecutive profiles (first "me," followed by "you," the hypothetical date) implies an exchange: Look, I have *this*, so you should have *that* to get me. In view of the long history of romance in capitalist society as an ethos opposed to the values of commercial self-interest, this seems odd, even chilling. Of course, the act of posting a profile is not shopping around a manufactured product of labor, it's the labor of shopping around, where the product is a crafted self.

When you think about it closely, the whole concept of "profiling" is more than a bit preposterous. Just imagine for a moment that you have many friends but for some reason you lack a *best* friend, one whose company you would enjoy more than any other's, and with whom you can share your most private thoughts. You decide that you will find a best friend by advertising for one online: WANTED: BEST FRIEND. Could you really pick out someone you could hang out with frequently and confide in by looking at pictures and reading short prose statements almost entirely composed of lists of traits? Think of those people you really do consider your best friends; if, before you knew them, you had first seen their photos and read a paragraph they had written online, would you have chosen them out of hundreds of other strangers? It's difficult to pick candidates for jobs without personal contact, never mind our most intimate and trusted relations.

Now, the fact is that if you were new in town and very lonely, you might very well find friends online, depending on just how needy for a social life you were and how discriminating you tend to be about the company you keep. Certainly there are a fair number of people who have relationships with or even marry those they dated online. Match.com advertises that 10 percent of subscribers "find a partner within a year." They also note that Match subscribers tend to be "better educated and earn a higher income," a population, not coincidentally, that marries more often.

But though these men and women might say they have found romance, there is no way to know reliably what they wanted. Do *they* know? Perhaps they were on the rebound, or were willing to date anyone who might provide reliably pleasant company and was attractive enough. (What *is* enough?) Were they desperate to escape aging alone? Did they feel a thunderclap, or did they do a mental and emotional calculation about what kind of life they might lead with this person?[16] Match.com would say they found "love"—but what is that? It's impossible to know whether the relationship was "romantic" in the conventional sense, or they were simply *ready* to have a relationship with an acceptable person who was agreeable to trying.

One thing is certain: Internet dating ads are enabled by the modern concept of romance as "finding a best friend," one you are attracted to enough to sleep with. The older definition of romantic love as passion, an overwhelming and irrational attraction, has little place here except as a highly abstract concept that guides the seeker the way a religious ideal might guide a pilgrim. Rarely does a profile produce rhapsody like this young woman's:

What is it I am looking for!!? A person made perfectly for you, your two souls become connected as one and are destined to be together until the end of time.... As butterflies fluttered in your stomach it was an explosion of emotions. As this invisible force draws you to this person you can sense a mutual feeling. A connection unlike any other you've experienced before, impossible to resist. You feel a burning, a fire from deep inside, that you can't ignore. This person becomes a part of you, your other half . . . your soul mate.

In contrast to the above, the term "soul mate" in most profiles seems to mean the romantic lover as best friend, or, if you will, the ideal of romance reduced to a banal compatibility of taste and values. It no longer means a Tristan-and-Isolde,

Werther-and-Lotte, Heathcliff-and-Catherine mingling of essences that erases boundaries between real and ideal, life and death, body and . . . yes, *soul*, a concept with a heavy linguistic and philosophical history that once brought to mind transcendent religious phenomena but now means something closer to "stuff about myself I only reveal to those I'm closest to."

Actually, psychology and marketing studies have shown that romance seekers practice what scholars unattractively call "positive assortative mating" or sometimes "homophily": the idea that you seek someone like you and, conversely, that you resemble the person you will attract.[17] No one says or writes, "I have no sense of humor, so I want someone funny who will have to work hard to amuse me," or "I'm chilly by nature, so you'd better be warm to compensate for my lack of affection." The irony is that while dating websites purport to offer the disclosure of the singular "real" heart (or, if you will, soul) for the purpose of finding true love, what struck me most about the profiles is how curiously similar they are, making the idea of "matching" on the basis of unique personality less than likely.[18]

The numbing act of reading copious quantities of these individual profiles reveals nothing more profound than that nearly everyone wants the same thing and has the same hopes for respect, loyalty, upbeat personality, and entertainment. And how will lists really help achieve these goals? Does *asking* for someone with a "wonderful personality" filter out nonwonderful personalities or, for that matter, particularly attract those who have them? Does *claiming* you have a great sense of humor without demonstrating it (as almost no one does) sell as a plausible self-assessment? (Apparently the most privileged group with the most social capital is not young women or older men but those who can impress with their wit, since this is the trait most often sought.) What, then, does this prose accomplish as an index of the unique individual's character? It's as if the profiler hopefully presents an ideal self and waits for the magic to happen.

Here's where Internet dating merges two seemingly incompatible discourses: one, the "mystery" of passion, fated meeting and connection, and the inexplicable attraction commonly metaphorized as "chemistry,"; the other, the supposed scientific principles of attraction that "explain" that magical, metaphorical chemistry as . . . well, *actual* chemistry.[19] The idea of complementarity is of course one of the most popular theories of attraction ("opposites attract"). The *New York Times* gushed about a wedding, for example: "Friends describe [the bride and groom's] personalities as complementary: He is calm and deliberative while she is passionate and spontaneous. Joseph grounds Esther . . . and she brings him out of himself."[20] This idea is rivaled only by the claim that we like mates with whom we have "so much in common" (homophily again).

The anthropologist Helen Fisher is a prolific author who is listed as chief scientific adviser for the dating website Chemistry.com, at which you can, in their words, "reveal your personality type and see what makes you tick." When the marriage of Arnold Schwarzenegger and Maria Shriver fell apart in 2011 amid much public scandal, Dr. Fisher was interviewed on a news show as an expert on romantic success: "I've studied personality and who is naturally drawn to whom on the dating site Chemistry.com," Fisher said. "I find that these two people are drawn to each other originally because the high testosterone type, as Arnold certainly is, needs the people skills, the verbal skills, the compassion, the nurturing, the intimacy of the high estrogen type, which is what Maria is, and that often needs the decision-making and the pragmatism of the high testosterone type." Why, then, if they were so well suited, did their marriage flame out so spectacularly? Here is Fisher's rather unscientific but apparently perfectly serious explanation of what happened to the relationship between these two beautifully compatible people: though their mutual attraction was so strong and rational, she admits, "after a while, [these same traits] can get on your nerves."[21]

It seems the ultimate commodification and rationalization of feeling—paying to meet a romantic partner through advanced technology—turns out to be quite irrational, after all.

What Do Women Want?

What version of "self" is deemed desirable for romance by women? What do women say they want, and in what way does this inflect the picture of what they believe love is?

I decided to do a small-scale comparative study of profiles on Match.com— the biggest player in the online dating business, with millions of worldwide subscribers—looking closely at the prose sections of the profiles of one hundred American women looking for men, and for comparison, one hundred American men looking for women. I selected the profiles at random as to specific geography (except for residence in the United States) and any other classifying information checked in boxes, such as physical facts, education, profession, religion, ethnicity, or income. I did, however, look for two specific age groups: "Older" (ages 50–70) and "Younger" (ages 25–35). From these I gleaned the fifty most frequently repeated descriptive terms in the profiles, and further distinguished these as either Description of Self or Description of Other (desired date/mate).

I did this because I was curious: what are the differences in the occurrence of these traits among the four groups, and how did each age/gender group use each trait to represent themselves and their desired romantic partners?[22] My goal was to compare the numbers of times the most popular fifty terms occurred in the profiles of the Older Women (ages 50–70), Younger Women (ages 25–35), Older Men (ages 50–70), and Younger Men (ages 25–35).

Older Women versus Younger Women Compared to Younger Women, Older Women described themselves as Accomplished/Successful more than they requested Accomplished mates:

"While I'm compassionate, playful, and devoted, I also have an MBA and work in management at a Fortune 500 company." Older Woman #10

"New Age Woman, successful, intelligent, attractive, creative. Sophisticated, well-traveled, multilingual." Older Woman #3

Older Women also tended to label themselves more often as Bright, Communicative, Creative, Fun, Romantic, wanting Similar Traits, liking to Snuggle, and interested in their Work than Younger Women did. Yet Passionate as a Self-description was about the same for Older Women and Younger Women, and given the difference in age, this is perhaps not what many would expect.

"I am very passionate and affectionate!" Older Woman #9

"I can be a little spitfire if I want to be but I also have a very passionate side." Older Woman #15

The most notable difference between Older and Younger Women was *what they said they wanted* in a date/mate. Besides their greater wish for an Attractive mate, Older Women also stated they preferred mates who are Giving, Loyal, and Listeners more than Younger Females did.

Though Match.com would never say so—maybe the Older Women themselves wouldn't either—the profiles seemed to imply that Older Women are advertising for solid, reliable relationships rather than spontaneous, passionate romances (yet remember that they describe *themselves* as Romantic more than Younger Women do, and just as passionate). One might speculate that as a result of age, their written desires for a mate reflect more what they believe they can expect rather than what they secretly want. But we can see how age, as opposed to gender, is associated with these similarities and differences by comparing Older Women to Older Men.

Older Women versus Older Men   The most interesting comparison, as it turned out, was that of Older Women and Older Men. Older Women clearly identified themselves less often as Romantic than as Accomplished, Creative, and Fun (Older Men had the highest number of self-descriptions as Romantic of all the groups). Looking at stated preferences in the Other, more Older Women than Older Men were interested in finding these traits in a date: Communication, Easy Going, Giving, Honest, Laugh, Listener, and Loving.

Older Women significantly outnumbered both Younger Women and Older Men in describing themselves as Attractive (20 percent of my sample for Older Women, compared to 8 percent of Older Men, 4 percent of Younger Women, and 2 percent of Younger Men).

"I'm told I do not look my age at all." Older Woman #41

"I've put on some extra lbs, but I still jet around campus." Older Woman #18

This complements Older Men's greater stated desire for Attractive mates (28 percent of Older Men versus 10 percent of Older Women).

"I know that looks aren't everything, but initial physical attraction is a reality, so please post a picture." Older Man #2

"Staying fit is important to me and it should be to you too. Skinny is great and fit is better. Please don't be overweight, ok? If you have a positive attitude about yourself you will probably not be." Older Man #11

Passionate is an interesting trait in Older Women and Older Men: while Older Women presented themselves as just as passionate as the Older Men did, they sought the trait less often in their potential date than did Older Men.

These results interest me in view of the postmodern idea that the surfeit of identities possible in electronic media and consumer society tends to erase dichotomies such as male/female and old/young. Since "anyone could be anyone," you would think that gender distinctions would be blurred, along with age disparities. Instead, Older Women's criteria for a date seem remarkably congruent with those cited by Shere Hite's complaining women in her best-selling sociological study *Women and Love*: listening, communication, and emotional availability.[23]

"It is also important that he [the potential date] be kind, generous, considerate, and a good listener, etc., etc., etc., the whole nine yards." Older Woman #2

"I would like to meet someone who is caring and a good listener, and has compassion for his partner, whether good times or bad." Older Woman #39

"You are romantic, affectionate, intelligent, educated and emotionally available." Older Female #49

When Romance Is Not a Story

The sociologist Elizabeth Jagger, examining gender and self-representation in online dating, has found that Internet ads are placed most by two groups: young men and older women.[24] Surely the abundance of young men posting online dating profiles are enacting their traditional role as youthful pursuers of young women, but what's in it for older women, as opposed to older men?

Romantic love can appear to be a utopia of democracy and meritocracy because supposedly there's "someone for everyone"; the ideology of *The*

Bachelor reality TV show, and American culture in general, is that everyone can expect romance and that even the most ordinary of mortals gets to be loved. Yet the hidden face of romantic love is that like it or not, it often comes down to an act of calculated valuation, not just selecting *whom* we desire, but *what*. Our idealization of romance includes the assumption that it is the very antithesis of material considerations ("marrying for love" in a Jane Austen novel) or commercialism (the resonance of the handmade, personalized gift over the store-bought object, or walking on the beach in the moonlight over walking around the mall). What we don't like to see is that there is a market value in the very personal identity whose uniqueness is the pivot upon which falling in love supposedly turns. Like *The Bachelor*, online dating is a cutthroat competition, though that element is covert rather than on display for entertainment.[25]

Online dating is the perfect expression of the modern dilemma of love. In theory, we are supposed to respond spontaneously and mysteriously to the most superior "object" of our heart's desire and are "naturally" selected in turn according to our own worth; in reality, the market is such that we have very limited choices predetermined by our own exchange value, and we are constantly made aware of the labor that must go into *finding* and *obtaining* the "right" selection. How ironic, then, that in our super-hyped-up romantic age, we have come full circle to our fictional Victorian hero's unromantic recipe for success in "love": "devote the time or make the effort to 'form an attachment'" and "adjust inclination to some object"! No wonder the profilers I saw on dating websites hesitated to describe themselves or the mates they sought as "exciting":

> "I'm not going to pretend that this whole process is exciting and fun and easy. Dating sucks for the most part, but it's necessary also, right?"
> Younger Woman #32

If modern romance is an emporium of desire and gratification, both metaphorically in general as well as more concretely and specifically in Internet dating, older women have a burden beyond that of sexual discrimination by age and perceived attractiveness. That is, unlike in sex ads, dating profilers must sell themselves emotionally as well as sexually. Whereas love in popular romance novels is frequently conceptualized as a "something," an essence to be gotten or denied, what is to be obtained is not necessarily that same "thing" when aging women conduct their everyday emotional lives in an economy of desire that appears to them in deep recession.

Whether or not cyberspace is an "egalitarian medium" where age differences matter less than in face-to-face relations, as some scholars claim,[26] the picture for older women and new love relationships in general is not a pretty one as far as statistics go. We know that the remarriage rate for women ages 45 to 64, for example, is half the rate for similarly aged men.[27] This probably reflects the relative scarcity of older men in proportion to older women, as well as the tendency for older men to (re)marry younger women, a practice that "becomes more extreme the older men are when they marry" and is linked to class and other forms of status, according to empirical analysis.[28] Then, too, as one study puts it, "high-status men have very few constraints in the remarriage market," whereas statistically, "divorced women tend to be unattractive marriage partners."[29]

Of course, it's also possible that older women have less desire to marry than older men. But even in dating, the difference is marked. It's not irrelevant that a typical magazine article on writing profiles urges women to "use sex to pique a man's interest" and "cut . . . years off their age" in the profile, advice that does not bode well for an equal playing field.[30] It's not just about age, either. Analyzing dating sites for gender preferences, the sociologist Günter Hitsch reported results such as the following: "Men typically avoid tall women. . . . Men have a strong distaste for women with a large BMI. . . . Men generally shy away from educated women."[31]

What the older woman may do in response to these depressed (and depressing) conditions is to "consciously create, manipulate, and compensate," as Hilary Radner suggests in regard to the modern consumer and her shopping choices.[32] The aging woman can't easily escape the realities of gender that throw back an unflattering image of herself as entirely unfit for the role of romantic heroine in a narrative. Though she may be more limited in her ability to choose her love relationship as she grows older, at least in escaping the story of love in the Internet profiles, she can straightforwardly give voice to what she wants. The irony is that this self-assertion contradicts the core principles of *The Rules* and other self-help literature aimed at women, where the latter are enjoined to consciously assume a pose of traditional modesty and utter (but manipulative) passivity to get a desirable man, on the grounds of inborn masculine and feminine principles: "Women who call men, ask them out, conveniently have two tickets to a show, or offer sex on the first date destroy male ambition and animal drive. Men are born to respond to challenge."[33]

You'd think older women would be the most conservative of seekers, yet the older women whose profiles I read openly flout the advice of *The Rules*. On the contrary, they are encouraged by a different set of rules, those of the profile genre rather than romantic story, to name their desires. This explains why they describe themselves as both more passionate yet also seeking a higher degree of pragmatic relationship traits, of the sort that would foster an enduring relationship.

> "At this stage of life, I feel that a successful relationship means giving each other the space to pursue our own interests, yet come together with shared values, common bonds, and acceptance of our different lives." Older Woman #13

> "I look for companionship that allows, without pretense or fear, expression of feelings." Older Woman #26

I would speculate that what we see in these representations of Self and desired Other in cyberspace is the freeing of the older woman from the *story of romance* to which she is told she does not belong because of her lack of feminine desirability. I am suggesting that the rationalized conventions of Internet dating profiles, however listlike and alienated, allow older women to escape the love story with its traditional heroine as youthful object of adoration (as in pop romance fiction or *The Bachelorette*) or needy, helpless figure who will do anything at all for love. Instead, the older women seem to look for the man who will *work for* them and also *work with* them (however this plays out after they post those profiles).

The art critic John Berger is famous for observing that in media, "men act and women appear"; as older women give online dating a try, it's as if their expectations are already so low that these women *can* act, after all. That is to say, they may finally speak in a way that perhaps they could not when young and romantic: to hell with passion, give me the guy who will listen to me. Neither desperate housewives nor those hot young things who have every reason to believe they will find the One, what do they have to lose?

THE REALITIES OF LOVE

In this chapter we have circled backward from the reality TV show *The Bachelor* to the courtship/marriage plot in Jane Austen, and forward from Victorian marriage advertisements to the profiles of Internet dating. One similarity in the modern intersections of reality genres with love stories is the hope for transformation of traditional and oppressive gender values. As Janice Radway and Tania Modleski have argued about popular heterosexual romance, romantic plots often emphasize mastering what is viewed as threatening about traditional masculinity. Male distance and the potential for rejection or the abuse of power are transformed through a benign, caring, and nurturing relationship in which the beloved's focus, both sexually and verbally, is on noticing, desiring, and valuing—or just listening to—the woman in love. When the Bachelor chooses the last woman standing, or the Bachelorette is pursued and adored, the story enacts both the woman's fear of rejection and humiliation and also its wishful opposite. By contrast, in the Internet dating profile, the older woman can directly request a caring partner (as opposed to an object of romantic passion) from a bodiless pool of possibilities because there is no romantic story in a profile.

Popular romance is often said to appeal to the readers' need for "unreality." My own premise is that all stories *do* something to or for us, and are meant for this purpose, consciously or not, by the teller, though what they are meant to do and what they actually do to the listener may be quite different. What we designate at the time as "real" or "reality" applies not only to the nature of romance but also to the idea and experience of self that frames it: romance is a *version* of our own "reality," a way to see ourselves and imagine others seeing us.[34]

All stories make life, and our own lives in particular, explainable. But romance in "reality" may especially render coherent what I *have done* for love (memory), what I *hope* will happen (Internet profiles), or what I *would do* if I found myself in fabulous circumstances (where I can pretend that I too am fabulous), as in *The Bachelor* or *Bachelorette*. When lived experience of love is fictionalized into story, told to others or told to oneself, when reality becomes "reality," we become both the creator and the consumer of romance. We both *are* lovers *and* play one on TV . . . or on the Internet, or in our own lives.

CONCLUSION

If the Glass Slipper Fits

Love stories are not timeless or universal. To the contrary, *pace* Shakespeare, love is a story that alters when it alteration finds.

Romance is often treated as generic narrative because we all know the popular mythic stories of love such as Cinderella. But historical and social conditions change the stories' meanings for us, and not infrequently their themes as well. Though their characters or plot points may appear the same across the ages, there can be no useful interpretation without a reflection of the time and place in which the story finds its life. As the psychologist Jerome Bruner says, narrative cannot be "placeless and timeless"; some "theory" of the world has to make it cohere.[1] I have tried to show, for example, that in the modern era, the difference between raunchy and romanticized sexuality is important to our own definition of romance, whereas in the Victorian era, when sexual pleasure was viewed with suspicion, the meaning of romantic love differed as well. Then, too, as we saw in chapter 5, versions of the "same" love stories in different eras say less about universal themes and longings than about the historical moment and its contemporary tensions.

Looking at love stories as historical representations of social issues rather than as the pure expression of primitive desires, it makes sense that their relationship to gender has been in flux as well. In the Victorian age, a time of transition for marriage as a "love-match," love itself was widely seen as a specialization of women's morally superior nature. But this idea more often referred to the (middle-class, Anglo, hetero) female's purported talent for nurturing and self-denial, qualities supporting conservative gender roles in the family, rather than for "romantic" love, which to many critics seemed self-interested and silly. In addition, Victorian magazines and novels did not worry about "keeping romance alive" or renewing lost passion, as do modern magazines, self-help books, and ads aimed at women; once love led to "success" (a well-chosen marriage partner), the basic anxiety and conflict that fuel the story were over.

One purpose in this book has been to show how the history of an idea like romantic love has a prolonged life that pushes into the present but is also transformed by new conditions. In a previous work, *A Craving Vacancy: Women and Sexual Love in the British Novel*, I suggested that individual fulfillment through love competed in the Victorian age with self-denying morality; here I have tried to illustrate a curious, distinctive mix of conservative and subversive in the fraught, complex, tangled view of love in much modern culture, loaded with unacknowledged history.

There was probably never a time in which romantic love was a simple and singular idea, but the multiple meanings contained within contemporary romance are especially rife with new implausibilities and self-contradictions. These are deeply muddled and confusing, though only when you think about it: love is selfless and selfish, real and illusory, identified by a certain kind of emotion-filled sexuality and yet also beyond sexuality within committed relationships. Somehow romantic love still bears the weary load (familiar to the Victorians in particular) of caring, moral commitment to fidelity and renunciation of all others, as well as the imperative to maintain and protect the family (all presented as essential to women's nature), while still taking part in the modern discourse of narcissism, self-gratification, and consumerism (shopping for the best, evaluating oneself in terms of the market—as we see in the personal ads discussed in chapter 10).[2]

These incongruous views are not universal, nor did they arise overnight. Socially, love is continually being reinvented. Historians have shown that by the eighteenth century and intensifying in the early nineteenth century, romance in Western cultures came to mean the kind of emotional attraction that is the basis for a rational companionate marriage, rather than a passion not connected to marriage except in extraordinary circumstances.[3] In the early twentieth century, greater access between the sexes, including in coeducation, coincided with the growing social acceptance of sexuality in romance.[4] And in our own time, sexual and emotional passion in courtship is expected to continue indefinitely, as marriage has become a lifestyle choice rather than a social compulsion, and we are exposed to the escalating use of media to sell and fix both romance and marriage.[5] Romantic love has become cultural capital as much as it is private experience; in fact, we could go further and say that the two are connected in an endless feedback loop that draws mass media, publicity, and celebrity into its orbit as well.

The full restoration of sex to the concept of romance in the twentieth century meant that women have come to place more and more emphasis on their sexual desirability even after the feminist movement, including a new "stripper" style and mentality. The latter was predicted to a remarkable degree by D. H. Lawrence in his "A Propos of *Lady Chatterley's Lover*," where he excoriated the modern "flippancy and vulgarity"—and essential sexlessness—of cynically exposing women's flesh. This is not at all what Lawrence had in mind when he called for a "blood-relationship" of passion as the foundation of the bond between man and woman.[6]

The new culture of feminine hypersexuality disorients women, who are understandably confused as to where their value and desirability lies. Sexual expression is one of our new freedoms, yet for many it doesn't replace the traditional privileges of being a certain kind of woman the Victorians called "ladies," who were featured as heroines of romance. Sexual liberty also doesn't harmonize comfortably with the growing idea that the apex of a woman's personal fulfillment is *emotional* intimacy and security.

The result, in my view, is that romance is now a kind of defense, a bulwark for contemporary women against the old fear of being sexually objectified and exploited, which has evolved into new forms. Romance has had a problematic and ambiguous relationship with sexuality in recent history, incorporating sexual passion in modern times as a necessary part of its nature, as opposed to the Victorian view, yet defining itself as opposed to "*just* sex" by definition. Perhaps modern culture hyperventilates about romantic love, understood as sexual passion with mutual emotional commitment, precisely because the traditional unequal relationships that came with limited safeguards for women hang in the balance, without assurances that the new model really works. It has apparently been an easy sell.

Since the sexual revolution and the recent explosion of exploitative sexuality in print and electronic media, it seems more important than ever for many women to hang on to romance as a way of defining femininity and women's surplus value beyond that of sex object. I see in contemporary love stories in all media a common fear of giving up traditional ideology, in which women will be respected only if loved by men. Popular culture in particular soothes these concerns by combining elements that are both modern and retrogressive into one reassuring anodyne.

For example, I argued in chapter 9 that while pornography and romance have been conceived as inimical genres, pop romance works by trying to conflate them, appropriating the sexuality of porn and the emotional protections of romantic love for its female audience. Hetero romance gives women the value and self-regard that used to be gained from rigid chastity, replacing the innate respectability of the Victorian "lady." This attempt to define feminine meaning appears more necessary when the line between the imperative to be "sexy" threatens to wash over into the contempt and mockery afforded to the "skanky" (see chapter 3 on modern magazines).

Some critics have theorized that formula romance was a response to the rise of "women's liberation"; if we think of feminism and romance as competing ideologies in the sixties and seventies, vying for women's attention and loyalty, then one solution has been the seemingly easy incorporation of feminism (or "feminism") into the traditional and conservative ideology of hetero romance. I have tried to trace, through a variety of texts and topics, how gendered concepts of romantic love cross over in multiple ways, from high to low culture, from public stories to private stories, and from the nineteenth century to modern society, replicating a deep ambivalence about feminism even while adapting it and exploiting its inspirational power as a position.

As a result, romantic love has evolved as a story that is in part regressive, often enacting all that Jane Austen and Charlotte Brontë deplored (women judged by their looks, marriage as a way to move up) while enacting claims to modern progressive feminism (equality through mutual devotion, women as sexual beings pursuing what they desire). In order to justify this mixture, feminism is interpreted to mean that women have a liberating "choice" to display their looks and hype their sexuality in order to catch or keep a man. Such a mix, holding out romantic love as the ultimate pot of gold at the end of every woman's rainbow, can be confounding and frustrating even as women are encouraged to long for it.

Feminism has triumphed in mass media in overcoming the Victorian imperatives of female passivity (then called "reserve," now called "being pushed around"), feminine modesty and chastity, and female duty above individual need and desire. But we can also see feminism co-opted as a progressive element of new womanhood in the celebration of the "strong" woman in reality TV programming who pursues "what she wants": namely, love, packaged with fame, money, and material goods. As ubiquitous as the push to romance is in contemporary culture, I would argue that there is also a strong countertrend that reveals how *unromantic* we really are.

In these reality shows and others such as those popular moneymakers created around trash-glam not-quite-celebrity women, issues of gender, class, ethnicity, and even region and nationality provide mocking laughter. This is true whether we envy the women's wealth and "lifestyle" or simply view them as heathens we inspect for the same horrified sense of connection and distance we have when we visit the monkey house at the zoo. The female stars of reality TV enact a deliberate cartoonlike femininity in their cultivation of "style" in a way that seems obviously retrogressive, and gender is emphasized as a clear and instinctive divide, yet the Kardashian sisters, for example, are "strong" women who have their own income as "businesswomen," and as such are the opposite of Victorian in many ways.

In much reality TV, this new femininity carries the same double message: while women are on display and live to attract males (the sport of extreme cleavage is the common ground of these programs, if anything is), the women are also brash and outspoken about men, are quick to put their own needs first, and overpower the men in their lives with mockery. The Victorian ideal of women as angels whose highest purpose is self-sacrifice is dead as a doornail here, as it is in modern magazines. If you define femininity as the Victorians did, by a "natural" modesty, dutiful submission, self-denial, chastity, or the capacity for superior morality, the stars of reality programming are neither feminine nor ladies. But neither are they exactly feminist heroines: these "real" women scorn men (as on *Jersey Shore*) but also attack other women (as do the Real Housewives). Instead they are avatars of self-marketing, Frankensteins forged by a mash-up of the progressive sexual and feminist revolutions of the sixties and seventies and the late-capitalist use of the development and spread of new media that widens the scope of celebrity.

In harmony with these ideals of self-expression and self-gratification is the emphasis the "real" women place on following their own liberated sexual desire. "I miss penis," mused one of the female stars of *Jersey Shore* winsomely during a particularly dry period. Her roommate JWoww is the modern strong and independent woman who asserts herself with a boyfriend who does not call her back: "Now I know where I stand, so fuck him" (though she quickly forgave him). Yet the sexual double standard is also rigidly conservative on *Jersey Shore*, where men speak with confident superiority about women as undesirable "grenades" and women categorize other women as "sluts" and "dirty whores." Meanwhile, the "fairy-tale" romance and wedding of Kim Kardashian occupied an entire season of TV and garnered huge publicity (and money). Like so much in popular culture, the result is a muddled picture that allows no clear path either forward or backward.

Since these days almost everyone purports to be in favor of equality, perhaps the most insidious aspect of modern romance is the idea that love equalizes gender. Though, as I have noted, the Western ideology of love tends to focus on the perfect equality of love as essential to its definition, mass media often continues to depict the man-in-love as an adorer who, as many songs say, "will do anything for you." Meanwhile, women still constitute the main audience for romantic movies, novels, magazine articles, self-help books, and advertising, which calls into question how "equal" romantic love is. In contemporary popular culture, men are afraid of loving and have to be caught and taught, but they are also still the ardent pursuers because if the woman actively (as opposed to manipulatively) asserts desire, romantic or sexual, she may be marked as less desirable.

On the one hand, men are given a pass because they supposedly have a distinct set of innate behaviors: they like to chase, they are prone to wandering, they are emotional babies. On the other, the modern belief is that every woman will be beloved by the man of her choice, and that dream is seen as a reasonable expectation, if not entitlement. A favorite romantic story is still the Glass Slipper, where the heroine is adored by the right man who chooses her above all others, but men are not much interested in consuming that story the way women are. To the contrary, women in our day are still, perhaps more than ever before, the audience for the story of romance.

The Romantic poet Byron famously said "Man's love is of man's life a thing apart/ 'Tis woman's whole existence" (*Don Juan*, Canto I). Though women's lives were expected to revolve exclusively around personal affection in the nineteenth century, in the Victorian era men both produced and read novels and essays about love and treated the topic seriously. Today, romance is assumed to be a female dream, while in media aimed at men, males mostly seem to have their minds on other matters (sex, work, and toys), and love appears as a cute joke about how they are inept at planning Valentine's Day or forget their wives' birthdays. This isn't perceived as inequality because it's supposedly "natural." But just as the idealization of motherhood enforces an unequal division of labor in the home, the greater investment of women in romance is directly related to an unequal division of emotional labor in relationships.

Perhaps this gender gap helps explain why there is a striking split between serious and popular views of romance in contemporary society.[7] In the Victorian age there was romantic fluff in novels and magazines, but also serious literary work such as *Wuthering Heights* that was romantic; even George Eliot's *Middlemarch*, for all its intellectuality, ends with a bright hope for the heroine's fulfillment in true love. In our own time the "happily ever after" has been largely relegated to popular culture, and award-winning literature more often reflects a satire and skepticism about love and marriage suited to our times. While pop romance for women (even in an adventure series for girls like *The Hunger Games*) abounds, pop culture for men and high culture for men *and* women has more or less abandoned that ideal of social and personal harmony through romantic love, as the writer Vivian Gornick has pointed out.[8] It's difficult to find a contemporary Jane Austen or Charlotte Brontë, whose work combines the traditional fantasies of happy-ending romance with literary genius and a serious artistic critique of society. Meanwhile, D. H. Lawrence's nightmare of alienated sexuality has come to pass, and his progressive dreams of social renewal through authentic passion seem almost as quaint as the Orgone Box in both pop and artistic cultures.

In sum, as I see it, romance has become a formidable part of contemporary Western culture because it is an easy response to genuine confusion over love and gender, aided by media and profit. We ought to think more carefully about romance, embedded as it is in a multimedia society that is increasingly complex and shifting in its gender values. In particular, we need further analysis of love that neither indicts nor trivializes what is so important to so many women in modern times, one that both appreciates women's needs and is clear-eyed about the price we pay for fulfilling them.

It should be mentioned that there is strong pushback from young feminists who are sometimes called the Third Wave, like the fearless Merri Lisa Johnson. These writers combine a strong sense of feminist history with a contemporary appreciation of diverse identities, changing needs, and the fluidity of both gender and sexuality. Online magazines like *Bust* or *Bitch* embrace conflicts in feminist thinking with a viewpoint they call "fierce, funny, and proud to be female" (*Bust Magazine* website) without degenerating into the silly-cute "Hi, girl!" tone that characterizes popular magazines for young women. Though they are very much minority voices in publishing and the behemoth of the e-verse, it is my wish that they would more often critically engage the nature and effects of romantic love for women as they do matters of sex.

Love is a genuine pleasure to many, and romance is a promise of that pleasure and a trace of its power. The future seems to hold a more generous inclusion of other subjects and consumers of romance, as more so-called alternative love stories with gay protagonists, or formerly taboo sexual pleasures, are written and filmed. There is much delight to celebrate in the genre of romance, both old and new, yet also much to understand and criticize. Many women still long for the Glass Slipper, but for now, in my view, its mixed messages for women are too often cleverly disguised, dressed up like Cinderella going to the ball.

NOTES

PREFACE

1 Laurie Rudman and Kim Fairchild, "The F Word: Is Feminism Incompatible with Beauty and Romance?" *Psychology of Women Quarterly* 31, no. 2 (2007): 125–136.

INTRODUCTION

1 I refer to the date (1971) when Harlequin Enterprises bought the publisher Mills and Boon and began its phenomenally successful mass-market publishing of category romances.

2 See Wendy Langford's overview in *Revolutions of the Heart: Gender, Power and the Delusions of Love* (London: Routledge, 1999).

3 For "postmodern" cynicism along with idealism, see Catherine Belsey, "Postmodern Love: Questioning the Metaphysics of Desire," *New Literary History* 25, no. 3 (1994): 683–705; Aaron Ben-Ze'ev and Ruhama Goussinsky, *In the Name of Love: Romantic Ideology and Its Victims* (Oxford: Oxford University Press, 2008), chapter 8; Eva Illouz, "The Lost Innocence of Love," *Theory, Culture & Society* 15, no. 3 (2001): 161–186.

4 See Yvonne Tasker and Diane Negra, *Interrogating Postfeminism: Gender and the Politics of Popular Culture* (Durham, NC: Duke University Press, 2007).

5 Susan Ostrov Weisser, *A Craving Vacancy: Women and Sexual Love in the British Novel* (New York: New York University Press, 1997).

6 Germaine Greer, *The Female Eunuch* (1970; New York: HarperCollins, 2008).

7 For the "competing discourses" of love, see David Shumway, *Modern Love* (New York: New York University Press, 2003).

8 My thanks to Eric Reinemann for his permission to use this passage.

9 bell hooks, *All about Love: New Visions* (New York: William Morrow, 2000), 196.

10 Mary-Lou Galician, *Sex, Love, and Romance in the Mass Media* (Mahwah, NJ: Lawrence Erlbaum Associates, 2003), 9.

11 Laura Kipnis, *Against Love: A Polemic* (New York: Vintage, 2004); Cristina Nehring, *A Vindication of Love: Reclaiming Romance for the Twenty-first Century* (New York: Harper, 2009).

12 Daniel Harris, *Cute, Quaint, Hungry, and Romantic* (New York: Basic Books, 2000), 84.

13 Jan Cohn, *Romance and the Erotics of Property: Mass-Market Fiction for Women* (Durham, NC: Duke University Press, 1987).

14 See Robert Sternberg, "Love as a Story," *Journal of Social and Personal Relationships* 12, no. 4 (1995): 541–546, for a psychological approach to this topic.

15 Fredric Jameson, "Magical Narratives: Romance as Genre," *New Literary History* 7, no. 1 (1975): 135–163. For a critique of Jameson's approach to gender, see Laurie Langbauer, *Women and Romance: The Consolations of Gender in the English Novel* (Ithaca, NY: Cornell University Press, 1990).

16 Gabriele Schäfer, "Romantic Love in Heterosexual Relationships: Women's Experiences," *Journal of Social Science* 16, no. 3 (2008): 189. In a review of recent scholarly books on romantic love, Virginia L. Blum says, "It is telling that none of these . . . grapples seriously with the role played by gender in one's experience of love"; Blum, "Love Studies: Or, Liberating Love,"

American Literary History 17 (2005): 335–338.

17 Chrétien de Troyes, *Lancelot: The Knight of the Cart*, trans. Burton Raffel (New Haven, CT: Yale University Press, 1997), 147.

18 See Merri Lisa Johnson, "Fuck You & Your Untouchable Face: Third Wave Feminism & the Problem of Romance," in *Jane Sexes It Up: True Confessions of Feminist Desire*, ed. M. L. Johnson (New York: Four Walls Eight Windows, 2002).

19 See Eva Illouz, "Reason within Passion: Love in Women's Magazines," *Critical Studies in Mass Communication* 8, no. 3 (1991): 231–248.

CHAPTER 1   THE ODD COUPLE

1 Kate Millett, Sexual Politics (Garden City, NY: Doubleday, 1970), 238.

2 See A. Walton Litz, "Recollecting Jane Austen," *Critical Inquiry* 1, no. 3 (1975): 669–682.

3 There is also a remarkable amount of fan fiction, as well as books that are "continuations" of Austen's novels, with titles like *My Dearest Mr. Darcy: An Amazing Journey into Love Everlasting (The Darcy Saga)*.

4 Frieda Lawrence, "*Not I, but the Wind . . .*" (New York: Viking Press, 1934), 165.

5 In R. P. Draper, ed., *D. H. Lawrence: The Critical Heritage* (London: Routledge and Kegan Paul, 1979), 96–97, 108.

6 Jane Austen, *Persuasion*, ed. with introduction and notes by Susan Ostrov Weisser (New York: Barnes and Noble, 2003), 22. Hereafter cited in text.

7 Juliet McMaster, *Jane Austen the Novelist: Essays Past and Present* (London: Macmillan, 1975).

8 D. H. Lawrence, *Lady Chatterley's Lover*, ed. with introduction and notes by Susan Ostrov Weisser (New York: Barnes and Noble, 2005), 300. Hereafter cited in text.

9 D. H. Lawrence, *A Study of Thomas Hardy and Other Essays*, ed. Bruce Steele (Cambridge: Cambridge University Press, 1985), 173.

10 Ibid., 203.

11 See Sarah Frantz, " 'If I Loved You Less, I Might Be Able to Talk about It More': Direct Dialogue and Education in the Proposal Scenes," in *The Talk in Jane Austen*, ed. Bruce Stovel and Lynn Gregg (Edmonton: University of Alberta Press, 2002), 167–182.

12 For an interesting reading of Mrs. Croft as a proto-feminist character, see Margaret Kirkham, *Jane Austen, Feminism and Fiction* (London: Athlone Press, 1997).

13 On the debate about the value of emotion, pleasure, and sex, see Wendy Langford, *Revolutions of the Heart* (New York: Routledge, 1999).

14 See Janice H. Harris for a discussion of the feminist critique of D. H. Lawrence, "D. H. Lawrence and Kate Millett," *Massachusetts Review* 15, no. 3 (1974): 522–529.

CHAPTER 2   WHY CHARLOTTE BRONTË DESPISED JANE AUSTEN

1 Letter to G. H. Lewes, January 12, 1848.

2 Letter to W. S. Williams, April 12, 1850.

3 Anthony Lane, "Parent Traps," *New Yorker*, November 14, 2005.

4 Mary Wollstonecraft, *A Vindication of the Rights of Woman* (1792; London: Unwin, 1891), 122.

5 Elizabeth Gaskell, *The Life of Charlotte Brontë* (1857; London: Dent & Sons, 1974), 215.

6 Virginia Woolf, "Professions for Women" (1931), in *The Death of the Moth and Other Essays* (1942; London: Chatto and Windus, 1970).

7 Charlotte Brontë, *Jane Eyre*, ed. with introduction and notes by Susan Ostrov Weisser (New York: Barnes and Noble, 2003), 295. Hereafter cited in text.

8 Daniel Wise, *The Young Lady's Counsellor; or, Outlines and Illustrations of the Sphere, the Duties, and the Dangers of Young Women* (New York: Carlton and Phillips, 1855), 234–235.

9 Quoted in Edward Benson, *Charlotte Brontë* (New York: Arno Press, 1978), 43–44.

10 Charlotte Brontë, "Mina Laury," in *Five Novelettes,* ed. Winifred Gerin (London: Folio Press, 1971), 143.

11 Letter of November 20, 1840.

12 Letter of September 20, 1851. Brontë believed the author of this article was John Stuart Mill, when in fact Mill was the editor of the article by Harriet Taylor.

13 For the new attitudes toward sexuality and identity in the "emerging discourse about marriage" in the eighteenth century, see Ruth Perry, "Sleeping with Mr. Collins," *Persuasions: The Jane Austen Journal* 22 (2000): 119–135.

CHAPTER 3 THE TRUE AND REAL THING

1 Roger's question and Chopra's answer are available online at http://www.oprah.com/spirit/Ask-Deepak-How-to-Feel-Real-Love.

2 See Francesca Cancian and Steven Gordon, "Changing Emotion Norms in Marriage: Love and Anger in U.S. Women's Magazines since 1900," *Gender and Society* 2, no. 3 (1988): 308–342.

3 For histories of magazines aimed at women, see Ros Ballaster, Margaret Beetham, Elizabeth Frazer, and Sandra Hebron, *Women's Worlds: Ideology, Femininity, and the Woman's Magazine* (London: Macmillan, 1991) and Margaret Beetham, *A Magazine of Her Own? Domesticity and Desire in the Woman's Magazine, 1800–1914* (Manchester: Manchester University Press, 1996).

4 The sociologists Anthony Giddens, Mary Evans, and Ulrich and Elisabeth Beck all relate Western ideals of love to democratic ideology.

5 See Michael Mason, *The Making of Victorian Sexual Attitudes* (New York: Oxford University Press, 1995).

6 See Alan Macfarlane, *The Origins of English Individualism: The Family, Property, and Social Transition* (Oxford: Blackwell, 1991).

7 The best treatment of this idea in modern magazines is Eva Illouz, "Reason within Passion: Love in Women's Magazines," *Critical Studies in Mass Communication* 8, no. 3 (1991): 231–248.

8 Judith Orloff, "Tips to Identify the Difference between Love and Lust," adapted from *Guide to Intuitive Healing* (New York: Three Rivers Press, 2001), http://www.drjudithorloff.com/Free-Articles/Difference-Between-Love-and-Lust.htm.

9 Eva Illouz, *Cold Intimacies: The Making of Emotional Capitalism* (Cambridge: Polity Press, 2007).

10 Kirsten Firminger, "Is He Boyfriend Material? Representation of Males in Teenage Girls' Magazines," *Men and Masculinities* 8, no. 3 (2006): 298–308.

11 Francesca Cancian, *Love in America: Gender and Self-Development* (Cambridge: Cambridge University Press, 1987).

12 Peter Stearns and Mark Knapp, "Men and Romantic Love: Pinpointing a 20th-Century Change," *Journal of Social History* 26, no. 4 (1993): 769.

13 Eva Illouz, *Consuming the Romantic Utopia: Love and the Contradictions of Capitalism* (Berkeley and Los Angeles: University of California Press, 1997). See also Jessica Van Slooten, "Fashionably Indebted: Conspicuous Consumption, Fashion, and Romance in Sophie Kinsella's Shopaholic Trilogy," in *Chick Lit: The New Woman's Fiction,* ed. Suzanne Ferriss and Mallory Young (New York: Routledge, 2006), 219–238.

14 For modern British magazines, see Angela McRobbie, "More! New Sexualities in Girls'

and Women's Magazines," in *Back to Reality? Social Experience and Cultural Studies*, ed. Angela McRobbie (Manchester: Manchester University Press, 1997).

CHAPTER 4   VICTORIAN DESIRES AND MODERN ROMANCES

1 Lauren Dundes argues that *Pocahontas* is a "step backwards" from Disney's *The Little Mermaid* (1989) because the latter features a heroine who "relentlessly pursues her goals . . . even if the goal is matrimony" in "Disney's Modern Heroine Pocahontas: Revealing Age-Old Gender Stereotypes and Role Discontinuity under a Facade of Liberation," *Social Science Journal* 38, no. 3 (2001): 357. I disagree; see chapter 5. See also Jill B. Henke, Diane Z. Umble, and Nancy J. Smith, "Construction of the Female Self: Feminist Readings of the Disney Heroine," *Women's Studies in Communication* 19, no. 2 (1996): 229–249; and Christine Holmlund, "Tots to Tanks: Walt Disney Presents Feminism for the Family," *Social Text* 2 (Summer 1979): 122–132.
2 Robert Waller, *The Bridges of Madison County* (New York: Warner Books. 1992), 62–63. Hereafter cited in text. Most of my remarks apply to both Waller's novel and the film that follows it closely.
3 Jeannette Henry, *Textbooks and the American Indian* (San Francisco: Indian Historian Press, 1970), 46.

CHAPTER 5   FOR THE LOVE OF MERMAIDS, BEASTS, AND VAMPIRES

1 See Helena Michie, *Sororophobia: Differences among Women in Literature and Culture* (New York: Oxford University Press, 1992).
2 For the idea of sexual dimorphism as "opposites," see Thomas Laqueur, *Making Sex: Body and Gender from the Greeks to Freud* (Cambridge, MA: Harvard University Press, 1990).
3 For a useful history of the Other as a cultural concept, see *The Fantastic Other: An Interface of Perspectives*, ed. Brett Cooke, George E. Slusser, and Jaume Martí-Olivella (Atlanta: Rodopi, 1998), especially Stephen H. Daniel, "The Lure of the Other," 51–70.
4 Hayden White, "The Forms of Wildness: Archaeology of an Idea," in *The Wild Man Within: An Image in Western Thought from the Renaissance to Romanticism*, ed. Edward Dudley and Maximillian Novak (Pittsburgh: University of Pittsburgh Press, 1972), 3–38.
5 Roland Barthes, *Mythologies*, trans. Annette Lavers (New York: Hill and Wang, 1972), 109.
6 See Joanna Russ, "Somebody's Trying to Kill Me and I Think It's My Husband," in *The Female Gothic*, ed. Juliann E. Fleenor (Montreal: Eden Press, 1983).
7 On the lover/villain/Byronic-hero figure in romance, see Deborah Lutz, *The Dangerous Lover: Gothic Villains, Byronism, and the Nineteenth-Century Seduction Narrative* (Columbus: Ohio State University Press, 2006); for the relationship between romance and the Gothic, see Fred Botting, *Gothic Romanced: Consumption, Gender, and Technology in Contemporary Fictions* (Hoboken, NJ: Taylor & Francis, 2008).
8 Carol Colatrella, "Overcoming Mourning and Melancholia: Redemptive Romance and the Supernatural in *Ghost* and *Truly, Madly, Deeply*," *Yearbook of Comparative and General Literature* 40 (1992): 91–104.
9 For an examination of androgyny in modern popular culture, see C. L. Harrington and Denise Bielby, "The Mythology of Modern Love: Representations of Romance in the 1980s," *Journal of Popular Culture* 24, no. 4 (1991): 129–144.
10 See Vivien Burr and Jeff Hearn, *Sex, Violence, and the Body: The Erotics of Wounding* (New York: Palgrave Macmillan, 2008).

11 There are excellent critical studies of Disney movies, among them *From Mouse to Mermaid: The Politics of Film, Gender, and Culture*, ed. Elizabeth Bell, Lynda Haas, and Laura Sells (Bloomington: Indiana University Press, 1995); Suren Lalvani, "Consuming the Exotic Other," *Critical Studies in Mass Communication* 12, no. 3 (1995): 263–286; Eleanor Byrne and Martin McQuillan, *Deconstructing Disney* (London: Pluto Press, 1999); and Jack Zipes, *Happily Ever After: Fairy Tales, Children, and the Culture Industry* (New York: Routledge, 1997).

12 Donna Haraway, *Simians, Cyborgs, and Women* (New York: Routledge, 1991), 21.

13 For historical treatments of mermaids, see Bonnie J. Leadbeater and Gloria Lodato Wilson, "Flipping Their Fins for a Place to Stand: 19th- and 20th-Century Mermaids," *Youth & Society* 24, no. 4 (June 1993): 466–486; and Laurie Essig, "The Mermaid and the Heterosexual Imagination," in *Thinking Straight: The Power, the Promise, and the Paradox of Heterosexuality*, ed. Chrys Ingraham (New York: Routledge, 2005), 151–166.

14 Hans Christian Andersen, "The Little Mermaid," trans. H. P. Paull (1872). All quotations are online at http://hca.gilead.org.il/li_merma.html.

15 *The Young Misses Magazine, Containing Dialogues between a Governess and Several Young Ladies of Quality Her Scholars*, by Madam Prince de Beaumont, 4th ed., vol. 1 (London: C. Nourse, 1783), 45–67. First published in 1756 in France. All quotations are online at http://www.pitt.edu/~dash/beauty.html.

16 Note that wit meant qualities of mind at this time, not mere humor.

17 Bram Stoker, *Dracula* (New York: NAL, 2007), 134. Hereafter cited in text.

18 See Alan Dundes, ed., *The Vampire: A Casebook* (Madison: University of Wisconsin Press, 1998).

19 See Freud's essays "On the Universal Tendency to Debasement in the Sphere of Love" and " 'Civilized' Sexual Morality."

20 The historian Ben Barker-Benfield called this the "spermatic economy" in "The Spermatic Economy: A Nineteenth-Century View of Sexuality," *Feminist Studies* 1, no. 1 (1972): 45–74.

21 See Carol Senf, "*Dracula*: Stoker's Response to the New Woman," *Victorian Studies* 26, no. 1 (1982): 33–49.

22 The vampire theme intersected with the genre of popular romance before the *Twilight* series, as in the television show *Buffy the Vampire Slayer* and Charlaine Harris's Sookie Stackhouse series of novels, which later became the TV series *True Blood*.

23 See Tania Modleski's classic analysis of this quality in mass-market romance, *Loving with a Vengeance* (New York: Routledge, 1990).

24 Cora Kaplan, *Sea Changes: Essays on Culture and Feminism* (London: Verso, 1986), 145.

CHAPTER 6   WOMEN WHO LOVE TOO MUCH . . .

1 Barbara Bross and Jay Gilbey, "How to Love like a Real Woman," *Cosmopolitan* 166, no. 6 (1969): 85; Sarah Ellis, *The Women of England: Their Social Duties and Domestic Habits* (1839). For Victorian women and gender ideology, see Elizabeth Langland, *Nobody's Angels: Middle-Class Women and Domestic Ideology in Victorian Culture* (Ithaca, NY: Cornell University Press, 1995).

2 See Philip Cushman, *Constructing the Self, Constructing America: A Cultural History of Psychotherapy* (Cambridge, MA: Perseus, 1995).

3 Elayne Rapping, "Hooked on a Feeling," *Nation*, March 5, 1990, 316–319.

4 For a related view, see Lucy Fischer, "Seduced and Abandoned: Recollection and Romance in *Letter from an Unknown Woman*," in *Issues in Feminist Film Criticism*, ed. Patricia Erens (Bloomington: Indiana University Press, 1990).

5 James J. Dowd and Nicole R. Pallotta, "The End of Romance: The Demystification of Love

in the Postmodern Age," *Sociological Perspectives* 43, no. 4 (2000): 549–580. The authors exempt musicals and screwball comedies as more about spectacle and comedy than about romance.

6 *Leaving Las Vegas*, directed by Mike Figgis, DVD (1995; MGM, 2000). Dialogue transcribed by author.

7 bell hooks, *Reel to Real: Race, Sex, and Class at the Movies* (New York: Routledge, 1996), 24.

8 Yvonne Tasker and Diane Negra, "Introduction: Feminist Politics and Postfeminist Culture," in *Interrogating Postfeminism: Gender and the Politics of Popular Culture* (Durham, NC: Duke University Press, 2007), 21.

9 *Breaking the Waves*, directed by Lars von Trier, DVD (1996; Artisan Entertainment, 2000). Dialogue transcribed by author.

10 Anthony Giddens, *The Transformation of Intimacy: Sexuality, Love, and Eroticism in Modern Societies* (Stanford, CA: Stanford University Press), 58. For a critique of the idea of "a democracy of equals," see Wendy Langford, *Revolutions of the Heart* (New York: Routledge, 1999).

11 Virginia Wexman, *Creating the Couple: Love, Marriage, and Hollywood Performance* (Princeton, NJ: Princeton University Press, 1993).

12 Ellen Fein and Sherrie Schneider, *The Rules: Time-Tested Secrets for Capturing the Heart of Mr. Right* (New York: Warner Books, 1995), quotes from 5–6.

13 *Sex and the City*, directed by Michael Patrick King, DVD (New Line Home Video, 2008). Dialogue transcribed by author.

14 *Sex and the City 2*, directed by Michael Patrick King, DVD (New Line Home Video, 2010). Dialogue transcribed by author.

15 Greg Behrendt and Liz Tuccillo, *He's Just Not That into You: The No-Excuses Truth to Understanding Guys* (New York: Simon and Schuster, 2004).

16 *He's Just Not That into You*, directed by Ken Kwapis, DVD (New Line Home Video, 2009). Dialogue transcribed by author.

17 Laura Mulvey, *Visual and Other Pleasures*, 2nd ed. (London: Palgrave Macmillan, 2009).

18 *(500) Days of Summer*, directed by Marc Webb, DVD (Fox Searchlight, 2009). Dialogue transcribed by author.

19 The TV show *Sex and the City* was judged by some critics as "postfeminist." See Jane Gerhard, "*Sex and the City*: Carrie Bradshaw's Queer Postfeminism," *Feminist Media Studies* 5, no. 1 (2005): 37–49.

CHAPTER 7   FEMINISM AND HARLEQUIN ROMANCE

1 For feminist hostility to popular romance, see Flora Alexander, "Prisons, Traps and Escape Routes: Feminist Critiques of Romance," in *Fatal Attractions: Rescripting Romance in Contemporary Literature and Film*, ed. Lynne Pearce and Gina Wisker (London: Pluto Press, 1998), 69–83; Lynda Crane, "Romance Novel Readers: In Search of Feminist Change?" *Women's Studies* 23, no. 3 (1994): 257–269; Joanne Hollows, *Feminism, Femininity and Popular Culture* (Manchester: Manchester University Press, 2000); Stevi Jackson, "Love and Romance as Objects of Feminist Knowledge," in *Making Connections: Women's Studies, Women's Movements, Women's Lives*, ed. Mary Kennedy, Cathy Lubelska, and Val Walsh, 39–50 (London: Taylor and Francis, 1993); Ann R. Jones, "Mills and Boon Meets Feminism," in *The Progress of Romance: The Politics of Popular Fiction*, ed. Jean Radford (London: Routledge, 1986), 195–218; Terry Lovell, "Nineteenth-Century Feminism and Fiction, I," in *Consuming Fiction* (London: Verso, 1987), 95–118; Pamela Regis, "What Do Critics Owe the Romance?" and An Goris, "Response to Pamela Regis: Matricide in Popular Romance Scholarship?" *Journal of Popular Romance Studies* 2, no. 1 (2011), accessed online at http://

jprstudies.org/2011/10/; and Jackie Stacey and Lynne Pearce, "The Heart of the Matter: Feminists Revisit Romance," in *Romance Revisited*, ed. L. Pearce and J. Stacey (New York: New York University Press, 1995, 11–45.

2 Pamela Regis, *A Natural History of the Romance Novel* (Philadelphia: University of Pennsylvania Press, 2003), 4, 6.

3 Wendy Langford, *Revolutions of the Heart* (New York: Routledge, 1999), 4.

4 See John Markert, "Romance Publishing and the Production of Culture," *Poetics* 14, no. 1 (1985): 69–93; Lev Grossman, "Rewriting the Romance," *Time*, February 3, 2003, http://www.time.com/time/magazine/article/0,9171,1004160,00.html#ixzz2IMzBt7fp; and "Romance Industry Statistics, 2011," Romance Writers of America website, http://www.rwa.org/p/cm/ld/fid-580.

5 Alex Witchel, "A New Romance," *New York Times*, June 12, 2005, reports that half of lesbian fiction sold is romance. James Buchanan, author of erotic male-male romance novels, estimates that 95 percent of her readership is female because "the word 'romance' throws gay male readers off" (personal correspondence with author).

6 See Ros Ballaster, *Seductive Forms: Women's Amatory Fiction from 1684 to 1749* (Oxford: Clarendon Press, 1992); and Janet Todd, *The Sign of Angellica: Women, Writing, and Fiction, 1661–1800* (London: Virago Press, 1989).

7 George Eliot, "Silly Novels by Lady Novelists," *Westminster Review* 66 (October 1856): 442–461; Mary Wollstonecraft, *A Vindication of the Rights of Women* (1792). Two well-known prescriptivists on female romance reading were Hannah More, "Strictures on a Modern System of Female Education" (1799), and Dinah Mulock Craik, *A Woman's Thoughts about Women* (1858).

8 Ann Douglas, "Soft-Porn Culture," *New Republic*, August 30, 1980, 25–29; Ann Barr Snitow, "Mass Market Romance: Pornography for Women Is Different," *Radical History Review* 20 (1979): 141–161.

9 Rosalind Coward, *Female Desires: How They Are Sought, Bought, and Packaged* (New York: Grove, 1985). For histories of romance novels, see Jay Dixon, *The Romantic Fiction of Mills and Boon, 1909–1995* (New York: Routledge, 1999); Margaret Ann Jensen, *Love's Sweet Return: The Harlequin Story* (Bowling Green, OH: Bowling Green State University Press, 1984); and Regis, *Natural History*.

10 Jayne Ann Krentz, ed., introduction to *Dangerous Men and Adventurous Women: Romance Writers on the Appeal of the Romance* (Philadelphia: University of Pennsylvania Press, 1992), 5. Hereafter cited in text.

11 Jayne Ann Krentz, "Trying to Tame the Romance: Critics and Correctness," in Krentz, *Dangerous Men*, 111.

12 Mary Poovey, "*Persuasion* and the Promises of Love," in *The Representation of Women in Fiction: Selected Papers from the English Institute*, ed. Carolyn Heilbrun and Margaret Higgonet (Baltimore, MD: Johns Hopkins University Press, 1983), 171–177. See Margaret Kirkham, *Jane Austen, Feminism and Fiction* (London: Athlone Press, 1997).

13 Nancy Armstrong, *Desire and Domestic Fiction: A Political History of the Novel* (New York: Oxford University Press, 1987).

14 Poovey, "*Persuasion* and the Promises of Love," 174.

15 Jade McKay and Elizabeth Parsons, "Out of Wedlock: The Consummation and Consumption of Marriage in Contemporary Romance Fiction," *Genders* 50, no. 1 (2009): 4–5.

16 See Rosalind Gill and Elena Herdieckerhoff, "Rewriting the Romance: New Femininities in Chick Lit?" *Feminist Media Studies* 6, no. 4 (2006): 487–504; and Rochelle Hurst, "The Barrister's Bedmate: Harlequin Mills & Boon and the *Bridget Jones* Debate," *Australian Feminist Studies* 24, no. 62 (2009): 453–468.

17 For example, http://teachmetonight.blogspot.com and www.romancewiki.com/Romance_Scholarship. Thanks to Sarah Frantz for her help with this information. See Sarah Frantz and Eric Selinger, eds., *New Approaches to Popular Romance Fiction: Critical Essays* (Jefferson, NC: McFarland, 2012).

18 Kay Mussell, in her influential article "Where's Love Gone? Transformations in Romance Fiction and Scholarship," *Paradoxa* 3, nos. 1–2 (1997): 3–14, mentions two innovations in evolving romance with potentially empowering effects: many types of romance that make one interpretation of romance problematic, and the influence of readers.

19 Sally Goade, ed., *Empowerment versus Oppression: Twenty-first-Century Views of Popular Romance Novels* (Newcastle, Eng.: Cambridge Scholars Publishing, 2007), 1.

20 Ibid., 10.

21 See Eric M. Selinger, "Review: *Rereading the Romance,*" *Contemporary Literature* 48, no. 2 (2007): 307–324.

22 Mairead Owen, "Re-inventing Romance: Reading Popular Romantic Fiction," *Women's Studies International Forum* 20, no. 4 (1997): 537–546.

23 McKay and Parsons see their work as "substantiating" Juliet Flesch's *From Australia with Love* of 2004.

24 McKay and Parsons, "Out of Wedlock," 7–8, 30. Rita C. Hubbard examines feminist changes in romantic heroines in this period in "Relationship Styles in Popular Romance Novels, 1950 to 1983," *Communication Quarterly* 33, no. 2 (1985): 113–125.

25 McKay and Parsons, "Out of Wedlock," 9, 11.

26 Ibid., 9.

27 Carol Thurston, *The Romance Revolution: Erotic Novels for Women and the Quest for a New Sexual Identity* (Urbana: University of Illinois Press, 1987), 8.

28 Kay Mussell, in her introduction to *North American Romance Writers*, ed. Kay Mussell and Johanna Tunon (Lanham, MD: Scarecrow Press, 1999), 1–9, additionally makes the point that the field has become increasingly professionalized.

29 See Markert, "Romance Publishing" and Dawn Heinecken, "Changing Ideologies in Romance Fiction," in *Romantic Conventions*, ed. Anne Kaler and Rosemary Johnson-Kurek (Bowling Green, OH: Bowling Green State University Popular Press, 1999).

30 Goade, *Empowerment*, 10.

31 McKay and Parsons, "Out of Wedlock," 23.

32 Ibid., 5.

33 Quoted in Witchel, "A New Romance." The definition on the RWA website is "two individuals falling in love and struggling to make the relationship work."

34 Goade, *Empowerment*, 2; Regis, *Natural History*, 30.

35 Goade, *Empowerment*, 1.

36 See Hollows, *Feminism, Femininity*, 86–87, and Hilary Radner, *Shopping Around: Feminine Culture and the Pursuit of Pleasure* (New York: Routledge, 1995), passim. For a more extended examination, see Eva Chen, "Forms of Pleasure in the Reading of Popular Romance: Psychic and Cultural Dimensions," in Goade, *Empowerment*, 30–41.

37 See Sandra Lee Bartky's thorough discussion of this in *Femininity and Domination: Studies in the Phenomenology of Oppression* (New York: Routledge, 1990).

38 bell hooks, *Communion* (New York: William Morrow, 2002), 174.

39 Alison Light, "Returning to Manderley—Romance Fiction, Female Sexuality and Class," *Feminist Review* 16 (Summer 1984): 22.

40 Regis, *Natural History*, xiii.

41 Shere Hite, *Women and Love: A Cultural Revolution in Progress* (New York: St. Martin's, 1987).

42 Jerome Bruner, "Self-Making and World-Making," in *Narrative and Identity: Studies in*

Autobiography, Self, and Culture, ed. Jens Brockmeier and Donal Carbaugh (Philadelphia: John Benjamins, 2001), 30–31.

CHAPTER 8 A GENRE OF ONE'S OWN

1 "This Summer Sizzles with the Launch of Kimani Romance: Bestselling Authors Pen Sophisticated and Sexy Novels for the World's Only African-American Romance Series," http://aalbc.com/writers/kimani_press.htm.

2 Gwen E. Osborne cites "industry figures" in " 'Women Who Look like Me': Cultural Identity and Reader Responses to African-American Romance Novels," in *Race/Gender/Media,* ed. Rebecca Ann Lind (Boston: Pearson, 2004), 6. See also Guy Mark Foster, "How Dare a Black Woman Make Love to a White Man! Black Woman Romance Novelists and the Taboo of Interracial Desire," in *Empowerment versus Oppression: Twenty-First-Century Views of Popular Romance Novels,* ed. Sally Goade (Newcastle, Eng.: Cambridge Scholars Publishing, 2007), 106.

3 See Gwendolyn Osborne, "How Black Romance—Novels, That Is—Came to Be," *Black Issues Book Review* 4, no. 1 (2005): 50, and "Our Love Affair with Romance," *Black Issues Book Review* 1, no. 4 (1999): 40–45.

4 For example, Laurie Likes Books #209, "Racism in Romance?" *All About Romance* (blog), October 15, 2005, http://www.likesbooks.com/209.html; Laura Vivanco, "African-American Romances—A Short History," November 1, 2006, http://teachmetonight.blogspot.com/2006/11/african-american-romances-short.html.

5 Angela P. Dodson, "Passion-filled Pages for Kimani Press," *Black Issues Book Review* 8, no. 5 (2006): 6–7.

6 See Charisse Jones and Kumea Shorter-Gooden, *Shifting: The Double Lives of Black Women in America* (New York: HarperCollins, 2003).

7 *The Greenwood Guide to American Popular Culture* (2002) defines romance fiction by its focus on courtship or marriage.

8 See Andrew Cherlin, *The Marriage-Go-Round: The State of Marriage and the Family in America Today* (New York: Vintage, 2010), chapter 5, "The American Way of Marriage."

9 Belinda Tucker and Robert Taylor, "Demographic Correlates of Relationship Status among Black Americans," *Journal of Marriage and Family* 51, no. 3 (1989): 655–665.

10 Anthony King, "Personal Characteristics of the Ideal African American Marriage Partner: A Survey of Adult Black Men and Women," *Journal of Black Studies* 39, no. 4 (2007): 570. See Averil Clarke, *Inequalities of Love: College-Educated Black Women and the Barriers to Romance and Family* (Durham, NC: Duke University Press, 2011).

11 David Brooks, "Pundit under Protest," *New York Times,* June 14, 2011.

12 Richard Fry and D'Vera Cohn, "Women, Men, and the New Economics of Marriage," January 10, 2010, http://pewsocialtrends.org/2010/01/19/women-men-and-the-new-economics-of-marriage/#prc-jump.

13 Tucker and Taylor, "Demographic Correlates," 657.

14 *Washington Post*/Henry J. Kaiser/Harvard University National Survey (2006); see Herb Boyd, "It's Hard out Here for a Black Man!" *Black Scholar* 37, no. 3 (2007): 2–9.

15 Anthony King, "African-American Females' Attitudes toward Marriage," *Journal of Black Studies* 39, no. 4 (2007): 434.

16 Melissa Harris-Perry, "Nightline Asks Why Black Women Can't Get a Man," *The Notion* (blog), *Nation,* April 4, 2010, http://www.thenation.com/blog/nightline-asks-why-black-women-cant-get-man#.

17 Natalie Nitsche and Hannah Brueckner, "Opting out of the Family? Social Change in Racial Inequality in Family Formation Patterns and Marriage Outcomes among Highly Educated Women," American Sociological Association, 2009, http://citation.allacademic.com/ meta/p_mla_apa_research_citation/3/0/9/8/0/pages309802/p309802-1.php.

18 Sam Roberts, "Black Women See Shrinking Pool of Black Men at the Marriage Altar," New York Times, June 4, 2010. See Kyle Crowder and Stewart Tonlay, "A New Marriage Squeeze for Black Women: The Role of Racial Intermarriage by Black Men," Journal of Marriage and Family 62, no. 3 (2000): 792–808.

19 Quoted in Gina Perales, "A Few Good Men: Scholar Notes Dearth of Black Males," Gazette (Colorado Springs), February 10, 2000.

20 Margaret M. Porter and Arline L. Bronzaft, "Do the Future Plans of Educated Black Women Include Black Mates?," Journal of Negro Education 64, no. 2 (Spring 1995): 162–170.

21 Harris-Perry, "Nightline Asks"; see also "Saving Black Marriages: Does It Take a Village?" CNN: Black in America 2, July 20, 2009, http://www.cnn.com/2009/LIVING/07/20/bia .strong.black.marriage/index.html.

22 Tucker and Taylor, "Demographic Correlates," 664.

23 See Patricia Hill Collins, Black Sexual Politics: African Americans, Gender, and the New Racism (New York: Routledge, 2004), chapter 8, "No Storybook Romance."

24 For views of this complex topic, see Sujata Moorti, "The Perilous and Imperiled Black Family of Romance," interview with Candice M. Jenkins, Genders 46 (2007), http://www .genders.org/g46/g46_moorti.html; and Rebecca Wanzo, "Black Love Is Not a Fairytale," Poroi 7, no. 2 (2011).

25 Norma Manatu, African American Women and Sexuality in the Cinema (Jefferson, NC: McFarland, 2003), 52.

26 Lynda Dickson, quoted in Perales, "A Few Good Men."

27 Kimberly Springer, "Divas, Evil Black Bitches, and Bitter Black Women: African American Women in Postfeminist and Post–Civil-Rights Popular Culture," in Interrogating Postfeminism: Gender and the Politics of Popular Culture, ed. Yvonne Tasker and Diane Negra (Durham, NC: Duke University Press, 2007), 249–276; Rachel Dubrofsky and A. Hardy, "Performing Race in Flavor of Love and The Bachelor," Critical Studies in Media Communication 25, no. 4 (2008): 373–392.

28 Manatu, African American Women, 53.

29 Kristie A. Ford, "Gazing into a Distorted Looking Glass: Masculinity, Femininity, Appearance Ideals, and the Black Body," Sociology Compass 2, no. 3 (2008): 1096–1114. See also Ann duCille, "The Colour of Class: Classifying Race in the Popular Imagination," Social Identities 7, no. 3 (2001): 409–419.

30 Jones and Shorter-Gooden, Shifting, 221.

31 Candice Jenkins addresses this history in Moorti, "Black Family."

32 Lisa Guerrero, " 'Sistahs Are Doin' It for Themselves': Chick Lit in Black and White," in Chick Lit: The New Woman's Fiction, ed. Suzanne Ferriss and Mallory Young (New York: Routledge, 2006), 92.

33 For example, by Ann duCille, bell hooks, and Claudia Tate.

34 Rita B. Dandridge, Black Women's Activism: Reading African American Women's Historical Romances (New York: Peter Lang, 2004); Belinda Edmondson, "The Black Romance," Women's Studies Quarterly 35, nos. 1–2 (2007): 191–211. Claudia Tate and Ann duCille argue that African American romance was constructed with political meaning, for the good of the community.

35 Ann duCille, Skin Trade (Cambridge, MA: Harvard University Press, 1996), 78.

36 Critics included Lerone Bennett, Addison Gayle, and Ishmael Reed. See duCille, Skin

Trade, chapter 2 for a discussion.

37 Carmen Coustaut, "Love on My Mind: Creating Black Women's Love Stories," in *Black Women Film and Video Artists,* ed. Jacqueline Bobo (New York: Routledge, 1998), 139–154.

38 Quoted in Osborne, " 'Women Who Look like Me,' " 61.

39 This is one of the parameters defining romance itself, according to the RWA website: http://www.rwa.org/p/cm/ld/fid=578.

40 Evelyn Palfrey, "Romance at Any Age," *Black Issues Book Review* 7, no. 1 (2005): 16.

41 It should be said that black authors who focus on relationships are not all female; Eric Jerome Dickey and E. Lynn Harris are two very popular black male authors.

42 Guerrero, "Sistahs," 88.

43 Ibid., 95. Hilary Radner views *Waiting to Exhale* as a renegotiation of the traditional romantic paradigm, rejecting the romance heroine as the "white girl" who submits to her lover or husband; see *Shopping Around: Feminine Culture and the Pursuit of Pleasure* (New York: Routledge, 1994), 115–128.

44 See Monica Harris, "Women's Fiction vs. Classic Romance," *Black Issues Book Review* 6, no. 2 (2004): 52–53, and Edmondson, "The Black Romance."

45 Melvin Thomas and Linda Treiber, "Race, Gender, and Status: A Content Analysis of Print Advertisements in Four Popular Magazines," *Sociological Spectrum* 20, no. 3 (2000): 357–371.

46 Psychologist Renée A. Redd and Donna Hill are quoted in Osborne, "Our Love Affair," 42.

47 Quoted in Jacqueline Bobo, *Black Women As Cultural Readers* (New York: Columbia University Press, 1995), 15.

48 Laurie Likes Books #209, "Racism in Romance?"

49 There is a long history to interracial romance, which has progressed more in reality than in film or genre romance. See Foster, "How Dare a Black Woman."

50 Osborne, " 'Women Who Look like Me,' " 66.

51 DuCille, *Skin Trade,* 63.

52 For example, at *Romance in Color* (www.romanceincolor.com).

53 For "racial vacuums" in both chick lit and sistah lit, see Guerrero, "Sistahs Are Doin' It," 100. Radner notes about *Waiting to Exhale* that "in this community it is the white race, in particular the white woman, who constitutes the racial and sexual other" (*Shopping Around,* 121).

54 Palfrey, "Romance at Any Age," 17.

55 Henry Louis Gates Jr., *The Signifying Monkey: A Theory of African-American Literary Criticism* (Oxford: Oxford University Press, 1989).

56 DuCille, *Skin Trade,* 78.

57 Quoted in Osborne, "How Black Romance."

58 See chapter 7, "Feminism and Romance."

59 See Candice Jenkins's notion of the "salvific" wish to "embrace bourgeois propriety," in *Private Lives, Proper Relations: Regulating Black Intimacy* (Minneapolis: University of Minnesota Press, 2007), 125.

60 Nancy Cott, "Passionlessness: An Interpretation of Victorian Sexual Ideology, 1790–1850," *Signs* 4, no. 2 (1978): 219–236, and *The Bonds of Womanhood: "Woman's Sphere" in New England, 1780–1835* (New Haven: Yale University Press, 1977).

61 Tyler Perry, *Don't Make a Black Woman Take Off Her Earrings: Madea's Uninhibited Commentaries on Love and Life* (New York: Penguin/Riverhead, 2006), 28.

62 Gail Stokes, "Black Man, My Man, Listen!" in *The Black Woman: An Anthology,* ed. Toni Cade Bambara (New York: NAL, 1970).

63 Collins, *Black Sexual Politics,* 21.

64 Ibid., 256.

65 Gwendolyn Osborne, "It's All About Love: Romance Readers Speak Out," http://aalbc
.com/reviews/itsallaboutlove.htm.

66 Ibid.

67 Patricia Dixon, "Marriage among African Americans: What Does the Research Reveal?"
Journal of African American Studies 13, no. 1 (2009): 29.

68 Laurie Likes Books #209, "Racism in Romance?"

CHAPTER 9   IS FEMALE TO ROMANCE AS MALE IS TO PORN?

1 Sherry B. Ortner, "Is Female to Male as Nature Is to Culture?" *Feminist Studies* 1, no. 2
(1972): 6.

2 According to Nielsen/NetRatings, "Approximately one in three visitors to adult enter-
tainment Web sites was female" in 2007. See Chris Pappas, "Sex Sells, but What Else Does It
Do?" in *Handbook of the New Sexuality Studies*, ed. Steven Seidman, Nancy Fischer, and Chet
Meeks (New York: Routledge, 2006), 236; and Bridget J. Crawford, "Toward a Third-Wave
Feminist Legal Theory: Young Women, Pornography and the Praxis of Pleasure," *Michigan
Journal of Gender and Law* 14, no. 1 (2007): 99–168.

3 See the discussion of this point in Pamela C. Gibson and Roma Gibson, *Dirty Looks:
Women, Pornography, Power* (London: BFI Publishing, 1993).

4 Steven Marcus coined the term "pornotopia" to describe the Utopian aspect of pornography in *The Other Victorians: A Study of Sexuality and Pornography in Mid-Nineteenth-Century
England* (New York: Basic Books, 1966).

5 See, for example, Walter Kendrick, *The Secret Museum: Pornography in Modern Culture*
(New York: Viking, 1987).

6 Linda Williams, *Hard Core: Power, Pleasure, and the "Frenzy of the Visible"* (Berkeley and Los
Angeles: University of California Press, 1999).

7 Feminist Anticensorship Task Force (F.A.C.T.), *Caught Looking: Feminism, Pornography,
and Censorship* (East Haven, CT: Long River Books, 1986); Lynne Segal and Mary McIntosh,
Sex Exposed: Sexuality and the Pornography Debate (New Brunswick, NJ: Rutgers University
Press, 1993); Jane Juffer, *At Home with Pornography: Women, Sex, and Everyday Life* (New
York: NYU Press, 1998).

8 See Gayle Rubin, "Misguided, Dangerous and Wrong: An Analysis of Anti-pornography
Politics," in *Bad Girls and Dirty Pictures: The Challenge to Reclaim Feminism*, ed. Alison Assiter
and Avedon Carol (Boulder, CO: Pluto Press, 1993), 18–40.

9 Nicholas Sparks, *The Notebook* (New York: Warner Books, 1992), 125–126.

10 Winn Gilmore, "Boca Chica," in *Herotica 2*, ed. Susie Bright and Joani Blank (New York:
Plume, 1991), 5.

11 Daniel Goleman, "Sex Fantasy Research Said to Neglect Women," *New York Times*, June
14, 1995; Bruce J. Ellis and Donald Symons, "Sex Differences in Sexual Fantasy: An Evolutionary Psychological Approach," *Journal of Sex Research* 27, no. 4 (1990): 528. Pamela Regan and
Ellen Berscheid studied subjects' beliefs about gender differences in sexual arousal triggers;
see "Gender Differences in Beliefs about the Causes of Male and Female Sexual Desire," *Personal Relationships* 2, no. 4 (1995): 345–558.

12 David Buss is a prominent example of such an evolutionary psychologist.

13 Debra M. Quackenbush, Donald S. Strassberg, and Charles W. Turner, "Gender Effects of
Romantic Themes in Erotica," *Archives of Sexual Behavior* 24, no. 1 (1995): 21–35.

14 Ellen Laan, Walter Everaerd, Gerdy van Bellen, and Gerrit Hanewald, "Women's Sexual
and Emotional Responses to Male- and Female-Produced Erotica," *Archives of Sexual Behavior* 23, no. 2 (1994): 153–169. See also Ellen Laan and E. Janssen, "How Do Men and Women

Feel? Determinants of Subjective Experience of Sexual Arousal," in *The Psychophysiology of Sex*, ed. E. Janssen (Bloomington: Indiana University Press, 2007), 278–290.

15 Lonnie Barbach, quoted in Goleman, "Sex Fantasy Research."

16 Meredith Chivers and Amanda Timmers, "Effects of Gender and Relationship Context in Audio Narratives on Genital and Subjective Sexual Response in Heterosexual Women and Men," *Archives of Sexual Behavior* 41, no. 1 (2012): 187.

17 Sai Gaddam and Ogi Ogas, *A Billion Wicked Thoughts: What the World's Largest Experiment Reveals about Human Desire* (New York: Dutton, 2011), 70–72.

18 See Leonore Tiefer, *Sex Is Not a Natural Act and Other Essays* (Boulder, CO: Westview Press, 1995), especially chapters 2 and 3.

19 Ariel Levy, *Feminist Chauvinist Pigs: Women and the Rise of Raunch Culture* (New York: Free Press, 2006), 33.

20 See Susan Weisser, "The Wonderful-Terrible Bitch Figure in Romance Novels," in *Feminist Nightmares: Women at Odds*, ed. Susan Weisser and Jennifer Fleischner (New York: New York University Press, 1994), 269–282.

21 K. N. Casper, *As Big as Texas* (Don Mills, Ontario: Harlequin Books, 2005), 83.

CHAPTER 10 MODERN ROMANCE

1 Baudrillard is only the most famous of these theorists and critics. See also David Shields, *Reality Hunger: A Manifesto* (New York: Alfred A. Knopf, 2010).

2 Ros Brunt, "Love Is in the Air," *Marxism Today*, February 1988, 19.

3 See Susan J. Douglas, "The Face of Post-Feminist Patriarchy," http://www.alternet.org/story/14670/the_face_of_post-feminist_patriarchy/; Katherine Frank, "Primetime Harem Fantasies: Marriage, Monogamy, and a Bit of Feminist Fanfiction of ABC's *The Bachelor*," in *Third Wave Feminism and Television: Jane Puts It in a Box*, ed. Merri L. Johnson (London: Tauris, 2007), 91–118; Lisa Lundy, "Simply Irresistible: Reality TV Consumption Patterns," *Communication Quarterly* 56, no. 2 (2008): 208–225.

4 Beth Bailey, *From Front Porch to Back Seat: Courtship in Twentieth-Century America* (Baltimore, MD: Johns Hopkins University Press, 1989); Ellen K. Rothman, *Hands and Hearts: A History of Courtship in America* (New York: Basic Books, 1984).

5 For modern dating practices, see Eva Illouz, *Consuming the Romantic Utopia: Love and the Cultural Contradictions of Capitalism* (Berkeley and Los Angeles: University of California Press, 1997).

6 Bill Albertini remarks, "[Romance reality] offers us . . . a false sense of order within the complications of dating rituals," in "So Wrong It's Right: The Guilty Pleasures of Reality TV," *Iris* 47 (Fall 2003): 12.

7 Judith Halberstam, "Pimp my Bride: Reality TV Gives Marriage an Extreme Makeover," *Nation*, July 5, 2004, 2–9.

8 For example, Beth Montemurro, "Toward a Sociology of Reality Television," *Sociology Compass* 2, no. 1 (2008): 84–106; Sujata Moorti and Karen Ross, "Reality Television: Fairy Tale or Feminist Nightmare?" *Feminist Media Studies* 4, no. 2 (2004): 203–231; Lynn Spigel, "Theorizing the Bachelorette: 'Waves' of Feminist Media Studies," *Signs* 30, no. 1 (2004): 1209–1221.

9 Frank, "Primetime Harem Fantasies," 91.

10 See Elizabeth Montemurro, "Fans, Fantasy, and Failed Romance: The Case of the Unhappy Ending on *The Bachelorette*," paper presented at the annual meeting of the American Sociological Association, Montreal, Quebec, Canada, August 2006.

11 See Diane Richardson, *Rethinking Sexuality* (London: Sage, 2000).

12 Celia Shalom, "That Great Supermarket of Desire: Attributes of the Desired Other in Personal Advertisements," in *Language and Desire: Encoding Sex, Romance and Intimacy*, ed. Keith Harvey and Celia Shalom (London: Routledge, 1997).

13 Eva Illouz, "Love and Its Discontents: Irony, Reason, Romance," *Hedgehog Review* (Spring 2010): 18–32, http://www.iasc-culture.org/THR/THR_article_2010_Spring_Illouz.php. See also Angie Burns, "Looking for Love in Intimate Heterosexual Relationships," *Feminism and Psychology* 10, no. 4 (2000): 481–485; Eva Illouz, *Cold Intimacies: The Making of Emotional Capitalism* (Cambridge: Polity Press, 2007).

14 Elizabeth Jagger cites its origin as the sixteenth century in "Marketing Molly and Melville: Dating in a Postmodern, Consumer Society," *Sociology* 35, no. 1 (2001): 39–57; John Cockburn specifies the mid-eighteenth century in *Lonely Hearts: Love among the Small Ads* (London: Guild Publishing, 1988).

15 Seventeen percent of couples married between 2007 and 2010 met on an online dating service, according to the Chadwick Martin Bailey Study of April 2010, commissioned by Match.com (cp.match.com/cppp/media/CMB_Study.pdf). See also "Online Dating Statistics, 2011," http://www.onlinedatingmagazine.com/onlinedatingstatistics.html.

16 Eva Illouz and Shoshannah Finkelman, "An Odd and Inseparable Couple: Emotion and Rationality in Partner Selection," *Theory and Society* 38, no. 4 (2009): 401–422.

17 For example, A. T. Fiore and Judith Donath, "Homophily in Online Dating: When Do You Like Someone like Yourself?" *Computer-Human Interaction* (2005): 1371–1374; Günter Hitsch, Ali Hortaçsu, and Dan Ariely, "What Makes You Click?—Mate Preferences in Online Dating," *Quantitative Marketing and Economics* 8, no. 4 (2010): 393–394.

18 Adam Arvidsson, who studied the "generally accepted normative model for self-presentation" on Match.com, also found them alike in "Quality Singles: Internet Dating and the Work of Fantasy," *New Media & Society* 8, no. 4 (2006): 671–690.

19 There are several websites that utilize the expertise of those who claim to predict love matches on the basis of science. See Lori Gottlieb, "How Do I Love Thee?" [cover story], *Atlantic Monthly* 297, no. 2 (2006): 58–70.

20 Kate Murphy, "Esther Kim and Joseph Varet," Vows, *New York Times*, April 24, 2011.

21 "Shriver, Schwarzenegger: Why'd They Split?" CBS News website, May 11, 2011, http://www.cbsnews.com/stories/2011/05/11/earlyshow/leisure/celebspot/main20061782.shtml.

22 Gay profilers may not be all that different from hetero profilers; see Richard Lippa, "The Preferred Traits of Mates in a Cross-National Study of Heterosexual and Homosexual Men and Women: An Examination of Biological and Cultural Influences," *Archives of Sexual Behavior* 36, no. 2 (2007): 193–208.

23 Shere Hite, *Women and Love: A Cultural Revolution in Progress* (New York: St. Martin's, 1989).

24 Elizabeth Jagger, "Is Thirty the New Sixty? Dating, Age and Gender in a Postmodern, Consumer Society," *Sociology* 39, no. 1 (2005): 96.

25 See Mary Evans, *Love: An Unromantic Discussion* (Cambridge: Polity Press, 2003).

26 See the discussion by Aaron Ben-Ze'ev, *Love Online: Emotions on the Internet* (Cambridge: Cambridge University Press, 2004).

27 "Remarriage Trends in the United States: A Fact Sheet," National Healthy Marriage Resource Center, 2009, http://www.healthymarriageinfo.org/docs/remarriagetrendsus.pdf.

28 See Paula England and Elizabeth McClintock, "The Gendered Double Standard of Aging in US Marriage Markets," *Population and Development Review* 35, no. 4 (2009): 797–816.

29 Kevin Shafer, "Gender Differences in Remarriage: Marriage Formation and Assortative Mating after Divorce" (PhD diss., Ohio State University, 2009).

30 Jeannine Amber, "The Profiler," *Essence Magazine* 35, no. 1 (May 2004): 182.

31 G. J. Hitsch, Ali Hortaçsu, and Dan Ariely, "Matching and Sorting in Online Dating," *American Economic Review* 100, no. 1 (2010): 130–163.

32 Hilary Radner, *Shopping Around: Feminine Culture and the Pursuit of Pleasure* (New York: Routledge, 1995), 178.

33 Ellen Fein and Sherrie Schneider, *The Rules: Time-Tested Secrets for Capturing the Heart of Mr. Right* (New York: Warner Books, 1995), 7.

34 Robert Sternberg, "Love as a Story," *Journal of Social and Personal Relationships* 12, no. 4 (1995): 541–546.

CONCLUSION

1 Jerome Bruner, "The Autobiographical Process," in *The Culture of Autobiography: Constructions of Self-Representation*, ed. Robert Folkenflik (Stanford, CA: Stanford University Press, 1993), 44.

2 See Eva Illouz, *Consuming the Romantic Utopia: Love and the Cultural Contradictions of Capitalism* (Berkeley and Los Angeles: University of California Press, 1997).

3 See Stephanie Coontz, *Marriage, a History* (New York: Penguin Books, 2006); and Peter Gay, *The Tender Passion* (New York: Oxford University Press, 1986).

4 Ellen K. Rothman, *Hands and Hearts: A History of Courtship in America* (New York: Basic Books, 1984); Steven Seidman, *Romantic Longings: Love in America, 1830–1980* (New York: Routledge, 1991).

5 James J. Dowd and Nicole R. Pallotta point out that love has become both more "hedonistic" and also rationalized and instrumentalized than before—in spite of the self-contradictions inherent in this; "The End of Romance: The Demystification of Love in the Postmodern Age," *Sociological Perspectives* 43, no. 4 (2000): 549–580.

6 D. H. Lawrence, *Lady Chatterley's Lover; A Propos of "Lady Chatterley's Lover,"* ed. Michael Squires (Cambridge: Cambridge University Press, 1993), 315.

7 Ann Douglas wrote about the "feminization of American culture" in the nineteenth century, connecting the transformations of capitalism to the formation of a "sentimental" mass culture promoted by women for the purposes of a kind of empowerment; *The Feminization of American Culture* (New York: Alfred A. Knopf, 1977).

8 Vivian Gornick, *The End of the Novel of Love* (Boston: Beacon Press, 1997).

SELECTED BIBLIOGRAPHY

Ben-Ze'ev, Aaron. *Love Online: Emotions on the Internet*. Cambridge: Cambridge University Press, 2004.

Ben-Ze'ev, Aaron, and Ruhama Goussinsky. *In the Name of Love: Romantic Ideology and Its Victims*. Oxford: Oxford University Press, 2008.

Botting, Fred. *Gothic Romanced: Consumption, Gender, and Technology in Contemporary Fictions*. Hoboken, NJ: Taylor & Francis, 2008.

Burns, Angie. "Looking for Love in Intimate Heterosexual Relationships." *Feminism & Psychology* 10, no. 4 (2000): 481–485.

Cancian, Francesca, and Steven Gordon. "Changing Emotion Norms in Marriage: Love and Anger in U.S. Women's Magazines since 1900." *Gender and Society* 2, no. 3 (1988): 308–342.

Collins, Patricia Hill. *Black Sexual Politics: African Americans, Gender, and the New Racism*. New York: Routledge, 2004.

Dowd, James J., and Nicole R. Pallotta. "The End of Romance: The Demystification of Love in the Postmodern Age." *Sociological Perspectives* 43, no. 4 (Winter 2000): 549–580.

DuCille, Ann. *The Coupling Convention: Sex, Text, and Tradition in Black Women's Fiction*. New York: Oxford, 1993.

Edmondson, Belinda. "The Black Romance." *Women's Studies Quarterly* 35, nos. 1–2 (2007): 191–211.

Evans, Mary. *Love: An Unromantic Discussion*. Cambridge: Polity Press, 2003.

Ferriss, Suzanne, and Mallory Young, eds. *Chick Lit: The New Woman's Fiction*. New York: Routledge, 2006.

Frantz, Sarah, and Eric Selinger, eds. *New Approaches to Popular Romance Fiction: Critical Essays*. Jefferson, NC: McFarland, 2012.

Giddens, Anthony. *The Transformation of Intimacy: Sexuality, Love, and Eroticism in Modern Societies*. Stanford, CA: Stanford University Press, 1992.

Goade, Sally, ed. *Empowerment versus Oppression: Twenty-first-Century Views of Popular Romance Novels*. Newcastle, Eng.: Cambridge Scholars Publishing, 2007.

Hite, Shere. *Women and Love: A Cultural Revolution in Progress*. New York: St. Martin's, 1987.

Hollows, Joanne. *Feminism, Femininity, and Popular Culture*. Manchester: Manchester University Press, 2000.

hooks, bell. *Communion: The Female Search for Love*. New York: William Morrow, 2002.

Illouz, Eva. *Cold Intimacies: The Making of Emotional Capitalism*. Cambridge, Eng.; Malden, MA: Polity Press, 2007.

———. *Consuming the Romantic Utopia: Love and the Contradictions of Capitalism*. Berkeley and Los Angeles: University of California Press, 1997.

———. "Reason within Passion: Love in Women's Magazines," *Critical Studies in Mass Communication* 8, no. 3 (1991): 231–248.

Ingraham, Chrys, ed. *Thinking Straight: The Power, the Promise, and the Paradox of Heterosexuality*. New York: Routledge, 2005.

Jackson, Stevi. "Love and Romance as Objects of Feminist Knowledge." In *Making Connections: Women's Studies, Women's Movements, Women's Lives*, ed. Mary Kennedy, Cathy Lubelska, and Val Walsh, 39–50. London: Taylor and Francis, 1993.

Jagger, Elizabeth. "Marketing Molly and Melville: Dating in a Postmodern, Consumer Society." *Sociology* 35, no. 1 (2001): 39–57.

Krentz, Jayne Ann, ed. *Dangerous Men and Adventurous Women: Romance Writers on the Appeal of the Romance.* Philadelphia: University of Pennsylvania Press, 1992.

Langford, Wendy. *Revolutions of the Heart: Gender, Power, and the Delusions of Love.* London: Routledge, 1999.

Levy, Ariel. *Feminist Chauvinist Pigs: Women and the Rise of Raunch Culture.* New York: Free Press, 2006.

Light, Alison. "Returning to Manderley—Romance Fiction, Female Sexuality, and Class." *Feminist Review* 16 (Summer 1984): 7–25.

Lutz, Deborah. *The Dangerous Lover: Gothic Villains, Byronism, and the Nineteenth-Century Seduction Narrative.* Columbus: Ohio State University Press, 2006.

McKay, Jade, and Elizabeth Parsons. "Out of Wedlock: The Consummation and Consumption of Marriage in Contemporary Romance Fiction." *Genders* 50 (2009): 1–13.

Modleski, Tania. *Loving with a Vengeance.* New York: Routledge, 1990.

Moorti, Sujata. "The Perilous and Imperiled Black Family of Romance," interview with Candice M. Jenkins. *Genders* 46 (2007), http://www.genders.org/g46/g46_moorti.html.

Mussell, Kay. "Where's Love Gone? Transformations in Romance Fiction and Scholarship." *Paradoxa* 3, nos. 1–2 (1997): 3–14.

Osborne, Gwendolyn. " 'Women Who Look like Me': Cultural Identity and Reader Responses to African-American Romance Novels." In *Race/Gender/Media*, ed. Rebecca Ann Lind, 61–68. Boston: Pearson, 2004.

Perry, Ruth. "Sleeping with Mr. Collins." *Persuasions: The Jane Austen Journal* 22 (2000): 119–135.

Radner, Hilary. *Shopping Around: Feminine Culture and the Pursuit of Pleasure.* New York: Routledge, 1995.

Radway, Janice. *Reading the Romance: Women, Patriarchy, and Popular Literature.* Chapel Hill: University of North Carolina Press, 1984.

Regis, Pamela. *A Natural History of the Romance Novel.* Philadelphia: University of Pennsylvania Press, 2003.

Schäfer, Gabriele. "Romantic Love in Heterosexual Relationships: Women's Experiences." *Journal of Social Science* 16, no. 3 (2008): 187–197.

Shumway, David. *Modern Love: Romance, Intimacy, and the Marriage Crisis.* New York: NYU Press, 2003.

Stacey, Jackie, and Lynne Pearce. "The Heart of the Matter: Feminists Revisit Romance." In *Romance Revisited*, ed. L. Pearce and J. Stacey, 11–45. New York: New York University Press, 1995.

Wexman, Virginia Wright. *Creating the Couple: Love, Marriage, and Hollywood Performance.* Princeton, NJ: Princeton University Press, 1993.

INDEX

ABOUT THE AUTHOR

SUSAN OSTROV WEISSER is a professor of English at Adelphi University. She is the author of *A Craving Vacancy: Women and Sexual Love in the British Novel, 1740–1880*, editor of *Women and Romance: A Reader*, and co-editor of *Feminist Nightmares: Women at Odds*.

CPSIA information can be obtained at www.ICGtesting.com
Printed in the USA
BVOW08s0919200913

331534BV00001B/1/P